Football - an Insider's Job

Dick
Chester

Football – an Insider's Job

Dick Chester

To, Nicola My one and only daughter

Love Dad xx

Escafeld Press

Escafeld press is an imprint of 1889 Books Ltd
www.1889books.co.uk

ISBN: 978-1-915045-09-6

Contents

Dedication

I was asked to consider who to dedicate this book to and it does give you the opportunity to seriously consider all those around you, particularly those that have knowledge of both yourself and your working life. It is therefore with pleasure that I dedicate this book with my personal thanks and gratitude to both Mum and Dad who gave me a very good grounding and to my two children, Nicola and Mostyn, my six grandchildren – Kelly, Ben, Charlotte, Henry, Darren and Richard, and my eighteen great-grandchildren – far too many to mention individually, and to special friends, Barry and Pat Ducker, who took to me as a person from day one after joining Sheffield United and remained my closest friends until their passing these last two years. I will forever be grateful to their family, particularly daughter Sue, for granting me the opportunity to deliver personal tributes for both at their respective funerals. That registers amongst my more privileged moments in my life and will forever be etched in my memory. Good friends lost but never to be forgotten.

In memory of Harry Gration 1950 - 2022

Foreword – Keith Hackett

I first met Richard Chester at Northwich Victoria in 1968 where I was about to officiate their Northern Premier League fixture against South Liverpool – a good old fashioned derby game! Richard had volunteered to run a line after his colleague and appointed linesman (assistant referee) had become ill on the way to the game. I was relieved and delighted and remember that day and the excellent performance by Richard, not an easy task in front of a very biased set of spectators who were not slow in venting their opinions on decisions.

Richard went on to hold the position of club secretary and CEO for many years with Lincoln City, Sheffield United and Sheffield Wednesday.

Our paths were to cross again whilst I was serving on the Football League's refereeing list and appointed to cover games at Sincil Bank whilst they were in Division Four. On three occasions I received calls from Richard regarding the state of the ground and possible early inspections, but with his previous experiences as a referee I was comfortable in relying upon his judgement. The games in question were an FA Cup tie against Nuneaton Borough, a Division Four game against Peterborough United and another league game against Torquay United. All of the ground problems were caused by the South Stand structure preventing any upturn in weather conditions getting through to this part of the ground, thereby leaving one half of the pitch playable and the other half always in difficulties. On each occasion I attended early morning on the match day and was received with a welcoming cup of tea and accompanied on to the pitch by both Dick and their groundsman with the decision being to declare the pitch playable. At the end of the games I was thanked by Dick and on one occasion received a telephone call from Graham Taylor a few days later thanking me and critiquing my performance. Such was the standard of hospitality and respect shown by two important members of staff.

The secretary of a club is the conduit between the chairman/owner, members of the board of directors, the manager, players, finances, contracts, police, media, fans, and the many companies that supply goods and services to the club. Richard like many other top administrators in the game in the era before the Premier League was the go-to person for everyone to contact. The total number of staff at a club could often be counted on one hand and Richard quickly earned a reputation for being one of the best administrators in football. He was also respected for his hard work and diligence and was always the first to welcome referees and officials to the clubs when he was in charge – an attribute not always equalled on the circuit. After the game he always came to the referees' dressing room to offer his sincere thanks whatever the result and calmly discuss any particular incident which may have occurred during the game – again another trait not always experienced with some other clubs.

The secretary must have a clear understanding of the Football Association and Football League regulations and employment law. The extra knowledge and understanding of the laws of the game that he had ensured that the task of marking the referee's performance or making the odd appeal against a sending-off to the Football Association never came into the area of a frivolous appeal or a mark not earned by the team of officials.

He would deal with who was invited into the various seats in the directors' box, and of course liaise with visiting owners, managers, and scouts. It's an onerous task, which he did with great aplomb. It was far from easy when dealing with so many issues in a highly pressurised match day situation.

Following the announcement of resignation by Keith Walker, a fellow refereeing pal of mine at Sheffield United, Richard moved into the hot seat at Bramall Lane, settled in well and was much appreciated by the media for keeping them, and the fans, well informed as to the happenings at the club, with the standards of hospitality to match officials still maintained and well-respected by all.

He then took that rare step of moving across the city of Sheffield, taking up a similar role at Sheffield Wednesday.

I distinctly remember taking a call from him inviting me into his office, whereupon he briefed me on a confidential paper he had been commissioned to develop based on revised refereeing criteria for the proposed new Super League discreetly being developed, and asking if I would be prepared to consider the initial draft before he submitted to the full working committee. The content was both far reaching, compared to existing operations, whilst at the same time precise and concise and little did I appreciate at that time how much influence this paper would have on what has now become the Premier League and one of the most successful leagues in the world.

Dick is one of the most reliable, hard-working, knowledgeable, and moral people I came across in my time in football.

I am so pleased to be able to open this book up with these few words.

Keith Hackett
Former FIFA International Referee

Chapter One: Who was I?

Whenever anyone asks my name, for the last 70-odd years I have told them, 'It's Dick – Dick Chester.' Of course, more formally, I'm known as Richard. If anyone were to ask me where I'm from I'd tell them it's near Lincoln. More correctly though, I was actually raised in the small village of Branston, a few miles outside of the city. This book tells the tale of how a lad from that small place and humble background went on to carve out a respectable career in football.

My work involved serving clubs from all four divisions of the Football League – not something that was common practice and maybe even unique. I worked at one of the biggest clubs of the day. I dealt with some eminent names and helped develop one of the most renowned stadia in the country. I've seen football at its best and at its worst. I learned how to rescue a club from imminent financial disaster and how to develop one to become one of the top organisations in the country. I've seen money used for good and I've had to try to stem the flow of money to players outside the terms of their contracts – known in the industry as 'bungs.' I've worked with honest, loyal and hard-working people. I've had to step in and counter people who have seen fit to be less than honest, and I've seen how football can metaphorically stab people in the back.

This then is my story. A story I never thought would ever be in print and one where, having kept a low profile in my working life, I found it very difficult: to open up and talk about both myself and my career. I hope that from this book readers will understand a little about me, but more importantly plenty of what I have learned about the business of football. I aim to share some of what I have been involved in and lessons I have learned. Football has remained a true passion of mine even as the years have passed me by and the industry changed beyond anyone's wildest dreams. There remains the firm belief in my own mind that the most important ingredient in the football recipe is the supporter. Every club needs them, and I fear most clubs don't truly recognise their importance. Without them the business would not exist, and today it has stepped far away from the local benefactor wishing to plough his hard-earned wealth into supporting his boyhood club. It now seems to revolve more around which wealthy overseas investor can stump up the most lolly for that ultimate control. More of that later on. But first, a little about my upbringing and journey into football.

My background stemmed from very humble beginnings, with both Mum and Dad very much categorising themselves as working class. In fact: poor working class.

Dad worked on the shop floor in a local engineering factory and Mum did housekeeping for the more affluent villagers. What both of them did have though was an immense degree of commitment to hard work and doing whatever they could to help others and where possible the community. That community in my early years was in the village of Branston, some four miles outside the Lincoln boundary. Even before school age I was expected to help with the large garden, producing crops and fruit which were sold to provide

Butter wouldn't melt in his mouth

the family with their holiday money. I assisted with the feeding of the chickens and ducks and the selling of their eggs, again to add to the holiday fund. Mother took control of the money, along with my father's wage packet every Friday evening, which he put on the kitchen table unopened for her to manage. When the egg production was over it was time for my uncle to visit, select the unlucky bird and pull its neck before it was plucked, drawn, prepared for the oven, and thereafter celebrated on the Christmas dinner table. It would be more than one unfortunate fowl, if it was the turn of my parents to host the family. This was often the case in my youngest years, as the family liked to see me opening my real presents in the evening. In those years I made do with a pillow-case on the end of the bed for me to wake up to early Christmas morning with an orange and a few sweets to tide me over.

The majority of the family who I grew up with were all Branstonians but during the summer months the house seemed to be full of family, down from Middlesbrough: the roots of my father's upbringing. I therefore experienced a mix of personalities. On the one hand most of my mother's side were fairly quietly spoken and I suppose partly reserved, whereas the visiting northerners were somewhat louder and outspoken, with strong left-wing and Labour Party-supporting views. At that time I didn't understand the differing cultures. Like most young kids, Grandmas

5

were a real favourite, spoiling me rotten but also tendering a level of care, bringing about a huge degree of love and affection. Mum's younger brother, Eddie Rowe, was the one who got me into cricket, football, and in particular playing the game of cribbage. He always doubted my calculations and would not allow me to score as many moves on the crib board as I thought I was due. Being a foreman in a large engineering factory he was more used to the shop-floor industrial language but he managed to express his disapproval at my calculations without using any swear words and stammered and stuttered his way through in his own unique way.

Sunday trip out to see Dad's friends in Lincoln

Once at school, dad stepped in and made sure I took things seriously and spent hours and hours with me before bedtime instilling the importance of the three Rs – reading writing and arithmetic. I still smile at how those three do not follow the three Rs when you look at the spelling! Mother meanwhile was the one more involved in the administration and deployment of discipline and punishments for any wrongdoings. Believe you me, there were plenty. The major lessons I learned were around honesty, trust, thieving and timekeeping.

As a young schoolboy, about eight or nine years of age, with virtually no pocket money each week, I went through a spell where a number of my school pals gave me some right verbal abuse because I didn't join in with their smoking habit. It got to the stage where, rather than being beaten up, I thought I may as well join them. With no pocket money to fund the purchase, I was stuck for cash. I knew, however, that there was the holiday money stored away in the heirloom, silver-plated sugar bowl in the corner glass-fronted display unit in the front room at home. When the chance came I pinched a two-bob coin then nipped off to the local shop and bought a packet of ten Park Drive. The result was a spell of sickness and feeling unwell, followed by telling my mates that I had tried and was going to give up.

They in turn said I'd been stupid I shouldn't have gone for Park Drive: you want John Players or Senior Service, I was told. They were more expensive, so a return trip back to the family heirloom pot provided me with a 2/6 coin, and another trip to the shop. If I went for John Player – these were what Dad smoked – so I thought I was on a good wicket there. Eh, you know what, I still felt ill smoking the damn things and threw almost the full packet away. Was that the end? Not on your nelly it wasn't. One evening, lying in bed in the two-bedroomed cottage, I heard my mother shout through from the front room to my dad in the kitchen. 'George, have you taken any money out of that pot?' Dad replied, 'Good God, Edie, you should know better than to ask that.' Mother replied with increased frustration, 'George I am going to ask you again. have you touched any of that money?' Dad replied again, 'I've told you before, don't be so silly as to ask.' With that reply I heard footsteps coming upstairs and I knew I was in real trouble. The outcome was the biggest thrashing imaginable, which seemed to go on forever. Mother used a leather strap – a level of punishment if rendered like that today would have serious consequences for the person administering it. Mother didn't speak to me for about a week and wouldn't feed me, although I did sneak up to my grandmother who always had something up her sleeve for me. Mother did break her silence before bedtime just to remind me that it would teach me a lesson.

It certainly did teach me a lesson as, from that day onwards, I have never touched any money that didn't belong to me. I would never ever go to my wife's handbag – instead always passing it to her for her to take out what she wanted. As I progressed through my working career and subsequently into football, systems of control for finances were pretty much non-existent and anyone wanting to adopt a "sticky fingered" approach could have made a pretty penny. More of the role that money plays in football later.

The other lesson I was taught by my father was one of honesty, arising from another misdemeanour of mine. Coming up to bonfire night I thought a good idea would be to sneak that leather belt from the cupboard under the stairs, which was its home, and mix it in with all the rubbish I had to carry down to the bonfire, which I did, and with a real feeling of smugness and satisfaction watched it burn down to its last remaining embers with no sign of the elusive belt.. Needless to say Mother needed the belt not long after for another of my misdemeanours, only to find it not there. Father stepped in, asking if I knew where it was, and, like any other kid on the block, I quickly said: 'I don't know,' but with an obvious guilty look on my face. He replied: 'Son – just remember one thing, you need to be a clever person to be a liar and you are not clever enough.' Another lesson learned that has stayed with me. Story closed – only to find the following evening Dad came from work in the local foundry, complete with a replacement belt, but this time wider and thicker.

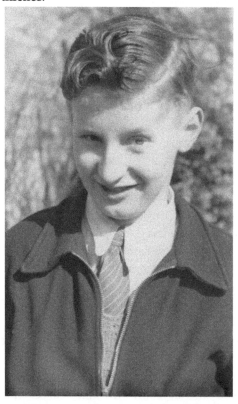

That belt soon came into action upon the young boy Richard again, who seemed to go from problem to problem not heeding the warnings. I was allowed out to play with my school pals after completion of household chores. I just needed to be home by eight. These games invariably ended up with a football match upwards of 15 or 20 a team. On one occasion, with our team losing, I decided that it was better for me to stay on and try to turn the result around. Although hearing the church clock chime eight, playing on seemed a better option than traipsing home with my chin down having lost. But, lo and behold, mother arrived, armed with the new weapon of punishment and promptly marched me home down the street whacking me every other step I took. Essential time-keeping was not only a lesson harshly installed in me but one that has stayed with me throughout my life, particularly in the working environment where I couldn't bear to be late for an appointment.

My early days, whilst being as well cared for as family income would allow, were not overcrowded with fun times and freedom. These seemed to be reserved for my pals who repeatedly called to see if I was 'coming out to play.' 'When he has finished his jobs,' being the reply from Mother. I cannot recall the home being full of love or child idolisation. Care and good standards, yes. When in need of love and cuddles, it was a short walk away for me at Nana's and Aunty May's – the latter of whom was a rock to me right through her life. Each Sunday evening it was a ritual for all of the family to gather at Nana's when many stories were related. Listening to those, and in my later life, I was able to understand a bit about Mum's growing up. She was a very intelligent girl but denied further education as, with family funds being very tight, any money that was available was earmarked for her younger brother. It was felt that, as a man, he needed an apprenticeship to set him up for life. In those days women very much played second fiddle. I think Mum felt very hurt and I do believe those frustrations carried on into my childhood.

The two-bedroomed cottage in which we lived was situated in the centre of the village, close to both the Wagon & Horses and The Plough public houses, with the gable end of the property running alongside the footpath, ideal for football practice. It was used quite a lot! The property seemed to attract many of the tramps journeying through the village with them calling at our back door, where Mum always had time for them, filling up their "dilly cans" with strong tea or hot water along with simple home-made snacks. On one particular day when Dad and I were preparing vegetables for dinner there was a knock on the door, which I was told to answer. Returning to the kitchen, I said, when asked, that it was only the bloody Sally Army. Dad dried his hands, faced up to me and, for the first time in my life, gave me a smack around my right ear. Waiting a while he then did similar around my left ear. Looking quite stern he said, 'the first clip was for swearing and the second was for showing disrespect to the Salvation Army who had stood by people in their hour of need during World War Two. No one should be rude to anyone when you know nothing about them. It is not becoming of anyone until you know much more about them and then there may be an opportunity for you to help and not be downright rude.'

Some harsh lessons and punishments were rendered, but these life lessons have worked well for me. Never in my working life did I swear to, or at, staff members, or not give them the opportunity to put forward their points of view. That's not to say that sometimes I didn't need to remind people who was boss and what was expected but there's a right way and a wrong way to do that in my experience.

You may be asking about brothers and sisters in such an upbringing. I tell people I was an only child who had two sisters and a brother – a statement that has dumbfounded many. Let me explain. Not long after starting primary school I got home one afternoon to be greeted by Mum who told me she had moved my stuff out of my bedroom. You will be in the spare bed in our room. We have someone staying with us for a few weeks. That someone was then a serving member in the land army – a unit set up to help the country get back on to its feet after the end of World War Two. Anne became a fixture in our home. She eventually married and, along with her husband Ernie, had two children, before Dad stepped in and suggested there was some sort of control put on the birth rate or that they should seek a place of their own. Sister Anne, as we called her, had endured a terrible life before moving to Branston. Along with two brothers and two sisters, they lost their mother to cancer and, when father was finding life difficult, he called all the children into their back garden put a shot gun in his mouth and died by suicide in front of them. Thereafter the family went their separate ways. It says something of the community and caring nature of my mother and father that Sister Anne was able to move on from such a horrendous event.

Not long after getting my bedroom back and beginning to believe I had gained some independence, lo and behold Anne's sister Lucy had moved into the area. She aimed to link up with her sister Anne once more and had begun a nursing career. She soon sought solace in our house with another bedroom shift for me. That wasn't for as long as her sister, but for both of them Dad became their father figure. He was proud to be asked to give each of them away at their respective marriages.

Moving on a year or two I had passed the 11+ exam and became a pupil at Lincoln Grammar School.

Present from Mum & Dad for 11+ success

I rapidly learnt a lesson in as much as my previous excellence at the village primary school counted for nothing when compared with some very intelligent classmates. Struggling to retain the same level of excellence from my primary school days, I very soon reached the conclusion that my aspirations of becoming a doctor were foolish to say the least. I regularly found myself struggling to maintain any sort of self-belief, having to work extremely hard to keep standards as high as possible. Whilst classroom work was challenging, sport seemed to come a little easier, gaining my school colours for football, being a goalkeeper for the U14s, U15s and first eleven and at the same time going on to play for Lincoln Boys.

I've mentioned two sisters but nothing yet of a brother. Soon after starting the Grammar School, I was making my way home after being dropped off at the local bus stop and was surprised to see my mother approaching. On the way back home she conveyed to me that I would be sharing my bedroom with a young boy who Mum and Dad had agreed to provide a home base for. This followed their agreement with the local childcare unit.

Friends then – like brothers now: Me, Keith & pet dog Snip

This was in 1951 and my relationship with Keith was far and above the norm for brothers, and to this day we have never had an argument or fallen out. I am still so grateful to my parents for making my life so different from a single-child family basis.

As a family we did everything together, with the special weekly treat being the trip to Sincil Bank to watch Lincoln City: one week the first team, the following week the reserves – never missed. Dad was an avid football fan and whilst a stalwart at Sincil Bank, always maintained space in his thoughts for Middlesbrough – the Boro were his home-town club. Keith, for probably the first time in his life, was very much a key part of a family, benefiting from parental interests in his well-being and educational development.

11

The 16th March 1954 is a day etched in my memory and one that took me a very long time to overcome. The evening before, Dad spent ages teaching Keith spelling and mental arithmetic, as he often did. My second sister's husband Tom was a lorry driver for the local haulage company and either he or one of his driver mates used to pick Dad up outside the house and transport him into Lincoln to start work at 7.30 a.m. This particular day he was picked up and dropped off, only to be a few minutes late clocking in. Instead of him going to his bench to start work before he qualified for any pay he sat down on a bench next to the clocking in station, opened his daily paper, and collapsed through the paper on to the floor. Unable to be resuscitated he died on the spot

I was at school and, following an announcement from the Headmaster in assembly, I was asked to report to the school office, wondering what I had done wrong. Nothing, but I was told to pick my things up and catch a bus back home as my father had been taken ill. When I arrived home the kitchen was full of relatives, all crying. Not stopping to ask any questions I ran upstairs to see my Dad, only to be followed by Sister Anne and told very gently that Dad had died at work.

Keith that night was terribly upset and was rather concerned that he would have to return into care, for he believed Mum wouldn't or couldn't cope. Following a regular private meeting with his childcare officer his concern was put to Mum with a prompt reply of: 'If it was suitable to give Keith a home, for Mr and Mrs Chester, it is suitable for Mrs Chester.' A total relief all round .

Mother, who lived to the ripe old age of eighty-nine, from this point on, became a rock to the family. She worked every hour God sent, holding down three or four jobs at the same time but always made sure that as a threesome we sat down together for meals and openly discussed what the day had given to each of us. That work ethic was a pleasure to behold and also served as a lesson to both Keith and I, who, within our own workplaces, were always committed and loyal to our employers. Alongside holding down her work commitments, Mum continued to put as many hours as possible into village life. Even up to her being almost eighty she still gave of her time for the benefit of others, running regular weekly events and organising coach trips. It was a real learning curve for me growing up. I was the recipient of many a good hiding but, forgetting the pain and suffering – and believe you me there was some, came through it on the right side and I believe a better person for it. Keith and I shared garden and domestic duties, preparing meals for Mum's return from work. Keith was a stalwart, and I am sure the work he undertook in our garden served him well when he went on to become a qualified horticulturist. Mum's pride and joy was looking at the photo prominently on show in her lounge when Keith was photographed talking to the Queen Mother at the annual Chelsea Flower Show. They were discussing the new varieties of clematis plants, which Keith had been heavily involved in developing whilst in the employment of Pennell & Sons. He is still the best brother I could have had and a very good friend. The best I could do to compete was a picture of me joining Lincoln City. At least at that time I thought football was more important than some flower or two. All I could get at that time from mother was: 'don't they know your name is Richard – you weren't christened Dick. '

Both my parents taught me the importance of community and of assisting others. Mum was involved in virtually every voluntary organisation in the village: Gardeners Association, Oddfellows, caretaker at the reading room, village hall committee, caretaker at the local fire station hall, whist drives, and the OAP Club, to name but a few. In between times, she assisted the local undertaker with the laying out procedures when villagers had passed away. My duty was to help her with anything deemed suitable and to do so before any play times could be enjoyed. That community spirit and involvement also rubbed off on me as, for many years, I became involved in community service. Branston Youth Club was formed during the 1950s, prior to me attaining the permitted age to join, with a local parishioner, Frank Walshaw – a former member of the local Royal Air Force who had settled in the village after marrying a local girl, being the driving force in its formation. It was through his connections with the Royal Air Force that he learned of a former barrack room building at RAF Skellingthorpe being surplus to requirements and available for the Youth Club on the condition that it was dismantled, transported, and re-built by the recipients. The Youth Club had been formed a few years earlier than this date and was accommodated in the old Fire Station buildings based in the car park immediately opposite the Wagon And Horses pub, for which mother was the cleaner and key holder, naturally making her an ideal member of the then newly formed committee. The work needed to secure the new youth club was supervised by Frank Walshaw and included help from members, some of whom had already gained practical work experience in the essential trades. The club went from strength to strength, enjoying a healthy membership and delivering good standards of activities and community involvement. Following the announcement that Frank was going to step down, I had reached an age where, with some advice being passed on by him and a few training sessions offered by the Local Authority, I assumed the role of Youth Leader. It has to be said that the level of training then, compared to the rigorous requirements of today, were poles apart. The Local Authority, once convinced that the new appointee was of a reasonable standard, reliable and prepared to give of their time, was approved with more or less the attitude of 'OK, we think you are the right one get on with it and tick the box for another position suitably filled.'

Branston Youth Club: Winners of Lincoln & District Sunday Football League

It was through the youth club that I had my first direct connection with Lincoln City Football Club. Looking for some sort of different activity in the calendar I wrote to the then manager, Bill Anderson, asking if he would be prepared to bring a few players to meet with the club members and spend an evening with them. To my utter surprise I received a reply simply agreeing and asking for some proposed dates, one of which was ultimately taken up. On their arrival I received him into the clubhouse and thanked him for his willingness to help us out. His response was quite surprising: it was the first time he had ever been approached to attend such an event. He thought potential new club players could benefit, so he would look to expand upon the initiative. The evening was a huge success, even going to demonstrations of ball skills and inviting willing volunteers to step forward and get involved. Turn the clock forward several years and what was included in future community programmes would be not too dissimilar from this evening.

The youth club itself, not registered with the local County Football Association, was not in the first instance able to play in local league football. To provide an activity for members, friendly fixtures were played against teams mainly from within the Lincoln boundaries. Some defeats were experienced – some heavier than others, and some where the mickey was being taken out of us by opposing players, which didn't go down too well. The competitive spirit was already there for all to see. Whilst undertaking the role of youth leader I was also a playing member of both the village football and cricket teams. As a relatively young and inexperienced player, life in the football team required a steely attitude: losing any sort of advantage was always pointed out to you by the senior players in quite industrial language! Comments would be on the lines of playing second fiddle being no bloody good to man or beast and would not give the team a win. If it came to being rough handed – or shall we say downright dirty – in our playing then so be it. We had to win.

Successful Branston Cricket Club team (Dick 3rd from right, middle row)

With the nucleus of the football team forming the foundations of the cricket team the same philosophy prevailed. For many seasons I was the wicket keeper and saw first-hand some of the dangers facing opposing batsman from an opening speed duo, both of whom were capable of much higher standards but who preferred to remain in the presence of their village friends.

As the seasons went on we formed a Sunday league side, both registering and affiliating with the football authorities and very soon becoming one of the teams that everyone was looking to beat. Combined with my duties in running the youth club I commissioned the help of a local character, Kelly Reid, to assist by taking over the football club. This he did with great aplomb securing success after success.

The combination of the standards imposed on me by my parents, and the will to win and team spirit from local participation, I am sure helped me considerably in my later managerial days.

Still involved with the youth club, I also became a member of both Saturday cricket and football committees, local parish councillor, secretary, and treasurer of the local social club and, much later in my life, treasurer, chairman and life vice president of the village bowls club, not forgetting being a founder member of a local Lions Club later on in my life. Community commitment, as displayed to me by mother in particular, is an excellent way of feeling good about yourself. Instead of adopting a selfish streak it can be quite rewarding to offer help and assistance to others. Of course there is always the risk of "let a few do it all for the benefit of the many" – something which will always apply I am sure. In football this left me convinced of the value of supporter groups and the importance of the various roles they play.

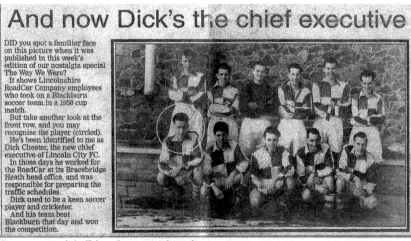

And now Dick's the chief executive

DID you spot a familiar face on this picture when it was published in this week's edition of our nostalgia special The Way We Were?

It shows Lincolnshire RoadCar Company employees who took on a Blackburn soccer team in a 1958 cup match.

But take another look at the front row, and you may recognise the player (circled).

He's been identified to me as Dick Chester, the new chief executive of Lincoln City FC.

In those days he worked for the RoadCar at its Bracebridge Heath head office, and was responsible for preparing the traffic schedules.

Dick used to be a keen soccer player and cricketer.

And his team beat Blackburn that day and won the competition.

Bottom row left. Played as outside right

At Lincoln Grammar School, I did not achieve the level of GCE results that was expected of me. This to a degree was due to long term absence caused by pneumonia after the shock of my father's death. I was invited to return for a further year to re-sit the exams. I politely declined and went out one Friday and secured a job with the local bus company – Lincolnshire Road Car – then started on the Monday as a trainee traffic schedules clerk. I progressed quite well and was invited to take some trade-related industry studies aimed at potential promotion opportunities, at what would have been a relatively young age. The company, though,

16

were in the grips of the National Union of Railwaymen, and in my early days of employment I had failed to see the benefits of union membership, ultimately withdrawing and deciding to move into pastures new. Each to their own I say!

Whilst with the Lincolnshire Road Car Company I had the opportunity to play football for them in the National Cadwallader Cup – a competition for national coach companies to enter. It was a successful venture, winning the two-leg final away to Southampton in the late season of 1958.

It was at the semi-final stage where my life could have gone in a different direction in football. At home in the first leg against Blackburn Transport I played in goal – a position not unfamiliar to me as I had previously earned my school colours playing in that position. The usual goalkeeper, who also played for my village side was a former semi-professional. This meant I was usually moved to an up-field position. He, though, was injured so I was selected to play in the number one berth. I had a very good game in the first leg and was complimented on my performance by one of the visiting officials. For the away leg I played in goal once more and had an even better game in atrocious conditions – so bad that I didn't even take my kit or boots off before jumping into the communal bath! After the game the teams were hosted in their social club where I was introduced to a Blackburn Rovers scout who had been alerted to watch the game. The essence of the conversation was to invite me to Blackburn Rovers for a trial and to be placed under the personal tutorage of the then England International goalkeeper, Colin McDonald. Not long after the chat I was approached by a very attractive bus conductress who promised me a good time if I chose to accept the offer on the table. Dick Chester, then, was very shy, naïve, and very much a home-bird and so declined both the trial and everything else on offer. What if?

My career path then took me to a privately owned group of companies where I graduated through both the accounting/management and sales roles. It was at this time that I married and became the proud father to two children: daughter Nicola, born in 1965, and son Mostyn born in 1967. Mostyn had health problems from birth, spending the first twelve months of his life in Great Ormond Street Children's Hospital before eventually being discharged after his first birthday. At that stage he weighed the equivalent to his birth weight. I like to think that I was brought up to recognise family values and respect for others and whilst I like to spend time with my family, I sincerely hope that they have enjoyed my love and affection and hopefully may have picked up on at least some of my principles

17

I subsequently moved on to work for a national organisation, Fisons Ltd. Here my management skills were developed further, along with the advantage of viewing life in a Stock Exchange-quoted company. At this time Lord Beeching was busying himself with the decimation of the rail industry and Lord Netherthorpe decided to follow suit with Fisons Limited. Splitting it into lesser units and the sell-off of departments deemed to be outside the scope of their newfound policies was the aim. That decision resulted in their drainage division being sold to their appointed employee representative who in turn persuaded me to join him as the senior administrator. This was handy for me as the base was less than 100 yards from my then home.

Sport was a large part of my youth. Football and cricket for the local Branston village team, who at that time were known for their competitiveness, if that's what you want to call it. Others might say steeped in bad sportsmanship but, whatever it was, winning was the key. Branston village football and cricket achieved an impressive array of league and cup titles. Games in both sports were fiercely competitive, or, as opponents would say: 'not played in the true spirit of the game.' With not a single member in either of the squads satisfied with second place, it always needed to be the top slot. I think some of that rubbed off on me in later years. After my time in football had lapsed I took up playing flat green lawn bowls, again played for my village side, ultimately becoming Chairman and now a Life Vice President of my 'home' Branston Village Club. However, along that path, and like other sports I had participated in, I also moved into the area of officialdom and passed all the appropriate exams to qualify as an English Bowling Federation Instructor. The badge, when awarded, was attached to a formal letter with some handwritten personal comments.

On top of that I qualified as a cricket umpire and as a football referee with both of the Lincoln Associations. The examination process for the refereeing was fairly straightforward. Attending weekly sessions held in the Black Swan pub (more commonly called in those days the Mucky Duck) it was essential to learn the laws of the game and their differing interpretations, all aided by drawing board examples. This was all to be completed over a few weeks. The advice then rendered by my particular tutor was: 'when you sit your test, answer the questions with 90% laws of the game and 10% common sense, and when you pass, which I am sure you will do, referee your first game using 90% common sense and 10% laws of the game, as it will be only on rare occasions that you have to bring into play the fine detail of the laws.' (In today's game, in my opinion, that has been lost by the reliance on the recently introduced VAR system.)

Thereafter, all that was needed was a successful final examination and interview by the leading representatives of the Referees Association and the Lincolnshire Football Association. In turn I was called to face the panel where it was confirmed that I had attained a good pass rating, following which the Chairman said: 'Well, it's not going to serve much of a purpose to question you on the laws of the game because as a player you must have committed every possible infringement so just accept this pass mark and enjoy your days as a referee!'

Starting at the bottom of the system with youth football then provided the pathway through Class Two to the ultimate Class One qualification. This provided opportunities to officiate at the highest level operated by the Lincolnshire Football Association and at that time made me eligible to officiate within the Northern Premier League. I officiated in the highest rated Lincolnshire League, was an appointed linesman for a Lincoln City friendly pre-season fixture and once was called upon to stand in as a linesman in a Northern Premier League match – Northwich Victoria versus South Liverpool. I had travelled over with a Lincoln colleague who had been ill for some time but thought he would be OK for the game. I was asked to take all my kit with me just in case. Travelling across it became quite obvious that he was not going to be fit enough, so on arrival he went to the officials' dressing room and came back to collect me saying I was to take his place. The referee for that game was none other than Keith Hackett. Keith went on to secure a first-class career and garnered much respect throughout his profession. The game went ahead without anything much to report but from Keith's pre-match and half-time talks it was clear he was a master at work and recognised that the match could only be sensibly managed by all three qualified referees working together. 'It is not all about the man in the middle – we are a team.'

Away from football, and to help supplement the family income, I spent evenings doing private accountancy work, leading me into the area of business/private taxation. This also helped me hone my skills and knowledge of an area which had previously been a weakness. Through one of those part-time jobs I renewed a relationship with an accountant who, apart from helping me free gratis with any tax advice, turned out to be the appointed auditor for Lincoln City Football Club. My life was soon to change dramatically.

His connection with Lincoln City was enough to get me an interview with a director, Heneage Dove, and their General Manager, Roy Chapman for the post of Company Secretary. I had been advised by my contact that they had received applications from their national advertisement but that none of them were deemed suitable The interview date was set for the same evening as a reserve team fixture at the end of the 1970/71 season. Arriving in time, I was received by Heneage, apologising for the non-attendance of Roy who had been delayed on his return from a London business meeting. He asked me to join him in the directors' box and to watch the game until he arrived. It was well after half-time and into the second half before Roy arrived, by which time I was perished through, and losing a lot of interest. At long last the interview started and for the first time in my life I really wasn't bothered about the outcome. I was instead delighted to have the chance to ask supporter-type questions, bearing in mind that the club weren't pulling up many trees. Courtesies exchanged and questions answered, I returned home, fully in the belief that nothing would come of it. About ten days later whilst sat on my own in the office I took a call from Roy. He told me he had board approval to offer me the job and the letter, confirming the same, was in the post. I began to ponder what to do for the best. Whilst I was excited by the prospect, I was conscious that I would be letting my new employer down badly. I read the offer when it came and, after putting forth some points regarding my recent new property investment in the village of Metheringham, and the fact that I would be required to move into the Lincoln area as a condition of employment, I was offered an improved deal. I accepted and commenced my employment with the club on 24 May 1971. My career in football was about to begin

That career in league football could have been very short lived. Little did I know, but the following Friday I was on the train to London to attend the Football League Annual General Meeting. An item on the agenda was the re-election to the Football League of the following clubs: Lincoln City, Hartlepool, Barrow and Newport County. As it transpired, despite being in a similar position during previous seasons, Lincoln were re-elected. It was a real eye-opener to me that, despite the potentially serious outcome of the vote, the directors in attendance were keener on getting into the Soho way of life the night before than staying behind at the annual dinner to lobby support. Travelling back on the Saturday afternoon, the conversation was more on the lines of 'for goodness sake don't breathe a word to the wives,' than what the new season would have in store and how the club were going to face up to it.

Along with those lessons from childhood this early experience in football taught me one further lesson that stayed with me throughout my career. It is an industry where it is difficult to decipher whether or not someone wants to befriend you because of who you are or what you are, or for privileges that can be gathered out of such relationships. I learned to keep my guard up.

What did I expect to find? That was a question I was asking myself right up to my very first day in work at Sincil Bank. As a "man on the terrace" supporter I had become accustomed to just reading about the club but, more to the point, all the demands, requests and broken promises thrust down our throats by press coverage from the board of directors. It was thought, despite outbursts of supporter opinions, that those at the top were fully in charge and totally in control of all club affairs. From the inside that assumption quickly proved to be a myth, when it quickly became apparent that their management was more or less from the headquarters of their own businesses, with the day-to-day management left to paid employees. Risky, to say the least, when investing personal funds, but, equally, not so much a risk if everything was running to order. Not always the case I may add!

From Lincoln City I moved to Sheffield United at the very end of 1978 and from the Blades I was headhunted and moved across the city to the Owls in 1983. At each club I was company secretary, but with varying areas of responsibility. The closest job title to that at many clubs in recent times would be CEO. The role I performed was one of extreme importance in terms of full compliance with statutory provisions and, if done correctly, was a very lonely existence. It is traditionally not a position that the general supporter is particularly interested in – they are more in tune with managers and chairmen. Most supporters will hope that their club is properly run, under good control and the backroom staff can support the team both in terms of need and development. In my day that is what I always tried to do and at the same time look at ways in which things could be enhanced for both club and supporters. It is a position where it is possible to have great influence on the direction of a football club and to some extent that of wider organisations such as the Football League. Whichever club, I had a job to do. I tried to be fair and equitable to all – not always popular but, I would like to think, always fair.

Writing this now I cannot really believe just how much I feel I have been able to achieve. There are times when I wonder, looking back on my very early days, if it really was me or whether or not I had a long long dream with some really enjoyable memories to reflect upon when waking up! To be honest I really did not know what I was letting myself in for.

Hopefully the foregoing will give an insight into the man who had that job to do, the lessons learned, and the values I held throughout.

The next chapter will show just how difficult times could be at two of my clubs. I needed to use every one of those lessons and hold my values very close to help me, and the clubs, through those times.

CONTRACT FOR CITY SECRETARY DICK CHESTER

LINCOLN CITY FOOTBALL CLUB have given a three-year contract to their 32-year-old secretary Dick Chester, it was announced by chairman Mr. Dennis Bocock today. Mr. Chester joined the club as assistant to the late Mr. Harry Pepper in May of last year.

Former pupil at Lincoln School, and a well-known figure in local sporting circles, Mr. Chester has rapidly established himself as an outstanding Football League administrator, and it is obviously with this in mind that City have engaged him for the next three years.

In announcing the agreement today, Mr. Bocock said the contract had been offered to Mr. Chester "in recognition of his abilities, hard work and determination to succeed in all departments."

Mr. Bocock told me: "As chairman, I would like to thank our secretary for the determined help he has given to the board and to myself since joining us.

HELPED

"No doubt his initiation into football was helped by our late secretary Mr. Pepper. But the Mr. Chester of today

by Maurice Burton

will rank as one of the up-and-coming authorities on all football matters, gaining knowledge daily.

"I am sure that one day he must become one of the leading authorities in his particular sphere. Like our manager, the board of directors and myself, Mr. Chester's eyes are firmly fixed on the progress being made by Lincoln City F.C."

Mr. Chester, married with two children, formerly lived at Alexander-close, Metheringham. He moved into his present home, at North Hykeham, soon after joining Lincoln City.

A mixed City side including amateurs and apprentice professionals was beaten 4-0 by

Tickets were going well and during the summer has been than half the month preparation of a new-look tickets for the match at City programme, supporting Wolverhampton on August 31 had last year's Red Imps already been taken up. Review which went down "Others have said they are well with the fans. going to book up for the trip This will sell at 7s and the on Saturday, and at present City secretary explains that there are fewer than 20 of the increased cost is due to the 52 seats left for the pub- the additional cost of print-lic," said Mr. Chester. ing a 20 page, magazine-type

Much of Mr. Chester's work of programme.

DICK CHESTER . . . given three-year contract by

Starting off my career

Followers of modern-day football will be well aware of the financial difficulties that some clubs find themselves in. Even a casual glance at football-related news over the last few years shows clubs who have struggled to pay the bills, gone into administration, and in one dreadful case been removed from the league altogether. In this chapter I'll show that struggles with money are not only a modern phenomenon. I'll discuss the position I found at my clubs and the steps that were put in place to improve matters. I'll show that there are some commonalities between those steps, and end by relating a few lessons that may be relevant even today.

Lincoln had struggled on the pitch for the previous decade or more. After a double relegation from the old Division Two into Division Four in the early 1960s, the club had bounced around the bottom half of the lowest tier, including occasional re-election campaigns. After 20 or more years on the terraces I felt that all the answers to the verbal abuse thrown at those sat in the directors box could be sorted out quite easily when on the inside. What an absolute load of balderdash and how wrong could I be!

---

2 Year Contract Dick Chester

As reported by Maurice Burton; Sports Editor; Lincolnshire Echo.

Lincoln City Football Club have given a three year contract to their 32 year old secretary, Dick Chester, it was announced by chairman Mr Dennis Bocock today. Mr Chester joined the club as assistant to the late Mr Harry Pepper in May of last year.

Former pupil at Lincoln School, and a well- known figure in the local sporting circles. Mr Chester has rapidly established himself as an outstanding Football League administrator and it is obviously with this in mind that City have engaged him for the next three years.

In announcing the agreement today Mr Bocock said that the contract had been offered to Mr Chester 'in recognition of his abilities hard work and determination to succeed in all departments'.

Mr Bocock told me: 'As Chairman I would like to thank our secretary for his determined help he has given to the board and to myself since joining us. 'No doubt his initiation into football was helped by our late secretary Mr Pepper but the Mr Chester of today will rank as one of the up and coming authorities on all football matters, gaining knowledge daily.

I am sure that one day he must become one of the leading authorities in his particular sphere. Like our manager, the board of directors and myself Mr Chester's eyes are firmly fixed on the progress being made by Lincoln City FC

Chairman's statement to Lincolnshire Echo when announcing the contract award

On appointment, I was immediately introduced to the current Club Secretary, Harry Pepper, who was suffering from a life-threatening illness. The club had decided to appoint someone (me) to work alongside him pending his retirement on medical grounds. After the first day, I was handed the job of opening and dealing with the club's post on the basis that it would give me a quick insight into affairs. What a baptism of fire to life in the 1971 fast lane of how to run a business without paying your bills! It's a small irony that this was to repeat itself some years later when moving up the ladder to one of the bigger clubs. What Harry really meant to say was – 'I'm at my wits end knowing how to deal with all these threatening demands for settlement of outstanding accounts.' There were enough final demand letters to paper the secretary's office walls, but seemingly not enough to worry the directors. The board remained oblivious to the day-to-day problems and demands, with no real detailed management reporting for consideration at their meetings. The immediate need was to get to grips with things and establish a precise understanding of the scale of the problem.

A club heavily in debt, not pulling up any trees on the pitch, not having any apparent management controls in place and no commercial drive wasn't really the right start for an inexperienced operator like me. 'Eh oh, give it a go' seemed to be the saying which fitted the bill. Ironically, again, such affairs within a club would repeat itself when my next appointment came along. At the time of my appointment, Lincoln City was operating to maximum levels on a £20,000 overdraft (today's equivalent being circa £300,000), not a massive amount one would say in today's marketplace but back then one could acquire quite a reasonable new family home for £2,500 to £3,000.

Signing a two year contract

With some initial work under my belt it seemed obvious that positive management controls were needed. A meeting with both the Chairman and General Manager, Roy Chapman, was convened. After about two hours thrashing around most areas of the business it was agreed that I could implement and deliver changes to enforce methods of control and development. Not a simple task for someone lacking in any sort of accountancy qualifications, but hopefully common sense would prevail. That started immediately with the matter of season ticket renewals, where at that time money was being received but no-one could reconcile cash taken to the number of tickets sold. Quite elementary you would think. A system of accountability was introduced. It was necessary to detail someone – me – with that responsibility. The employee previously responsible gave notice, citing that the club was becoming too dictatorial in trivial areas when more attention was needed for "on the field matters." At least that was his explanation at the time although later gossip suggested it was more related to the cash from season ticket sales. This first "dipping your toe in the water" experience quickly led to a review of the accounting functions and the need for a better form of monthly controls in the shape of some management accounting functions. Previously I had been on the periphery of such processes but now I was well and truly in at the deep end. In no time at all it was apparent that the part-time wages and accounts clerk was there just to process the functions needed but not to get involved any further. Another transfer of responsibilities inherited by me.

There then followed some late-night candle burning to put together a cash-flow forecast for the forthcoming 1971/72 season. I worked using the simple thought process that the club should only spend on football matters that which it had coming in from match day and other related football income streams. I bet that doesn't happen in today's game! At the same time, commercial income was allocated to cover administration and running costs – I bet that doesn't happen either, although I can imagine owners would relish that outcome. I didn't need to be Einstein to see that nothing really worked. Everywhere or everything I looked at needed time, management, and some clear thinking to try and give the club a chance. Believe you me, it needed a few cages to be rattled and changes made. These ultimately followed, although as a relatively new senior, but inexperienced manager, I found some discomfort in administering them. However, I never let my worries detract from my responsibilities.

One area of control which was of personal interest to me was the distribution of the club's allocation of cup final tickets, made available via the Football Association. The reason I say 'of personal interest' was that my father used to enter every possible sweepstake or raffle to secure for my mother and himself two cup final tickets, just to be able to soak up the atmosphere. Here I was, given the responsibility of dealing with our allocation, with an open offer from the board of directors to include myself for any two tickets of my choosing – paid for, of course. It gave me the greatest pleasure to hand these over to my mother and then wife to enjoy their day out together whilst I had the kids for the day. What struck me was how much those tickets were enjoyed, what memories it brought back to me of my father, and just how much the same allocation to a true supporter would have meant for them given the chance. After that I used to take up my annual allocation and, on several occasions, pass them on to supporters who I felt were deserving causes. Another lesson delivered from my early days of growing up and respecting others.

The major area for concern was the deplorable situation with both bankers and creditors. Following the annual change of chairmanship in 1972, Dennis Bocock was now at the helm and there were soon to be some significant improvements. It became clear that he wanted meaningful up-to-date reports and regular weekly discussions on a one-to-one basis at his home in Bracebridge Heath. In one of our earliest meetings I persuaded him to take the initiative and seek a change of bank, taking the club's business to the one used for his own business. His exceptional relationships with them would provide confidence to the bank and aid the club, as they would realise the true value of his bank guarantees already held by the club. Welcome on-board Barclays and some breathing space.

With that breathing space, thanks to the chairman, and time to consider new internal controls I took it upon myself to telephone everyone who was owed money by the club. I explained that the club would pay off the debt, but it would be in staged payments, as and when funds were available, and that I would personally keep in touch with them to advise. Alternatively, to help both the club and themselves, they could enter into some sort of amicable arrangement with the club. The idea was that they would take out suitable commercial arrangements with the club and defray the outstanding balance on their accounts or pay any surplus to the club. This would help the club and reduce the risk of a re-occurrence. The reactions were unbelievable. In the first instance they appreciated the honesty and open lines for them to communicate and secondly the surge in advertising and sponsorship support was very positive indeed. Another practice and lesson learned that I would use again later in my career.

This improvement to the commercial side of the club was also important in keeping costs in check. One area of expenditure which previously tended to run away with itself was hotel and travel costs. This included the hiring of a team coach to transport the team to all of its away games and also the cost of hotel accommodation and meals, either as a day trip or an overnight stay. At the time of my joining, the club had always used Hudson's Coaches, largely due to the business connection between Charles Warner and that company. In my mind there needed to be a fresh approach, so, during the close season, competitive tendering was a priority, following which a new and improved contract was secured. A similar tendering process was adopted with the major UK hotel groups. Again, not only were improved deals secured, but all of our hotel reservations were handled by their head office personnel. This meant that the club no longer needed to search through all of the options in advance.

This saved money, time, and effort. It provided positive outcomes and a system which I used later on at the Lane and Hillsborough.

My time at Lincoln City coincided with improved performances on the pitch – not my doing I may add! The team improved from perennial relegation battlers to mid-table and even a push for promotion. This helped build an awareness within the working community of the importance a national football league club in the City of Lincoln. With this came the opportunity of enhancing commercial involvement in the club and a general desire for businesses to become associated with the club. The final piece of the jigsaw in developing the club was the revamping of the board of directors. Heneage Dove was not enjoying his days as just a member of the board; having had a period as chairman to whet his appetite he decided he needed to make some changes on the board. He had manoeuvred to a position whereby he was able to force the withdrawal of existing members. The missing piece in his jigsaw was to appoint alternative members to fill the gaps. His approach to me was one of seeking advice and recommendations for suitable prospective members, based on the knowledge gained from the new and wider marketing network that I had been able to create. Following my recommendations, a board reshuffle was finalised with Harold Sills, Alan Davey, Reg Brealey, Dennis Houlston, and Gilbert Blades all taking their seats around the boardroom table. The reshuffle saw the departure of previous long serving director: Charles Warner, Roy Chapman, and George Cook. More later around the machinations that led to this.

The new board brought about new investment and a positive approach. This was aimed solely at success and open support for the manager to secure the best possible tools for the trade. Rather than rotating the chairman each year, the new board opted to change the vice-chairman annually. The first appointment to that role was Reg Brealey. It soon became evident that his aims and objectives were targeted towards progress. At the same time, the Chairman made a press statement on 11 December 1975 via the *Lincolnshire Echo* lauding the fact that the club had now cleared their £40,000 overdraft at the bank and at long last were free of debt. So, a new board, a chairman and vice-chairman looking positively to the future and improved financial circumstances. It certainly seemed that things were looking up at Sincil Bank.

Unfortunately, for the club and its supporters, after a time of tasting success it didn't quite turn out that way. More as to why later on. So what had I learned from my experience at Sincil Bank? A grounding for which I will always be grateful, but I can't help but mull over the 'what might have been' had the set-up not been so agonisingly destroyed by the then chairman's apparent insecurity and obsession.

Before that, let me explain how I believe a football club should run. In very simple terms a football club is a business and should work in a none too dissimilar way to any other business. All businesses have mainstream incomes whether it be the sale of professional services, or tins of beans from a corner shop. Football's mainstream income is from season tickets, match day takings, levies paid out by the Footballing Authorities (including what used to be pools income but more recently major TV shares). In terms of internal management processes I always had the aim that this income should be sufficient to cover footballers wages/salaries, management staff costs and training costs.

A second level of income can also be derived from the football business – that being: commercial, marketing, sponsorship, advertising, licensing rights, hospitality and voluntary bodies' activities. Again in terms of internal management I always aimed for this source of income to cover all administrative functions – admin salaries, office supplies, repairs, both ground and general, light, heat and telephone, travel and motor costs, rates, bank charges, together with other general items of expenditure.

For the greatest part, these principles seemed to work at Lincoln. All of this could be upset considerably though by transfer fees, which, in Graham Taylor's time, were quite expensive for a Fourth Division club. In this case they were well supported by directors' loans and investments. This at times forms a third level of income for a club.

All of these practices should come together and reflect in an annual profit. If only it was that simple! Poor results, bad weather, lower crowds than forecast, need for change of players all come into play but with a football club, on most occasions, all countered by added bank support.

All of the above, apart from the banking issue, is virtually no different to general commercial businesses. Of course other businesses have competition from similar local and national enterprises to contend with. In football, often there is only one club in any given town or city and where the fanbase have been indoctrinated through previous generations to support 'their' club as if it was God-given! Businesses in general need to ensure quality of both product and customer service. In football it is not uncommon for boards of directors to feel that they have the divine right to treat supporters poorly with little or no regard to the quality of service or results they are offering at that time. Welcome on-board Dick to Lincoln City Football Club 1971, and Sheffield United Football Club 1978.

I was pleased with the progress made at Lincoln City. From Graham Taylor's first full season of 1973/74 through to his leaving, there was an average increase in football income of almost £21,000 per season. Offset against that was an increase in football salaries of £6,250 per season.

Transfer dealings accounted for a shortfall of £65,000, which in turn was balanced by the investment of £50,000. Commercial revenue had shown significant increases, producing a 398% increase from my first season through to my leaving. All of which combined to provide a healthy outcome, leaving the club with a healthy balance in hand and investments on the London Money Market. Overall, therefore, I felt I left having achieved some positive outcomes.

Sheffield United was the next club on my football journey. My route to Bramall Lane was one where my past connections with footballing people stood me in good stead. During my earlier days at Sincil Bank we had a referee, named Keith Walker, to officiate at one of our home games. One practice I insisted upon was that the club needed to properly recognise the presence of the match officials. So instead of shutting them in a small pokey room and forgetting them, they were regarded as important to our club and afforded equal hospitality facilities. Part of that was down to me and for each game I made sure that I spent sufficient time with them to ensure they were comfortable. On one such occasion Keith Walker arrived rather earlier than expected which afforded me some time to spend with him. He stated that he wished he had a job in football like mine and wondered if he ever fulfilled that ambition would I help him if he were to ask?

Sometime after, I took a call from reception saying that they had a Mr Walker on the line who wanted to speak with me. When put through it transpired that he was already in the hot seat at Bramall Lane. He needed the help which I had indicated I would give him and which I duly provided. To say it was a regular occurrence was an understatement, as it seemed at times that I was already working for the Blades! That friendship proved extremely valuable to me as, when Keith was appointed as Lead Referee Officer for the North American Soccer League, he called to ask if I would be interested in meeting his chairman with a view to succeeding him at the Lane. That interview was arranged with John Hassall at his Castleton home. John immediately asked if I had any experience in handling debt and creditor problems. My answer was in the affirmative, but little did I know then what he meant by that question. We exchanged pleasantries, shared a cuppa or two and I enjoyed some good home-baking before heading back to Lincoln through the snow and difficult road conditions over the top after leaving Hathersage. A real baptism of fire into the Derbyshire weather! My appointment was ratified by the board of directors at their next meeting some two days later. I was warmly welcomed by the directors: Albert Bramall, Bert Jackson, Prof Frank O'Gorman, Alan Laver, Ken Lee, and Dick Wragg and was assured of their support.

Before taking up office, and after shaking hands with the chairman and directors, I arrived home and took a call from a colleague called Eddie Plumley who had just left Leicester City to join up with Graham Taylor at Watford. Eddie asked that I ring his ex-Chairman, Mr Sharpe, as his old position at Leicester City was being held open for me. I duly telephoned and when offered the position I asked if he would speak with John Hassall and explain the circumstances surrounding the nature of the call but was told that that would have to be done by myself. Having shaken hands and agreed to work for the Blades I was not the sort of person to go back on my word and I remained happy to honour our agreement. Sheffield United with their huge debt and declining results on the pitch would be my new working home.

The formal contract was completed on 5 January 1981 and confirmed a starting salary of £15,000 per annum with provisions for the supply of a company car, telephone and recovery of expenses wholly and necessarily incurred in the performance of duties. There was a further clause which restricted me from indulging myself in any other business and requiring me to devote the whole of my time to promote the interests and welfare of the company. The hours I was to embark upon took care of me having any time available for anything else with an average workload of between seventy and eighty hours per week – a repeat of my Sincil Bank days.

At Lincoln City I managed a situation where the club was up to its limit in terms of bank borrowings and creditors were screaming for settlement. Over time, the work that I and others completed was instrumental in overseeing a positive transformation. At Sheffield United I was faced with precisely the same issues, but the numbers were far different. The first bank statements I opened, between the differing accounts held at National Westminster Bank, Sheffield, showed an overdraft just short of one million pounds. At that time I think I was struggling to realise how many noughts there were in a million, let alone how to tackle it!

If you were to talk about action replays then my early days at Sheffield United at the end of 1978 were an identical scenario to that at Lincoln City but this time with a larger and more respected club in a much bigger city. I had moved from a club with a catchment area of some 60,000 to one where you could add a nought and take that to 600,000. Sheffield United were higher up the league ladder than Lincoln but were struggling. Relegated from Division One in 1976 the club would fall as far as Division Four in 1981 before beginning a steady climb back up the leagues in the 1980s.

It was evident from the first staff meeting that they had found things quite tough but like all "Unitedites" they were clearly committed to their tasks. The fundamental need for me was to get my feet under the desk, fully appraise the situation and then get to work. With a staff of eighteen to run the office, commercial/lottery office, ground and maintenance staff, laundry and social club it was always going to be 'all hands to the wheel'.

As with my earlier days at Sincil Bank there was a need for enhanced financial controls and careful monthly management, followed by direct reporting to the board of directors. It would be fair to say that John Hassall was extremely hands-on. He visited on a daily basis, was fully appraised of the financial problems but he did not necessarily have the detailed information he needed to fully and precisely present to the board of directors. Along with Geoff Smith, who sometime in the future was to assume full responsibility, we devised a really tight budget where each item of expenditure was closely monitored. I can honestly say that that particular policy worked extremely well until it came to the playing side of the business where it seemed there was always a good reason to spend money! The essential early work and responsibility was to get to grips with the scale of the problem and then put some management controls in place.

The severity of the position became clear early on, when the chairman, John Hassall, and I were summoned to visit the Inland Revenue to discuss the issue relating to non-payment of our monthly dues from salary deductions taken for tax and national insurance liabilities. The tone of the meeting started off in a very frosty manner but given the opportunity, I, as the new man on the block, was able to provide a fair and reasonable report of the magnitude of the club's financial position. The response was quite encouraging as she was prepared to be patient. As long as the club paid its current payments when they were due she would allow the backlog to be paid off on a 'drip basis'. Leaving the meeting both of us breathed a sigh of relief and were ready to report to the board of directors at their regular board meeting that afternoon.

The process adopted for board meetings was that the first item on the agenda would be the manager's report and once delivered the manager was excused and free to leave the meeting. In this instance Harry Haslam, the then manager, had negotiated a deal to sign Les Tibbott from Ipswich Town, with that being the first item on his agenda. In those days the Club Secretary was not permitted to talk on football matters, but I sat there thinking 'Harry you've got no chance after the grilling we had been subjected to by The Revenue'. As discussions developed I was becoming somewhat bewildered, believing that the deal was going to get the OK from the directors. The chairman had not yet advised the directors of the Inland Revenue meeting. I was thinking and worrying that Harry was going to get the vote to go ahead without the directors knowing the full state of affairs.

Before the decision was put to the vote I asked the chairman if I could just ask the manager one question which was: 'how can you equate the value of this asset to the club's balance sheet assets. What will he provide to the team and what figure would you put on his future valuation?' 'Mr Chairman', Harry said, 'I have been in football for almost forty years, and I've never heard such a load of bollocks in my career.' He was asked to elaborate more on his proposal which he tried to do without being at all convincing, but the decision to complete went ahead. At the end of the meeting I spoke with the Chairman in the privacy of my office suggesting that when this hit the press tonight the first call in the morning would be from the Inland Revenue. Sure enough it was. I provided the caller with the chairman's business number, which resulted in quite a dressing down, undoing all the ground we had achieved. From that moment onwards we were on their "watch list." We dared not step out of line.

Working on the pretence that it may have some benefits I took it upon myself to contact all creditors. Another repeat of my Sincil Bank days. I explained to each the full plight of the club by being upfront and honest and ended by saying, 'please don't ring me. I will ring you as soon as I am able to pay something.' It would be fair to say this was a somewhat more difficult exercise than I had experienced previously, as many that I spoke to were both true Yorkshire Cricket supporters, still unhappy at the removal of cricket from the Lane. Others were also upset that the club was in decline after dropping out of Division One. My advice was again an action replay, suggesting that if the club were to go into administration the chances of getting anything would be very remote indeed. Again similar outcomes were achieved, with thanks received for my contact, honesty – and some element of hope. I suggested to many of the creditors that they could always help us as well as themselves by reducing the outstanding balance by taking up some commercial involvement. The intention being to lift the profile of the club, put to bed the disappointment of losing Bramall Lane as a home ground for Yorkshire County Cricket, and to enhance the club's image. The longer-term plan was to become the leading club in the city – at least off the field.

As with Lincoln, changes at boardroom level were also needed. With the size of the debt, all the internal workings and financial controls which had been put in place earlier were going to be somewhat toothless unless a way could be found to inject a substantial intake of fresh investment.

The financial controls saw every single area of income and expenditure assessed prior to the start of every season and then closely monitored against actual transactions on a week-by-week basis. Every purchase was subjected to competitive tendering and monthly reports submitted to the directors. We cut costs, virtually all around. For example, for away trips, hotel chains were quite insular with their national or group rates. I managed to develop close working relationships in this industry. In one instance for an away game to Bournemouth, the group waived all charges for the rooms. With the best will in the world the only area where controls were variable was within the actual playing of the game – the club's prime activity. A good run of results would make controls far easier. In contrast, and what occurred more often than not in my early days at the Lane, was the complete opposite – disappointing performances, poor results, and declining attendances. This would all lead to reduced match day income and my job becoming that bit more difficult.

On top of this, the club were relentlessly paying substantial amounts of income to fund the Nat West Bank's demanding terms for the club's overdraft and loans. The carefully controlled monthly expenditure was bearing very little substantial fruit on the branches. It seemed to me, therefore, that major investment in the club was the only option. At this time John Hassall extended an invitation, at my instigation, to host Reg Brealey in the directors' lounge. Reg duly accepted. He returned once more to my total surprise. The first I was aware of his return was when his name cropped up when allocating match day visitor passes. He was to be the chairman's guest in the directors' box. This time, after the game had finished, the two of them spent a good deal of time in conversation. The outcome was me taking a phone call from Reg the following Monday, advising me that he had been invited to join the board. He had the chairman's authority to ask me to arrange for Harry Haslam, Derek Dooley, and myself to be available for a meeting to go over things before making his decision. That took place, seemed to go OK, and was followed with an evening call at home, asking me to provide a paper for him on what I visualised to be the best route forward. The salient points of that report included: the need for major investment but not in the form of loans, the need to complete the outstanding work under the recently completed South Stand to provide enhanced facilities for both players and staff, match day administration, hospitality/catering development, maximisation of the uses of the ground to provide all the year round income rather than just from home games, better policies to recognise the value and importance of the massive supporter base, giving supporters the chance to become closer to the club and to play their part in future community involvement, closer affiliation with local and national press and the need to ensure that the right level of work goes into the acquisition of players rather than the manager signing them from information contained in the then Rothman's Annual Yearbook and without currently viewing them in action. A comprehensive list! I am pleased to say that the paper was taken on board and his approval was given for me to adopt all of the recommendations and work alongside him in their implementation.

The outcome was his confirmation to the Chairman that he would be happy to join the board. He duly did and then using the offices of a London based firm of Solicitors – Allen and Overy – introduced and paid for by Reg – the club went ahead with the convening of Special General Meetings to create an additional £1 million pound share issue. This was on a joint and several basis and agreed by all members of the board. A joint and several undertaking is one where the board of directors undertake to buy up any unissued shares once existing shareholders have been given the opportunity to take up their proportionate entitlement. Those resolutions were presented and approved in a General Meeting, but the take up of the offer for each shareholder to retain their equivalent equity stake failed quite miserably. When the directors were called upon to honour their undertaking there was no take up other than Reg. He took up all unsold shares and thereby ultimate control of the club. The directors who declined to contribute to the joint and several undertaking resigned in the days following. Professor Frank O'Gorman, Ken Lee, and Albert Jackson became part of Sheffield United history.

The new chairman and I were soon invited back to see the lady at the Inland Revenue having let some monthly payments slip by, pending a successful outcome of the new share issue. Again emphasis was made of the need for the Revenue to be regarded as a preferential creditor, and the requirement for that to be recognised and honoured by the club. After much deliberation she asked for our proposals, to which the chairman offered a schedule of payments which deep down I knew, if things didn't go well, we would be unable to honour. The look on my face must have resonated with her as she promptly replied, asking for my suggestions which, being more realistic, were made and accepted. The debt was cleared long before the end of the proposed schedule.

Credit has to be expressed to Reg Brealey here, who not only soaked up the unissued shares but also provided funds for the completed works of the ground floor level of the South Stand, the demolition of the pavilion, renovation and re-painting of floodlight pylons and completion of works relating to the car parking facilities. He also provided the funding for subsequent transfer activities prior to and during the promotion year. I think it would be fair to say that had it not been for these huge investments, Sheffield United at that time could so easily have folded. Football is a heavily opinionated business and whilst fans have their own beliefs they should in no way detract from the true value of Reg Brealey's financial contributions. His investment helped rescue the club in the short term, develop the facilities in the medium term, and help drive the club back up the football league ladder. More of Reg later.

From an administrative point of view, it was a Football League regulation that within five working days of a home fixture the club concerned had to provide a completed match day return. This must show both the breakdown of the attendance, both in numerical and financial terms, and set off all match day direct costs. This left a nett day-take, from which cheques were raised to cover both the required levy to the Football League and the visitors' share of the match day receipts. The system we had designed and developed allowed us to complete those transactions well within any imposed time frame. Wanting to impress his counterparts, the chairman asked if it would be possible to complete all relevant checks, agree the gross match day takings, and deliver to him in the hospitality area the cheque for the visiting chairmen to take away with them. This was done and created a standard not previously, and I doubt subsequently, deployed, with the visiting chairman invariably leaving the ground with such comments as: 'Well we're not going home with any points but at least I've got a few quid in my pocket sooner than expected!'

With both Lincoln City and Sheffield United, the methods used were of a very similar format. Both clubs, on a pro-rata basis, were heavily in debt working up to maximum borrowings. In the case of the Blades it was a much bigger problem by virtue of the values concerned. On the one hand the bankers at Lincoln City seemed to be more relaxed about the situation, whilst still being concerned about their security, whilst at Sheffield United the manager at National Westminster, George Street, pressed much harder for a continued reduction in borrowings. The club had arrangements with Securicor to collect match day takings, store overnight and transport into the bank on the next working day. On occasions I would be advised by the then manager that as the receipts were greater than expected and that we had additional fixtures in the following weeks that he had decided to reduce the overdraft facility by whatever sum he saw fit. This situation was completely out of our control, and in my opinion outside of any binding agreement. It resulted in me meeting up with the manager of Yorkshire Bank, the husband of one of my staff members, and with all necessary approvals opened up an account with them purely to receive match day receipts and to use for the benefit of a more flexible working arrangement. It also meant that at the same time we could deal with creditors as promised. After all, the general creditors, many of whom were natural supporters, were, in my opinion, just as important to the club as the appointed bankers. Following the first match where the takings were deposited into the new account, I received a call mid-Monday afternoon from the Nat West manager advising me that they had not yet received any deposited funds via Securicor. After a brief conversation it was left to be followed up the next day. Duly that call took place. When I advised that alternative arrangements had been made with an alternative bank, his response was far from professional or comforting.

Around about the same time I had taken it upon myself to thoroughly check the quarterly charges imposed on the account by the bank. After hours of calculations based on day-by-day payments in, and payments out, I failed to come anywhere near the level of charges imposed. The task was immense – no such things as computers in those days to aid you. It was down to manual calculations per transaction. Consequently I took it a step further and went back over the previous three quarters, thereby making it a review of an annual basis. The end result was constant – absolutely nowhere near the charges imposed. Prior to any season starting, the club endeavoured to sell all of the available programme advertising, ground advertising, player sponsorship and match ball donors. However, for one particular match there was a vacancy for a match ball sponsorship. Luckily for me, I had managed to sell the space to the Area Manager of Nat West Bank.

After the match I asked the Area Manager if he could give me a few minutes of his time, which he kindly did. After about half an hour in the privacy of my office there was a consensus that I had a justifiable basis on which to lodge a complaint, but he needed to spend time on it back at HQ. He agreed to preserve page upon page of my handwritten calculations and took them away with him for their own review. Within a week he came back to me with apologies, confirming it was the first time he had witnessed such detailed accurate calculations, and a credit of some £75,000 plus. At the same time he expressed the value in terms of their own public profile at being associated with such an important client in the City of Sheffield and a profile they wished to uphold. It came as no surprise that shortly afterwards there were some managerial changes at Nat West, George Street, Sheffield 1 – with the manager being moved to a less prestigious Nat West Bank.

I think it must have been my days at Bramall Lane when hair loss first began to appear. I am sure the same would apply to many Blades fans witnessing the demise of their club: from Division One down through the ranks to Division Four. Much though was achieved during my days at The Lane – largely through a combination of new investment consolidating the financial position, a promotion season and careful management controls. My time there saw an 82.1% increase in turnover with more than half of that being attributed to a growth in commercial income, a reduction in borrowings of 41.3%, with creditors now enjoying normal trading terms with the club. Overall a satisfactory outcome, highlighting a combined commitment throughout the Club. I have said numerous times that no one person could justifiably take all the accolades. These achievements were as a result of total commitment from all departments and the massive supporter contributions. Much to be proud of! I'll return to my relationship with Reg later on, along with the circumstances of me leaving Bramall Lane.

Jason Dickinson's 'Sheffield Wednesday: The Complete Record' includes coverage of my moving to Hillsborough in 1983 as follows:

"Already well-known in professional soccer and a familiar figure on the local football scene. He mastered the techniques of football administration in seven years as Secretary/Commercial Manager at Lincoln City FC, and then joined Sheffield United as Secretary in 1979. In fact he was just embarking on a career as a football consultant when the opportunity arose to join Wednesday. It is of interest to note that Dick

Chester is not only unique in having been Secretary of both Sheffield clubs, but can claim a special place in the record books as being with both city clubs at different stages in Sheffield's double promotion season of 1983/84."

They are very kind words. I am not sure if anyone ever truly masters the job of club secretary. Joining the Owls saw my work move in different footballing circles than before. The role at Sheffield Wednesday might at first glance appear to have involved a very different job to the one I undertook for the Imps and the Blades. Wednesday were in a strong financial position, having turned the losses of the mid-70s into profits by the end of the decade. Turnover was also up, along with home match attendances. Those fans were watching a team on the up. Jack Charlton as manager had returned the team to Division Two in 1980. At the time of my joining at the very end of 1983, Howard Wilkinson's team were well on the way to returning to Division One for the first time since 1970. Time at my previous clubs had largely been devoted to elements of serious financial positions, whereas I was aware through press coverage and mutual associations between each club's hierarchy that Wednesday had been in a not too dissimilar position years earlier and had turned things around.

Tony Pritchett reported in a lead story in *The Star* in April 1982 how the two club's fortunes had been mirrored in an article headed "The Haves and the Have Nots." In that article he had compared the latest two balance sheets for each club highlighting the Blades sizeable borrowings whilst the Owls showed healthy bank balances. Prior to the building of the new stand at Bramall Lane, it was seemingly the opposite with the Blades having reserves and the Owls showing hefty borrowings and having increased overdraft facilities turned down: a function that both Sheffield clubs used at this time.

Football clubs in the early 1980s collectively owed the banks £160million with the Blades probably owing as much as many First Division clubs, whilst the Owls were one of the strongest ten clubs in the Football League in terms of financial stability. The contents of the article in *The Star* highlight the fickleness of the industry and how things can change. I have always said that once the ball starts rolling in any particular direction it is difficult to stop. At Lincoln City, for instance, had the chairman been more positive towards potential promotions the ball was still rolling that way with Graham Taylor at the helm and delivering results on the pitch. That didn't happen; important staff members left, and the direction of the ball suddenly changed to downhill with no one able to stop it rolling until it hit rock bottom and out of the Football League.

My job at Hillsborough was both similar and different to those I'd held before. My work involved building a club, ready and able to challenge in Division One. Of course day-to-day essential financial control could never be overlooked. The longer-term aim was for the club to become a powerhouse in that top league. Different therefore to my previous clubs. The methods I used that I felt were strategic, logical, practical and fair, were broadly similar to those I'd used before. I have always been one to learn lessons from my life and work. We'll also see how my childhood lessons influenced me in my work at Hillsborough. Wednesday, I was always told by Owls directors visiting the Lane, was the place to be and I always held in the highest esteem the management and foresight of Eric Taylor, a true visionary.

Looking down on the task in hand with Eric England

Before I relate the internal affairs of Sheffield Wednesday let me start by clearing the air as to how I finished up being the only person to have served both clubs in a two club city as a Chief Executive Officer – that is the current name for the position I held. Once I departed from The Lane I had established myself in a football consultancy role. Having dealt with indebtedness and general lethargies in supporter recognition, I believed I could offer some positive direction to those clubs based in the lower levels of the football system who had become largely dependent upon the investment of loans by any local entrepreneur interested in maintaining

39

the status of his local club. I aimed to share some of the experiences and methods of resolving the many problems likely to be encountered.

On a rare day off I was busy bringing up to scratch a plot of land acquired at the bottom of my existing property. I was hoping to create a self-sufficient vegetable garden and greenhouse to cultivate a few plants. With a degree of sweat swilling around I took a break for a much-earned cuppa only to take a telephone call. The voice at the other end said, 'Hi there, Dick, Cliff Woodward, here.' Now football was a right place for take offs and mimicry. So somewhat on my guard I was quizzical about a Wednesday director ringing me at home when I had nothing to do with a club at that time. I replied by saying, 'Oh yes, now please tell me exactly who it is, as I've got a bleeding big plot of garden to attend to!' The reply came back, 'I've told you it's Cliff Woodward. If you don't believe me you have my home telephone number from your time at Bramall Lane, ring me back and you'll know it's me when I answer.' I duly did and his response was, 'Now do you bloody believe me!' After I apologised, he came straight out with: 'Now then, what about you coming to work for us at Hillsborough?'

The offer was a total surprise, I must say, for, having had a good working relationship with their then secretary, Eric England, I had no inclination that he had left. In fact he hadn't – he just wanted to retire, not fancying the demands of life in the old Division One. This was a situation looking more and more likely to happen that season. I was briefly lost for words until Mr Woodward jumped in and asked whether I would be prepared to meet the chairman, Mr Bert McGee, to talk things over. Whilst involved at The Lane I had been accustomed to boasts of how well managed and organised they were and immediately felt it was worth a fact-finding meeting. I asked if he had any idea when such a meeting would be convened. The reply was instant: 'Yes, this evening at the Chairman's home address in Brincliffe, Sheffield.' Not often it happens but, somewhat lost for words, I said, 'OK, let me know the time,' which he already had up his sleeve.

Later that evening I visited the chairman at 7.00 p.m, when I learnt of Eric England's departure. After over 40 years of loyal service he would get a pay-off once a replacement could be found. It transpired that whilst this had been going on, my resignation from Sheffield United had been announced. This instantly prompted the chairman to put my name at the top of his wish list. During the interview he said that he was absolutely fed up with being the biggest club in Sheffield and yet being outdone completely by press coverage from the other side of the city. He went on to say that he had no need to seek references as the Hillsborough directors were all in unison. If he could secure my services I would be welcomed on-board, as they had already spoken to serving members of the Blades board and had received their unequivocal assurances. There was very little time taken to finalise terms and conditions. A major part of the meeting became the requirement for me to be in full charge of all areas of the business other than the usual responsibilities associated with the training and playing elements. Player's transfers, contractual terms and conditions would be finalised through both the chairman's and my own direct involvement.

It was requested that this agreement to my appointment should remain totally private and confidential until such a time as I was introduced to the staff. Arrangements were made for me to visit Hillsborough. When I arrived at reception, I was to ask for the chairman and Mr McGee would be there waiting to greet me. This was followed through and both of us made our way to Eric's office where there was quite a quizzical look on his face when we entered. Without any delay the chairman simply said, 'Meet your successor Eric.' The look on Eric's face was one of utter bewilderment. After a relatively short chat the chairman made his exit and left Eric and I to talk things over. I gave assurances to Eric that I was more than happy to be at his side, to try to pick up the ropes and for him, in his own time, to introduce me to his appointed staff.

I agreed to report for work 48 hours later, giving him some time to reflect and giving myself some time to advise my consultancy clients of my change of circumstances. Each one was fully understanding , endorsed my decision, and was happy to carry on their dealings on a short-term, part-time basis as and when needed. Eric ensured that I was properly introduced to all of the staff, although those included in the commercial office were omitted, as his duties excluded any direct involvement with them, although that would now change with my appointment. Separately, therefore, I took myself off to meet the then commercial manager, Dennis Woodhead who sat me down for quite a long time opening up with quite a blunt introduction. 'Thank the f—k you have joined us. At least it will keep the chairman off my f'ing back every time he picks up *The Star* and reads of the happenings at the Lane. He's a right pain in the arse for me!' Whilst I couldn't concur with those comments it did lay down some markers for me to pick up on. Firstly, it re-affirmed that the planned publicity campaign emanating from my stay at The Lane had worked. Secondly, it left me worried that there was a real problem looming for me, with Dennis being content to drift along and not wanting his feathers ruffled. Luckily the latter did not apply, and he was quite willing to go along with changes although he also was approaching retirement. He had given good service to the club both as a player and also in his involvement in both the lottery and commercial operations.

During the time working alongside Eric I was introduced to the match day police commander, Supt. Brian Mole, who instantly made reference to the respect I had gained from his counterpart at Bramall Lane and asked how I wished their operations to be organised. My role as company secretary carried full responsibility for crowd control and safety aspects relating to admission and management of crowds. The way in which the police operated was, in my opinion, dependent upon the intelligence gathered and the discipline imposed by the match day commander. I agreed that he had ultimate control over the duties of his officers, but that I wished to have a close working relationship with him. I asked if we could together conduct joint reviews of crowd behaviour and security issues both outside and inside the ground. These operations allowed both of us to observe any event as it unfolded and to be on the spot to take any necessary actions. My first game, whilst Eric was still in situ, was against Cardiff City. On a tour of the inside of the ground we moved up to the top of the terracing overlooking the Leppings Lane turnstiles when we spotted supporters gaining admission into the ground without any exchange of money. The natural reaction of the long arm of the law was to enforce an arrest. Thinking quickly on my feet I asked for him to let things go until such a time as Eric had retired, for I knew he would not want to be involved in any police actions just prior to his retirement. This was accepted and left pending. We both remarked that this was unlikely to be a one-off and that there may be some difficult situations ahead of us. Brian Mole did say it was the first occasion he had had the opportunity of viewing the ground with a club official in attendance and saw benefits from such an arrangement. I had done similar at previous clubs firmly believing that you could not properly perform these duties and responsibilities sitting on your bum in the office or enjoying a pre-match meal in the hospitality areas.

At the end of that first game working alongside Eric, with me having no after-match processes to complete I wandered into the chairman's hospitality room to be confronted by a packed room all congregating around the TV set to wait for the match day results to come through. At this point in time I could say I made two errors. The first was to enquire how Sheffield United had got on – a question which fell onto very stony ground! The second was to sit in a high-backed Victorian chair, the only one not being occupied, which turned out to be the one used solely by the chairman. I was promptly advised what not to sit on the next time I came into the room. Well, at least in words of differing syllables!

Upon assuming full control, my first objective was to meet all of the staff. It seemed there had been some trepidation having a 'Unitedite' in the middle of Wednesday territory. My message was simple. Do the job for which you are paid, treat customers fairly and respectfully, treat your fellow colleagues with respect and above all be aware of the fact that I expect honesty and integrity. If all of that is delivered we will get on fine. Step outside of that and I think you will soon learn who is the boss. Their trepidations, it was explained to me, came from a belief that their jobs would be in jeopardy as I would be bringing Bramall Lane staff with me. Quite taken by surprise I responded by asking them to consider their cumulative knowledge of the Owls and how valuable that would be for me going forward. Those assurances seemed to have the desired effect proven by the fact that not one member from The Lane made the journey across the city. What I found was that football within the city was akin to a religion. You were a stalwart in your belief, and nobody would take that away from you. Your support of either club had often been ingrained in you since early years and that loyalty had probably been passed down through several family generations. Devoted loyal supporters of both Sheffield clubs will, I am sure, question how one person can have their feet in both camps. For me, the employee, I found it not too difficult to recognise who my paymasters were and to dedicate total commitment to the betterment of their affairs, all of which should create supporter advantages. It may of course have been a benefit me moving from outside the city and not coming from the tribal family background of Blade or Owl.

One of the policies of the board at Hillsborough was that each director should have a responsibility for a separate area of the business. For one director, Matthew Sheppard, it was the accounts function and management. My first meeting with any director was with him and his interest quickly turned to how I had managed the function at the Lane. I immediately keyed into his request and detailed the minute way each area of expenditure was under constant review and how the targets were established for each department. He then went on to deliver what could be summed up as a back-handed compliment. 'That is what one would expect in any business, particularly where there is a loss-making situation to contend with, but, believe you me, you are wasting your time. The simplest and most effective way of managing such affairs is to ensure that the money in the bank is at a constant level and that at all times your debtors are greater than your creditors. That being the case you will always produce a healthy balance sheet at the end of each year.' That was another lesson for me which I must confess I carried with me in my later business life. Having said all of that there was always the risk that some malpractices could go by undetected. A little more of that to follow.

Before I got too ingrained in the detailed management of what was clearly going to be a Division One club, I approached my counterpart at

Liverpool FC, Peter Robinson. Peter had previously been in a similar position with Scunthorpe United, meaning both of us had come from similar backgrounds. I wanted to ask if he would pass on to me some of his knowledge, bearing in mind he was with one of the top six clubs in the country. During a meeting with him and his chairman, John Smith, he talked me through the workings of a successful club, together with supporter demands taking up almost half a day of his time. I had arrived at lunchtime, enjoyed some hospitality, and eventually arrived back in Sheffield late the same evening. My views at the time were quite simple. If you are going to compete with the best, then, if they are willing, I should try and learn from the best. Certainly Peter Robinson was one of the best, who remained a very close ally throughout my footballing career, along with Ken Friar at Arsenal FC and Jimmy Greenwood at Everton FC.

One of the practices I tried to follow was to be able to do whatever job I expected from each staff member and to actually work alongside the staff and not be isolated in an 'out of reach' office. Joining the Owls when I did meant that, with the team aiming for Division One, there would be several occasions when the demands on the ticket office staff would be considerable. It required a degree of flexibility to allow all selling points to be open throughout a working day to satisfy the expectations of the supporters. After all it was the supporter who paid our wages.

The impression coming out of Hillsborough during my time in football was that, thanks to the respected contribution and forethought of the late Eric Taylor, this was a club on top of its affairs. I first met Eric when he visited Lincoln City in a league game against Sheffield Wednesday very early in my time at Sincil Bank, and after the game he asked if he could spend some time with me to offer his advice. We duly met after the game, whilst the rest of the directors were enjoying the hospitality of the boardroom. He opened up by saying he had heard on the infamous football gossip train good reports of my abilities and generously spent the next half hour advising me in all areas of responsibilities.

Eric Taylor had often been nicknamed 'Mr Sheffield Wednesday' after managing the club between 1942 and 1958, before moving behind the scenes. His title of 'general manager' does, in my opinion, a disservice to his influence as he redeveloped the stadium including the building of the then world-class North Stand in readiness for the 1966 World Cup. Eric was involved in a near fatal car crash in 1967 and retired in 1974. He was in ill-health and died a few months later at the relatively young age of 62. By my time, nearly a decade had passed since Eric's untimely passing and I must say nothing very much appeared to have been developed and the club was quietly resting on its laurels.

The classic telephone pose: settled in at Hillsborough

Unfortunately, following meetings with each staff member, it became apparent that the club was now not on top of its affairs. A few fingers were pointed in different directions, and I quickly formed the opinion that there needed to be a 'root and branch' review. This was something that was not in my line of thinking the night I shook hands with the chairman. My working arrangements with the chairman, though, were excellent. We held a meeting every Monday lunchtime either in his office at his business or in mine at Hillsborough. Every single thing that he had been privy to was conveyed to me and likewise I to him on the strict understanding that all would remain in total confidence between the two of us and if ever either of us broke that code then the relationship would be terminated. That never happened from the day I joined to the day I left. He told me that he assumed the chairmanship at a time when the club was in debt to the bank and, when seeking some additional overdraft facilities, the bank turned down his guarantees. That hurt and he declared he would never ever be put in that position again, meaning that he was going to adopt strong handed means of managing, both in terms of the club's operations and also with his board of directors.

One concern about the running of the club's operations related to the sale and reconciliation of pre-match ticket sales. On one such occasion, whilst covering for lunchtimes, I cashed up the transactions for what had been a quite busy morning but retained a sum of £200. I left that with the chairman and asked him when he came down to the game on Saturday to bring it with him. We could then jointly review the pre-match ticket sales report from the relevant staff member. Sure enough the report confirmed an exact balance. With the chairman's agreement the staff member was called into my office, handed the £200 and was asked to go back to review, and revise, the said report. The chairman instantly asked for an explanation and advised that an entry would be made on his personnel records and signed by himself.

It would be fair to say that this was one of the areas where in the previously mentioned staff meetings the fingers had been pointed. From then on, all staff engaged in ticket sales ensured they cashed up their own transactions after each session thereby tightening controls. However, that did not put an end to the problem. Thanks to a confidential call one Friday evening from a staff member, it was suggested that when arriving at the ground the next morning, usually before any other staff member on match days, I took a look in a desk drawer where I would find a batch of tickets readily available for distribution as gifts and favours. The tickets were effectively stolen from the club. The Police were informed and instantly the surveillance operation resulted in the employee being called into my office, spoken to by the officer and led away. The chairman took over the disciplinary issues surrounding this incident. As the employee was aware of previous similar misdemeanours by very senior employees before my time with no action taken, the chairman accepted his resignation and agreed that the matter would be closed. Total confidentiality would be retained and the club would decline to complete any subsequent references

The outcome was twofold, in as much as it resulted in some serious staff changes and the bench-mark set for any other member of staff desirous of adopting a sticky fingers practice.

This situation ran in parallel with match day operations. On the occasion of my first home game – 2nd January 1984 – I arranged to address all of the match day stewards and turnstile operators. I knew some from my Bramall Lane days, as they operated at both grounds. I advised them of my way of working and the close links I would have with the police. I also said that if they had any concerns I would be available. My responsibility was the safety, access to and egress from the ground for all spectators, and to ensure that all of us needed to work together. At the same time, all must be aware that all monies paid through the turnstiles belong to the club and any infringement of this simple philosophy would be dealt with accordingly.

Having previously mentioned the instance seen by Chief Supt Brian Mole and me, I spoke with him and assured him that if anything similar occurred I would support him in his actions. There turned out to be a string of incidents culminating in several arrests. Such was the scale of the problem that I was faced with a deputation from my chief steward and fellow operatives – who held responsible positions in Sheffield – in my office offering their help to identify potential offenders. All of these incidents were reported to the chairman on a match-by-match basis and, after one game had finished, my duties and responsibilities completed, I entered into the boardroom hospitality area where I was greeted by the chairman and a round of applause from other directors thanking me for sorting out this problem which they felt had been going on for some considerable time without ever being addressed.

Prior to the chief steward and his staff coming to see me in my office I was beginning to feel that I would be ultimately faced with a deputation from the gatemen threatening to refuse to take up their positions and putting a game in jeopardy. With this in mind I took a call from the chairman one Monday morning saying that our normal meeting would be in my office, but he wanted some time with me beforehand. Upon his arrival he asked me to join him on a trip round the ground. At each suitable point he left me to inspect the toilet blocks. Believing that someone had reported a deficiency in our cleaning I came out of each one saying nothing wrong at all. On our route back to my office I asked him what the purpose of all that was. Quite bluntly he said he would address that when back in the office. We duly arrived and, sitting opposite sides of my desk, he asked if he could advise me of a customary Yorkshire industrial saying. I agreed. He went on to say 'Remember this: you've never made it in management until your name is on the shithouse wall, and I am totally gobsmacked that yours is not on every shithouse wall in this ground. But never mind that, carry on with what you are doing. You have mine and the board's total approval.'

Hillsborough, in my days, had a total of 88 turnstiles, so it was difficult to keep an eye on all at the same time. It was left to the naked eye to spot any problems or issues. It called for a radical re-think. In collaboration with a local Sheffield based company, Phillips Electrical, the combination of my requirements and their IT qualifications allowed us to install a comprehensive computerised gate counting system, which became one of the first such systems in the footballing world. In simple terms the existing turnstile operation, which recorded one admission per turn of the mechanism, was supplemented by the supporter breaking an infra-red beam on entering into the ground, collated by a centrally situated computer system managed by a dedicated member of staff. This verified numbers in attendance and also entries per section of the ground with an alarm system alerting any potential overcrowding. Additionally, a bank of CCTV cameras were installed covering each block of turnstiles, which, after the game, and over the weekend, were viewed for any operatives' misdemeanours. This brought about some very unexpected things. One of which was young kids turning up on the inside of the ground, collecting small bags from turnstile operators and then exiting the ground via a steward-controlled exit gate.

The system proved to be of immense interest to visiting clubs and on several occasions I allocated some time to show visiting chairmen and/or officials these operations with additional business coming the way of the contractors. The basis of this system was the forerunner to existing operations. Of course, technological advances in IT mean that modern systems far exceed that which we installed. In addition to the information and camera operations contained within the central control room, further cameras were installed in my office. A further set of units were installed in the police control box. This made it possible for all to be viewed at all times. With the availability of use of the police radio system I was, at all times, linked into all of their conversations. I cannot recall any one home game when I had occupied my seat in the directors' box and actually saw the kick-off. Without being at all smug, it would be fair to say that there were very few incidents of any serious nature that occurred. However, many of the conversations on the police system were pretty much unrepeatable! On the occasions I was with the match day commander, it was always possible to review any incidents from within the police box located between the Leppings Lane terracing and the main stand. The combined system had been designed to cater for all eventualities, ease control, and make decision making much more definitive.

One of the biggest problems to overcome in terms of supporter admissions is confined to the last period prior to kick off. We took it upon ourselves to monitor the ratio of admissions to ultimate gate attendances and, over a four game period, figures showed that 67% of the crowd entered through the turnstiles in the 20 minutes period prior to kick off. With crowds hovering around the 30 – 35,000 level, the demands at the turnstile gates were considerable. Despite many efforts to incorporate pre-match activities, this failed to reduce the level of demand, a lot of which was down to the supporter having his last drink in his chosen pub and then getting down to Hillsborough. This applied to both home and away supporters and, in the case of the latter, the Leppings Lane end became even more difficult to manage with, on many occasions, the need for police intervention. I will return later to this topic.

My role at Hillsborough, although ostensibly the same as at previous clubs, proved to be somewhat different when it came to essential qualities of control. From totally negative starting points with my previous two clubs, I started at Hillsborough with surplus balance sheets and a team aiming for the highest league status possible. My responsibilities necessitated the control of that positive position but at the same time use those strengths to further develop the club in terms of facilities, commercial development and working alongside the very professional Howard Wilkinson to maximise successes on the field. At the end of my time at Hillsborough the team had secured, and stabilised, their position in Division One, seeing match day revenue increase by 24.76% and, alongside that, commercial income had increased by 55.23%. Combined, it provided the cushion to cater for a 40.86% increase in wages and salaries and sufficient to carry the deficit in player transfers of £177,150.

Off the field of play the club secured the major development of the Kop and significant improvements in catering and hospitality, and enhanced office developments costing in total £944,000, allowing for the sizeable grant secured from the Football Grounds Improvement Trust towards the £1million Kop development. At the start of my reign, the club showed a healthy surplus between assets and liabilities on their balance sheet. However, I am pleased to say that I was privileged to be part of a well-managed and controlled club, able to enhance that balance sheet figure by a further 49.7%. It had proved to be completely different, but completely rewarding, and I can truthfully say that the benefit of working with that board of directors was the best encountered throughout my football career.

The footballing world is a far different place than when I was part of it but the principles remain exactly the same. In my time there was no safety net in terms of passing on the responsibility, no spare capacity within the workforce, and, at all times, there was a strict accountability issue in front of you. It was my responsibility to ensure all areas relating to financial practices, company law, statutory obligations and football regulations met the stringent requirements of the various regulators. Furthermore, it was my intention to think outside the box as regards football trends, looking for opportunities to ensure and develop solid marketing and commercial practices. Not in any way, shape, or form did I at any time look for or expect accolades. It was just my job, and a simple fact that someone within the clubs needed to do that bit extra and live up to what was expected from their supporters.

To that end, it would be fair to say that it is doubtful that my working week was less than 70-80 hours per week. The footballing calendar ensured that I worked weekends and many of the statutory bank holidays. Today it is my considered opinion that the football business seems to operate with a volume of staff far in excess of what is fundamentally required. After all, the game hasn't changed in terms of its basic fundamentals: there is a game this Saturday, all arrangements for admission have to be in place to comply with a 3 o'clock kick off, all players have to be correctly registered, and the match officials and, where applicable, television crews installed. At the end of the 90 minutes arrangements need to kick in for safe egress for the supporters. The formalities in terms of required procedures from the authorities must then be completed. That has been the case since football began.

Presentation made by South Yorkshire Police in recognition of my close and effective working arrangements with them

Looking back on my experiences with clubs served in terms of management processes and controls, I can't think that I would have done much differently than I did. I do believe I served them well, gaining but not demanding the respect of all my staff, and just as importantly left clubs in a far healthier position than when I embarked upon my employment with them. Of course my part was very much that of being a careful and thorough administrator, but the main thrust of each turn around was down to the sizeable investment by newly appointed directors and the massive support received from Joe Public, without whom all would be in vain. I have always worked on the belief that a pound saved is worth twice the amount of a pound earned. A club should only spend what you would have done had it been related to your own personal housekeeping. The sums involved in today's football are eye-wateringly huge at the higher levels of the game. It is my opinion that the principles employed at Lincoln and Sheffield all those years ago were sound ones. A football club facing the financial abyss in the 21st century would still find it helpful to adopt the step-by-step approach used back then. As the old adage says: 'the more things change, the more they stay the same.'

Alan Biggs

Don't anyone dare dismiss Dick Chester as old-fashioned or a throwback. Much of what he did as a club administrator - not least as an innovator - should be thrown forward to improve the running of the modern game.

He and others were referred to as "secretaries" back then. Effectively he was much more of a chief executive than many of those now titled with that job. Dick, while preferring a low profile, was also far more available and accountable to the media than the almost invisible, yet immensely powerful, CEOs of today.

I speak from experience of that, having had the pleasure – and it was – of dealing closely with him when he uniquely had spells at both Sheffield clubs in the 1980s. Such was Dick's integrity, he was as trusted at Hillsborough as he had been at Bramall Lane previously.

Beyond that, and most importantly, he is a very nice man with who you can share confidences – in fact, trust with your life.

I wish Dick the success he deserves in shining a light on a little understood aspect of football and on an era which can still teach us lessons for the future.

Chapter Three: Community Charged

I am unflinching in my belief that a football club is the centre of its local community. The beating heart, as it were. The word community, though, may have different meanings to different people. To me, the community that a club is part of includes the supporters – match-going or not – local businesses, sponsors, the local press, and elements of the wider population who a successful club can support. In this chapter I recount how I tried to ensure that all my clubs were at that central point in the community. The clubs came from differing starting points and were at different places on the journey, but my overall perspective remained the same.

I'll start by looking into my work with club communications and programmes. Early in my time at Lincoln City I was given a baptism of fire into that world as Harry Pepper dropped a right bombshell saying to me, 'Don't forget amongst all those changes you seem to be making you need to leave yourself enough time to write the match day programme and renew the ground and programme advertising.' Not that there was that much! Never before had I done anything like editorial work. As a supporter I had criticised the programme in which there appeared little meaningful or readable material so again here was a chance to do something about it.

Prior to my involvement it was the case that material required for the forthcoming Saturday's programme had to be with the printers by the previous Monday evening. It was to use the cheapest paper possible. This meant that interesting issues that came to light in the week could not be included in the programme. I soon found out that a local printing firm, Bargate Printing, was based only a short distance from the ground. Luckily for the club and I they were owned by the Eccleshare Group, and through the direct connection of Roy Chapman, at that time general manager and director at the club, a new arrangement was established. This resulted in a much-improved design, better material, presentation, and content. Importantly it also gave the opportunity to include anything of interest which occurred up to the Thursday evening before a Saturday match. The aim was to provide the supporter with something of more interest but allowing us to keep the cost at an affordable level. At that time it was five pence per programme. A bargain!

Included in the new design was an article written by Maurice Burton, *Lincolnshire Echo* Sports Writer, giving as much information as possible on the opposition. The combination of more thought about what was included along with improved presentation and production gained general public support. We received many letters and comments acknowledging the huge improvement. There is a danger of complacency after success of course. Future productions needed to continue to show a similar pattern of improvements and interest. In preparation for my second season, with the price increased to seven pence, I ran a competition to find a suitable young person to contribute as a junior editor. His or her article was to be aimed at the young supporter. That junior editor was Chris Travers who in later years became a director at the club.

An announcement in the *Lincolnshire Echo* 14 April 1973 reported that the club programme had been voted as best in the Fourth Division, but after that we were destined to be always the bridesmaid and not the bride. The time spent on new designs, new ideas for articles and presentation, was with the ultimate aim of satisfying the needs of the supporters. It was to give them something which wouldn't prove a laughing-stock, as had, so many a season, been the case on the field, unfortunately. New ideas which stood out included the inclusion on the programme cover of the match day team. Then there was the presence of the Red Imps Girls, sellers of Golden Goal and Match Draw tickets, in smart, newly designed costumes kindly donated by a then leading Lincoln Fashion Store, Mawer & Collingham. This also ensured that there were many photos to be included in subsequent programmes.

During my days at Bramall Lane the processing of the programme material and liaison with the respective printers was part of Derek Dooley's remit, although as a collector of the information he had no desire to be responsible for the production of the content. Historically the programme had always been produced locally but with the serious creditor position prevailing at that time it had not been possible to conclude a satisfactory deal. The decision was made to enter into commercial arrangements with an Essex based business, Maybank Press. They already had dealings within the football world and ultimately prove themselves to be more than capable and reliable. With them undertaking production and sales the club were also able to eliminate a loss-making item from their trading. It is interesting to note that in those days FAX machines were beginning to penetrate the market. Their use was becoming widespread in business. This meant we could download material as late as 24 hours before a game and not hamper production timelines.

The Owls programme was already a well-established and supported magazine when I joined and apart from a bit of tinkering about and some added material it proved more than satisfactory so leave well alone and let things take their course!

Another essential challenge, although initially not a complete success, was to improve relationships with supporter groups. Lincoln City was fortunate enough to be supported by two fund raising sections. In the first instance the Lincoln City Football Supporters' Club, who were a totally independent organisation originally formed in 1952 but with deep roots with the football club. They had the presence of an ex-director, Vic Withers, on their governing committee. They also had a delegated member of the board of directors serving as a liaison officer. The second organisation was the Red Imps Association who operated from the club's headquarters but were also managed by a voluntary committee and, in essence, were seen as the poor relations in terms of fundraising. In the two years prior to my engagement the Supporters' Club had donated £14,500 and the Red Imps £11,950. Very early on in my time, and particularly with the club struggling for cash, the Supporters' Club began to hold back on any sort of regular contribution other than if the donation was to be used for their declared specific purpose.

One consequences of the Supporters' Club keeping hold of their donations was the distinct possibility of a fall out at some time in the future. The club felt that the name of the Lincoln City had been used to raise funds and therefore any proceeds should be handed over for the club to determine their best use. The fall out with what had been a previously well-trusted organisation carried on for some time. The truth of the matter was quite simple in as much as both the football and supporters' clubs needed each other. However, each organisation needed to leave the management and objectives to those responsible for the other body. Unfortunately that was not the case, but in my opinion using the name of Lincoln City Football Club should have given the edge to the club. With egos and past history being the dictating factors an impasse did seem to be on the cards. Another consequence was the greater focus by the club on the Red Imps Association in an attempt to increase revenue and to make a more direct connection with the fan base. Influence was brought to bear with significant changes to their management committee including the appointment of a new voluntary chairman, Mr Brian Bundy, with whom I soon developed a close working relationship. 1972, being the first year of the Red Imps Association's new operation, saw their contribution lifted to £9,575 whilst the Supporters' Club dropped to £7,000.

Lincoln City Football Club operated a system where the role of chairman operated on a twelve-month rolling basis. The inevitable fall out with the Supporters' Club, largely fuelled by Charles Warner, ex-Chairman, Roy Chapman, General Manager, and a fellow director George Cook, all fell during the term of Dennis Bocock's year in the hot-seat. In a spate of newspaper articles he took the brunt of the criticism. From a personal point of view I could never really see the benefit of the rotation of chairmen on an annual basis. It seemed that you got started on a working relationship with one chairman and no sooner had it started than you were moving on to another one and so on. I always believed that from their point of view it must have felt an honour to hold that position only to step down after a very short period in office. This must surely have detracted from the prestige of the position and leave you disappointed and frustrated. In my time, particularly at Sincil Bank, I felt the presence of a regular under-current of disenchantment and perpetual blame being put on other people's shoulders. I am not at all sure if that represents the true feelings of each of the chairmen involved but it was an issue which in my mind led to many political manoeuvres, one of which led to a change of manager. It is safe to say that, at Lincoln, although I tried my hardest to link supporters groups with the club, there were still some frosty relationships.

In terms of the Lincoln City Football Supporters' Club, I have to say I had mixed feelings. As a young supporter on the terraces it was inevitable that you would see a member of the Supporters' Club selling their wares. They were seen then by almost all on the terraces as an organisation whose profits were going to benefit the football club. In addition to their presence on the ground they also held very well supported bingo evenings in the Lincoln Drill Hall – a city council-owned building. These were a sort of an attraction in city life. With both the success of the evenings and the fact that the building was not directly under their control, the Supporters' Club management committee decided that the future of the organisation would best be served by owning their own headquarters. Their future decisions were limited by the forecasted expenditure of £88,000. This no doubt also influenced the decision to retain funds rather than continue with their valued contributions to the club. Directors of the football club deemed it to be not in the best interests of the football club and there was deadlock. Previous donations, I was advised at the time, seemed to have strings attached in terms of what they wanted their donations to be spent on. Like any other disagreement there had to be two sides to the story and for my part I was not in a position to take any other view other than that of my employers. My terms of engagement were to maximise income to the club and thus enhancing the performance of the Red Imps Association was first and foremost on my list.

When I moved to Bramall Lane it was time to try a different approach. To garner all possible opportunities for supporter involvement, I was responsible for the development and creation of a new company called Bramall Lane Aid and Development Enterprises (1981) Ltd together with several associates. The aim was to create a network of affiliates appropriate for whatever standing or desire the supporter may have and to encourage them to become part of the club and equally raise money for the benefit of their club.

Before the launch of BLADES 1981 there was an which highlighted to me the true feelings of supporters' commitment to their club – whether in the case of Sheffield it be blue and white or red and white, the same depth of loyalty and feeling existed. Having moved into a new home in Dronfield, I was taken by my next-door neighbour to the local pub, Hyde Park Inn, where both sets of supporters enjoyed their pints and banter. I instantly became a member of a games table – either playing dominoes, fives and threes, or cribbage. My partner was a rank and file Wednesdayite which meant that, before we started any of the games, if there were red matches on the marker board, they had to be lit, blown out and then used. Although still at the Lane, I arranged tickets for the directors' box at Hillsborough for their game against Watford in the 1980/81 League Cup. This meant I could meet up with Graham Taylor once more. With a spare ticket I asked my games partner if he would like to go with me as my guest. He couldn't believe it, almost kissing me in the process – not an event I would have relished! He too lived in Dronfield and on the night of the match I called for him at about 6.15pm – met at the door by his wife who told me he had been ready since 5 o'clock watching for me to come down the road. He was panicking that we would not have enough time to get there before kick-off, but I assured him there would be more people going to Tesco shopping than Hillsborough – a bit of banter! Arriving at the ground, the car park attendant who I knew greeted me saying, 'Evening, Dick, let me take you to your car parking space' – just opposite the main entrance. My pal looked aghast that someone at Hillsborough knew my name and was so friendly. After parking up, we made our way to the main entrance and were handed the tickets with another warm welcome. I accepted them and walked through into the reception area, but when I looked round my pal was nowhere to be seen. Backtracking I found him standing outside the main entrance gazing up at the 'Welcome to Hillsborough' sign, mouth wide open in disbelief that he was going into the inner sanctuary of his beloved club.

At the end of the game – having lost 1-2 – we enjoyed the hospitality on offer within the guest room. Graham Taylor soon walked in and came over to me, whereupon I introduced him to my pal who joined in the chat. Within a few minutes a beleaguered Jack Charlton came in, made his way to the three of us, giving me the chance to introduce my pal to him. I have never seen a grown man, not known for his quietness, so lost for words and so full of admiration. The whole event made my night and reaffirmed my belief as to the true feelings of staunch supporters who deserved far more recognition than had previously been shown. I took this belief into my work.

A not too dissimilar story centred around a Unitedite. During the very difficult season of 1980/81 the Blades travelled to Newport County in January. A bleak mid-week fixture which no club director fancied travelling down to! To retain our representation I decided to travel down, not on the team coach but leaving by car, mid-afternoon. I duly arrived but not without some difficulties with the car's electrics. Luckily for me their chairman took the keys off me and said the car would be waiting for, me after the game. I say game, but that might be stretching it a bit, for going in at half time luckily just one goal down, we conceded three more goals in the second half, making it a thoroughly miserable evening. Ready to leave for the journey home, I told Harry Haslam I was using the same route back as their coach and, if he were to see a car broken down on the side of the road, not to go past without checking if it was me.

I set off back on the road to Ross-on-Wye and no sooner had I left the Newport boundary than I came across a man donning a red and white scarf thumbing a lift. It had to be more than a coincidence, so I stopped and offered him a lift: 'anywhere a bit further up the road north' being his request. He settled down and got warmed up with the car heating. I then asked: 'What is that scarf you are wearing?'

'It's a Blades scarf,' he said.

To which I replied, 'Well who or what are the Blades?'

'They're Sheffield United mate – the best team in Sheffield,' he replied.

'Ah. Well, you are a long way from home so what are you doing down here?' I asked.

'Bin to see them play against Newport County, mate – well, they didn't play, they just turned up, they were bloody awful!' he replied with a real sense of disappointment and frustration.

'How did you get down here, then?' was my next question.

'I walked as I always do, as I'm unemployed, left home about 8.30 this morning and thumbed lifts down and got here just before kick-off – sometimes wish I didn't with the way they are playing. Harry Haslam wants locking up and someone to throw the keys away, he will ruin this club and all that it stands for!'

Not long after this we travelled past Ross-on-Wye and picked up signs for M5 North, when I said to him, 'Well, I'm going north so I suppose you are OK and wanting to carry on sitting comfy.'

'Too bloody true, mate – it's brill of you,' came his reply. From this point onwards he went through the team and the management staff using descriptions not suitable for inclusion in this book but all adding up to the fact that the team wasn't good enough. The journey continued, ultimately finishing up on the M1 North and then picking up on the signs for Sheffield.

'Well, looks like you won't be long before you are on home soil – I'm going to go down the Parkway and heading for John Street – is that any good for you?' I asked.

'Too bloody good to be true. I live within a stones' throw of the Lane, so anywhere near there would be great,' he replied.

I eventually pulled up outside the main entrance to the ground and told him, 'I live at Dronfield but hoped that my detour may have helped him and would I see him at the next home game against Gillingham?' He looked absolutely bemused, wanting to know if I was a Gillingham supporter who had moved to live in the area. 'No, I'm Dick Chester, the Club Secretary!'

'Bloody hell – don't tell Harry Haslam or the players what I have said about them will you?'

'Your secret is safe with me,' I said!

At the Gillingham game I was walking round the inside of the ground with the Police – an action I always undertook so that we could observe any problems – and no sooner had we reached the Kop than I saw a bit of a scuffle amongst the crowd and this guy who I had given a lift to cried out, 'Hi there, Dick – thanks a lot for my lift – I've told all my mates.' I duly acknowledged with a smile and continued my duties. When I returned to the offices the receptionist said there is a parcel for you – well, not you, it's for Mrs Chester – and when it was opened it was a box of Thornton chocolates with a thank you inscription from this self-same supporter. How nice was that!

To highlight that the Blades wanted to be seen to be part of the Sheffield community a further opportunity came our way to meet that desire and also to recognise the achievement of other leading Sheffield high profile sports people. Through some personal connections of Tony Barrington, a press announcement was released on 17th April 1982 that unbeaten Graham Ahmed would challenge for Bomber Graham's light middleweight boxing championship in an open-air contest to be staged at Bramall Lane. Herol 'Bomber' Graham was a product of the Brendan Ingle stable and had proved himself to be a worthy champion, so with a major outdoor event to stage, at a time when work was required on the main pitch, arrangements had to be made to cater for both events, which, I am pleased to say, went all according to plan.

As supporters it is important that there should be no under-estimation of your value to your club. The thinking behind the formation of BLADES was that supporters didn't necessarily have to come through the turnstiles. There might be quite understandable reasons why this was the case. In forming this organisation there was the opportunity for supporters in that position to become involved in other associations where that support could, with the necessary commitment by the club, be converted into a financial benefit. Football is a very committed and emotive game, with supporters' eyes firmly fixed on their own club's successes or failures. The margin for success is very limited indeed. In the era of my involvement you had two opportunities out of twenty-four to succeed with a promotion – not particularly good odds – but before any of those seasons started optimism was invariably expressed and more often or not any or all prices increased.

BLADES was hopefully designed to give both an involvement and a voice to the supporter and to develop a greater network from within the City of Sheffield. As part of a 'two club' city, Sheffield United had to make themselves a prominent feature of city life and, whilst being aware of its competition, the aim was never to be overawed by them but to be determined to be the best. The constitution was simple in outline but had to be done properly to provide for its viability, sustainability, and future development. To this end Bramall Lane Aid and Development Enterprises Ltd became the holding company to which all of the subsidiaries had to report and lodge any income. The following subsidiaries were placed under their immediate control: Blades Executive Club, Senior Blades, Junior Blades, Blades Travel Club, Blades Supporters' Club and Blades Future Players Fund. This provided an opportunity for supporters of all walks and creeds to become directly associated. The only exception was that the proposal for a Blades Ladies Luncheon Club was declined by the chairman and to this day seems to have been left on the shelf. To enhance our community profile a magazine entitled Blades News was produced and distributed free of charge throughout the city. It was designed to keep the public up to date with club affairs and to give them the opportunity of writing to the editor with stories, comments, and views. This also served to give the supporters a few bragging rights over their city competitors.

From a personal point I enrolled my new-born grandson into the Junior Blades. I think he was the second member registered. As far as the Senior Blades are concerned I have reached the age where I can take advantage of a club, basically formed by myself, and for which I can enjoy the benefits derived by their very hard-working committee. The 1981/82 Portrait of a Championship brochure published in recognition of the Blades promotion back into Division Three contained a full article describing the details and purposes of each organisation. I was advised some years ago that such was the success of this group formation that the

Football League used this template when putting together their Football in the Community programme. It is something that I remain very proud of, given its continuing success over the last 40 years and to this day I am indebted to the commitment of their differing committees to ensure it still remains an integral part of Blades life.

I mentioned that the wider community should be of importance to a football club. Work with the community is mutually beneficial for the club and community. It may lead to greater engagement from the fan base or more sponsorship from businesses. To ensure this happens, though, it firstly needs engagement and leadership from the club. Graham Taylor's appointment at Sincil Bank in 1972 allowed for greater development of links with that local community. It is, in my opinion, an essential factor that in the successful management of your duties with a club you need to totally respect the contribution your customers make to you, and in many cases their support is unstinting, whatever may be thrown at them. Do they deserve your thanks? Of course they bloody well do!

I was delighted to have the opportunity of being part of the lead management team with Graham. I had previously been given the chance to spend time with him, during his absence through injury, talking about the club and the role it played within the community. This did not interest his predecessor David Herd one little bit; I think he thought we were just another smaller version of the Old Trafford publicity machine. In my days as a local referee I had also had the opportunity of witnessing Graham's influence and coaching abilities on the local Lincoln Nalgo football team and at the same time being on the receiving end of some "touchline advice" when decisions made were contrary to his opinions. A characteristic he would carry forward into his managerial days! In my various discussions with Graham, reference was made to my work in terms of major ground development proposals, and the need to break the mould that was so apparent in football at that time. From our first working days together an immense amount of time was spent talking about the route forward and his willingness to front promotional community schemes. His thinking was quite clear. Leave me to the football side of things, talk any scheme through with me to ensure I have a full grasp of what you are trying to achieve, and I will front them for you. I will use the players where necessary and make sure we maximise the club's profile. After all the supporters would at all times be more interested in the words of the manager than an administrator. It was in him and his team that they entrusted their confidence. It was both interesting and a sign of belief that many of the schemes were repeated in his Watford days. He was a very good ambassador.

Kevin McCabe

I first became involved as a director and shareholder of Sheffield United back in the mid-1990s, ultimately becoming the Owner and Chairman of a team I began to support in the 1950s having been born but a cricket ball's throw from Bramall Lane. Thus, with my feet under the table I started to pick up papers and glean information from the then Senior Executives of the Blades, and in particular the Company Secretary, David Capper, to better learn as to how the Club – rather than the football team – had progressed in recent past years. My aim was to simply learn more about its business and ethos, recognising that one has had to be a custodian of an Institution that was so important to the City of Sheffield. The Blades have an intriguing history and heritage with the roots of its stadium stretching back to 1855 and thus my desire was to understand anything and everything that was required for it to be run properly and become a modern true family and community football organisation run with pride and distinction.

What I quickly discovered and enjoyed was that there was a hidden jewel situated at the Lane in the form of the Senior Blades, an initiative that was established in 1981, with George McCabe (no relation) and Derek Dooley, two highly profiled Sheffield men of football – fronting it particularly well.However, in time I learnt more about Dick Chester – a quiet individual who behind the scenes had so much to do with properly overhauling and reorganising the management of one of England's longest serving clubs situated in Sheffield, itself the 'home of football'. Yes, it was Dick Chester, who was the creator of BLADES 1981 that became the Senior Blades, a quiet and studious gentleman who simply understood the fundamentals of running a football organisation in a sensible and economic way, never forgetting the need to protect it from overspending on first team football to the ultimate detriment of the club itself. He also kept Sheffield United on the straight and narrow linking in with the officials at the Football Association and Football League to ensure that our Club complied with all its obligations.

The Senior Blades have in themselves become a mini-institution with their members representing South Yorkshire people from all walks of life, and of course also including ex-players and their families for whom the Blades meant so much. To this day, the continuing leadership of the Senior Blades sees regular use of the club's facilities at the Lane, none more so than holding their monthly lunches with special guests present in the prestigious Platinum Suite which can accommodate up to 350 attendees.

To trace back the management and guidance of Sheffield United FC from the 1960s to this day one recognises the important role Dick Chester played in so many aspects of the day to day running of the Club undertaking a variety of duties encompassing those required by a Company Secretary and Financial Operating Officer – two key roles that are still required to this day.

Dick was an unsung hero – vital to ensuring that the stability of the Club was a key priority.

Kevin McCabe

The 1972 profile of Lincoln City Football Club was one where the supporters were expected to accept the club for what it was, rather than the club seeking ways in which it could become part of the community and be seen to be serious about it. Graham's appointment ensured that this began to change. Many promotional marketing programmes were devised, developed, and promoted on the back of the team. Organised school visits were arranged. Differing initiatives were presented to the schools particularly aimed at supporting proper conduct and learning, both within the classroom and the family home. Students who successfully responded to the programmes were rewarded with a supply of complementary tickets for both pupil and an accompanying parent. It was a win-win-win situation. Win for the schools with an increase in motivated students. A win for the students with greater academic success and tickets to the games. Finally it was a win for the club with the priceless effect of building community engagement and the fan base.

Season 1973/74 saw the club become the first team in the Football League to introduce a "sponsor a player" scheme. Chatting the idea through with Graham, this could not be just a sheet in the programme with names of individuals or businesses sponsoring a player's kit. It had to be more personal than that. Before launch we had decided that the best way forward would be to host a special evening for all of the sponsors at the club and for each player to be allocated both a table and time to spend with their sponsors so that each could get to know the other properly. To say it was a success would be an under-statement with everyone leaving the evening in good spirits and from the club's point of view they already had confirmation that the sponsors wanted to continue the following year. That scheme was noted through the infamous football grapevine and became a feature with many other clubs.

One such occasion where the club received massive supporter involvement and financial commitment was in 1974/75. In October, Graham and I made another long journey deep into the heart of South-East of England. Having been to Southend-on-Sea to sign Dennis Booth we returned to Upton Park, London, to complete the loan signing of Peter Grotier from West Ham United. Peter was on the fringe of breaking through as a regular first team keeper but just couldn't quite make it. In our discussions with him at the club, he confirmed he was willing to come for first team football but had no desire of making that permanent. Upon his arrival in Lincoln he found himself in the position of having his accommodation provided for within my home. He quickly settled in and was brilliant with my children and spent time with my very young son teaching him the art of goalkeeping. He also knew how to upset the neighbours by regularly kicking the ball over the boundary fences into their gardens!

Slowly his attitude towards Lincoln and Lincoln City began to change, particularly as he became a massive favourite with the crowd. That favouritism resulted in the supporters undertaking all sorts of fund-raising activities to contribute towards the £20,000 transfer fee. At that time the Imps fans were one of the earliest sets of fans to commit to such a campaign, but their belief in Peter was more than justified as his service to the club was exemplary. He made 223 appearances over the next five seasons and was included in the PFA team of the season twice.

In addition, Graham and I came to a mutual understanding that, whilst the club expected the working members of the community to pay to come and watch the players at their place of work come 3.00pm Saturday afternoon, the club had not previously considered going to see the same people working at their place of work. Therefore we made several visits to the business premises of leading local employers, all of which had an immediate impact on mutual understanding and respect for each other's professionalism and difficulties.

Commercial development was one of paramount importance, with little or nothing in place when I started at Sincil Bank. Initiative, thought, development and launching of each area of both advertising and sponsorship was needed. Luckily success came in abundance and covered virtually every area of the club. It was nearly a case of "if anything in the club moves then can it be sponsored" – providing of course all parties could equally share in the feeling of success. No good at all just taking money off a sponsor and for them to become unhappy after one instance. Not only is that a lost client but they have the potential to be a dangerous one in terms of spreading bad publicity.

1975, therefore, was a busy time in terms of sponsorship and commercial development, with a wide range of initiatives many of which saw the club leading the way for others to follow and, I believe, giving the fanbase a degree of confidence and pride that both on and off the field the club was doing its level best to achieve the successes the club so desperately needed.

It was inevitable that given Graham's work ethic, depth of enquiries into player's strengths, weaknesses and characters, and additional funding to support the signing of quality players, promotion would be delivered. It was in 1976 when the team finished champions of Division Four. On the back of all our marketing efforts I secured an appointment to see the managing director of Smith Clayton forge to discuss some element of involvement by them. This was arranged across lunchtime with the customary training session fully completed. On our way to the appointment Graham asked, 'What are we going to talk about?'

'No idea mate, we'll wait and see how it goes.'

'What the f'in hell are we doing here then.'

'Don't worry we'll pick up any threads and go from there – we know our business and once we get to know theirs a bit better, I'm sure something will lead us into some sort of a deal.'

Reporting to reception we introduced ourselves and advised that we had an appointment with Dr J S McFarlane, Managing Director, Smith Clayton Forge Ltd, and were instantly ushered in by his private secretary into the designated meeting room. He came into the room and broke the ice by confirming he wasn't sure what he could do to help which brought a big smile on Graham's face and a comment saying, 'I don't think you are on your own I'll leave it to Dick.' The outcome was an instant positive response when he learned of our desire to incorporate businesses within the club's profile and a willingness to bring players to see the shop floor at work. After a general chat over the impressive marketing impact we had made within the city and considerations of possibilities of his company playing their part, it very quickly ended with an agreement to sponsor the production of the 1975/76 Yearbook. The book included contributions from both parties and the establishment of a genuine friendship between the three of us.

Within the 1975/76 promotion book I had the opportunity to include a section simply headed "secretarial comments," within which I was able to sum up the thoughts behind my thinking in the area of sponsorship and finance in football. I made the point that sponsorship, in varying forms, had certainly become a very important aspect of football club finances. It was, and is, my fervent view that this source of income should in no way be abused. All too often it has been said that the attitude prevailing in society has been to "take" and very little effort is made to "give."

In my opinion football has the necessary platform from which to launch itself to the fore. We at Lincoln City were adamant in our views that sponsors at Sincil Bank should be given all possible considerations and co-operation as a result of their support to the club. We should aim to ensure value for money for their investments. Unlike the leading clubs in the First Division the strength of pull towards Third and Fourth Division clubs is somewhat weaker, thereby making any tangible proposition a "much harder sell" and whilst their local club is invariably the only option suitable for their business it doesn't give the club carte blanche to abuse them. On this basis, therefore, no useful purpose can be served by sitting back and hoping that the richer and bigger clubs will agree to divide the lion's share of the cake among us small fry, or in fact think that remedies will automatically descend from above as an act of charity. Certainly the scarcity of money within the game – disregarding any other factors – will nullify any such actions. With very few shoulders available to cry on, Lincoln City accepted the situation and tried to provide a club which the city and community could feel was aiming in the right direction.

Those thoughts and processes, I believe, stood the club in very good stead and certainly provided the benchmark for me in my career. I felt frustrated in meetings with the associate member clubs. The thinking seemed to be about how they could present an argument to get more money out of the bigger clubs. I cannot remember attending any one of those meetings where there was any positivity shown towards supporting new initiatives for the lower clubs to follow and any discussion as to how they "cut their coat according to their cloth." I always sensed a "Gi me! Gi Me!" attitude. In reality it should not be at all surprising that the bigger clubs got fed up or reluctant to help when they could see that these clubs weren't doing much to try and remedy their own positions. The only real remedy that presented itself was, which I suppose is similar to today's market, to bring in a new investor who could stabilise the finances and provide money for new players.

This, in my mind, put a definitive emphasis on trying to provide a deep-rooted community programme whilst at the same time endeavouring to encourage commercial businesses to come forward in their support of the club. Whilst there may have been instances where, like at school and reading your end of year report you read, "tried hard but could do better," it is my sincere belief that I left Lincoln with an improved community programme and increased sponsorship. That sponsorship money was gained in the correct way with benefits for all involved.

Sheffield United's outlook upon supporters was virtually no different to what I had encountered previously. The board generally felt that having taken Yorkshire County Cricket away from them in 1971 they wouldn't be able to overcome that disappointment, particularly with football results being on the decline. Why bother and waste our time, seemed to be the message. I had many discussions with John Hassall over this. My view was that it was precisely for those reasons that the club had to bother. This hardcore base of fans were too important to the future of the club to treat this way. Apart from which in today's world you wouldn't regard that attitude as being in the best interests of customer relations. I can honestly say that not all of our discussions were calm and serene; one or two finishing up with the chairman saying, 'We'll pick up where we have left off today when I come in in the morning – I'm leaving now."

What I couldn't get my head around was, whilst adopting this sort of attitude to the supporter, they were at the same time filling the directors' box and hospitality areas with friends of directors or supposed friends of the club, some of whom would not even buy any of the half-time raffle tickets. On many occasions, I was unable to allocate seats to visiting dignitaries or senior football personnel. I spoke with the chairman who, quite understandably, felt I was 'treading on thin ice but if you want to take steps to change that then be it on your head.' Working closely with Derek Dooley, who was both lottery and commercial manager, we identified a number of potential sponsors who could well be interested in being approached. We hosted them and assured them of what they would receive from the club. All this before they needed to commit themselves or their companies to any real level of investment. This worked a treat with no backlash from the "hangers on" and importantly increased turnover and profit from the in-house golden goal raffle, a recognisable increase in both sponsorship and advertising revenue and an opportunity to defray the over-burdening creditor list.

At Sheffield United, change to community relations proved much more difficult to achieve than at Sincil Bank. Further much-needed work was essential to change the outlook of the board in terms of supporter and community values. At this time there was a deep feeling that the supporters needed the club and not vice versa. Again, whilst enjoying a close working relationship with the chairman, John Hassall, his views relating to the importance of the supporters were somewhat at odds with mine. Indeed the same applied to Derek Dooley, who, as a footballing icon in the city, felt that his name and reputation was enough to bring the supporters to the club and it was not necessary to chase them. I have to say that once supporter groups had made contact, Derek was excellent in terms of extending warm welcomes and developing continued associations. In my very early days at the Lane, that sort of change of approach was not of interest to Harry Haslam either. He felt strongly that the role of the players was to perform on the pitch, having been trained sufficiently well, rather than becoming involved in airy-fairy schemes such as school visits or attending supporter club evenings. These, in my mind, are the essential tools to impress on a young mind the virtues of supporting the club. Once on board the chances are they will be there for life. For the more mature supporter it is the opportunity to join the players and management in a social setting, to seemingly become one of them for the evening, take and give the banter, and see the players as people and not just an image running around a rectangular piece of grass kicking a bag of wind and seemingly playing god. They need to be on the same level to relate to them. Once that's under the belt the support will become stronger. I think it would be fair to say that Harry's negativity to become more closely associated came home to bite him on the bum sometime later.

Sponsorship was another important area where the club could

identify with local businesses and where there could be mutual benefits shared and enjoyed. At the time of my start at Bramall Lane, the club could not provide a company car as part of my terms and conditions, due to it still being used by Keith Walker, the incumbent. By agreement I was granted the use of the vehicle for the marketing manager's role at the White Hart Hotel, Lincoln, a role given to me by Reg Brealey the hotel's owner.

I suggested to John Hassall that in order to eliminate future capital expenditure and reduce monthly motoring costs, we could seek to secure our company vehicles from local traders in exchange for sponsorship/advertising opportunities. Such deals are known as "contra" deals – you give us something we want, and we'll give you what we can to satisfy your marketing needs. A simple theme. The chairman and I convened a meeting with Derek Dooley and he was asked to approach a suitable motor dealer to try and secure such a deal. In words of single syllables he suggested the idea was 'f'ing idiotic' and said no. The chairman's response was equally as blunt. 'Derek I am not asking you. I am telling you,' following which the meeting rapidly concluded. A couple of days later the chairman was once again present in my office. Derek re-appeared with a smile all over his face saying, 'I secured a deal and have agreement for a new car for both Dick and myself.' From that point on the transactions rolled in until all of our vehicles were supplied, maintained and subject to regular change by differing Sheffield-based franchises. This system was also repeated at Sheffield Wednesday via the kind cooperation of Stephen Monfredi, with sponsored vehicles for both Howard and myself. If you ever saw a player's name plastered all over a car supplied by Monty's Motors, these private arrangements were a great example of club management: players and sponsors working together for a common goal.

However, before those days at Hillsborough, the whole issue of sponsorship and company corporate identity was to rear its head at an Annual General Meeting at the Lane. When the normal business on the agenda had been completed the chairman threw open the meeting for any other business. One of the club's shareholders at that time was a Mr Bernard Proctor, a staunch Unitedite and a car dealer by profession. He stood up and asked if he could address a question to 'this country bumpkin who the club has engaged as secretary and who clearly knows nothing about Sheffield football or indeed Sheffield.' The chairman asked him to moderate his speech but allowed the question to be addressed. I was asked: 'Do you have any idea what you have done, allowing a company to advertise on the ground and plaster blue and white all over?'

My reply: 'That's right, those are their corporate colours and with the deal completed, as it is, they have every right to incorporate their company colours.'

'Well tell them to take them down,' was the response.

'Sir, the best thing I can do is to invite you tomorrow to accompany me to a meeting on their premises, when I would be willing to discuss a cancellation of the deal on the basis that you will completely replace the deal and provide us with the volume of cars that they are willing to supply,' was my response. He immediately sat down and left the issue well alone. Many years later Mr Proctor became a director of the club. I had left by then, but I doubt very much if he went on to pooh-pooh such good commercial deals presented to the board of directors!

This whole issue was a clear message to me that I quickly needed to take heed of the commitment of the Blades fans and the real feeling of opposition to our Sheffield based counterparts. It also showed me that for a strong marketing policy to work there also needed to be some reasonable level of flexibility from our supporters. I felt that if there was any occasion in the future when they were not prepared to recognise the effort being made to turn things around then a little more understanding of the severity of the cause wouldn't go amiss.

Leadership and engagement from the club are vital. At Hillsborough following the retirement of Dennis Woodhead as commercial manager I engaged the services of Bob Gorrill who at the time had experience dealing with similar affairs at Chesterfield FC and also had previous involvement within the sales department of G T Cars, one of the earliest sponsors of company vehicles to my previous club. Bob very quickly got to grips with the commercial side of things, enhanced the performance of that department considerably and was still in position when I ultimately moved on. This role, particularly with the emergence of the team as Division One contenders, was extremely important and many of the schemes and ideas presented to him were instantly acted upon and fully delivered. This in addition to his many new clients and successful conversions to the Hillsborough scene. Many a time when called upon he received the support and backing of Howard Wilkinson and his players.

I mentioned that we needed the support of the press. I aimed to be open with both press and media outlets with the aim of ensuring positive coverage for the club, enjoying particularly good relations with the Sheffield Newspaper Group, Radio Hallam, Radio Sheffield, BBC Look North and Yorkshire ITV. At the same time it was essential to recognise the confidentiality of the information to hand and protect the rights of each club and the particular issues to hand. The very first test of press relationships came quite early in my time at the Lane. It was brought about following the signing of Les Tibbott from Ipswich Town. Tony

Pritchett, Senior Sports Writer for the *Sheffield Star*, was at the ground with his photographer and notebook to conduct the usual interview and photo session. He then popped into my office to check that all the processes had been completed and that no complications were likely to arise. At the same time he asked me what the player's top line salary would be – a question I declined to answer but was told by Tony that it was in the public interest. My response was quite definitive, saying, 'when you get back to your office ask the editor if he will give you permission to print the details of your earnings. If he says yes, then I will consider it again.' His response was, 'I am sure the editor would not sanction the release of such confidential information and it would probably not be of any interest to our readers.' 'In which case don't ever ask me any such question again,. Such detail is private and confidential and will remain so, as far as I am concerned.' What transpired from that meeting was an amicable understanding that at monthly intervals we would sit down together during which I would provide for him a lead story on each and every area of potential coverage to ensure that collectively we could keep the name of Sheffield United first and foremost in the *Star* on a daily basis. It was designed to instil confidence and bragging rights for our supporters. This continued right up to my leaving and consolidated the respect amongst all.

Maurice Burton was the sports editor for the *Lincolnshire Echo* during my days at Sincil Bank. It was through our good working relationship, and his personal contributions in many of the ideas designed for inclusion in the club programme, that mutual trust and cooperation was established. I did not feel that this had been the case before the start of my employment. Moving to Hillsborough, my relationship was with Paul Thompson at the *Sheffield Star* and *Green Un*. I endeavoured to ensure that the club gained similar coverage to the Blades. Paul was helpful to me, and we received positive coverage about various changes that were made at the club. One which could have proved difficult related to the introduction of CCTV cameras. The *Star* published a positive article about how it was a state-of-the-art system – helping avert any 'Big Brother' worries from supporters.

I have spoken previously about my working relationship with the chairman at Sheffield Wednesday. Bert McGee and I discussed during car journeys and meetings the position he wanted the club to be in. He was at all times completely besotted by his true Wednesdayite feelings and the importance he knew that the club played in the City of Sheffield. I recall one car journey home from a Football League regional meeting where it had been mentioned that there was an impending vacancy for a seat on the Football League Management Committee. I asked him to consider submitting his name for the same. Bert was a straightforward-speaking, blunt, dour Yorkshireman who could bring a new dimension to that particular committee. He was not sure, in fact adamant that he wouldn't, but ultimately had a change of heart and was duly appointed. Such was the confidence we had in each other that when their minutes and agendas were issued he would always ask me to read and comment and where applicable offer a guide for him to follow. I can truthfully say that we never breached any confidences placed in each other, never had a cross word or a fallout. We didn't always agree on everything but talking things through came to a workable compromise – and at all times aimed to put the club first before any personal gain. Bert was the chairman who was closest to my views in the importance of delivering the club's links with the community. He was well-supported by Howard Wilkinson and the players. I was fortunate to work alongside them, and to be given the freedom I needed to do my job well.

This brings me to my *mea culpa*. There was one occasion where his delegated powers left me in the firing line. On the occasion of our good cup run in season 1985/86 we were drawn out of the hat to play Everton in the FA Cup Semi-Finals at Villa Park on 5th April. The long-standing club policies meant that once the ticket allocation had been received from The Football Association the distribution saw shareholders have first option, followed by season ticket holders and then the general supporter. During this particular season the club had been faced with heavy demands for tickets driven by the success on the pitch. Whichever options the club deemed appropriate to put any surplus tickets on sale, we were constantly faced with supporter complaints. It was good to some supporters if the ticket office stayed open for evening sales but to others that was no good at all as they had shift patterns to contend with, for example. Other options were on a Sunday but again complaints came in as many were not available. In one of the weekly meetings between the chairman and myself it was considered, and ultimately agreed, that for the FA Cup Semi-Final we would reopen the ticket office at the conclusion of a home game when supporters would have been present. Good idea it seemed at the time. Not so good an idea when the chosen game was against Liverpool on 29th March.

As usual I arrived at the ground for that particular home game quite early, before normal opening times and prior to any staff arriving, only to be faced with queues of supporters. In the first instance I assumed that they would be wanting tickets for the Liverpool game, that being a big attraction in those days. But alas, no, they were all there for a possible semi-final ticket. As the day progressed the queue grew and grew until it became quite unmanageable, stretching out of the ground onto Penistone Road and making admission to the home game very difficult indeed. Chief

Supt Brian Mole came to see me asking for the club to re-think its decision and allow the purchase of the tickets to go on sale before the game ended, as there was a risk of a potential disturbance. That is what happened and in next to no time the limited number of tickets available for sale had all been snatched up.

Come the end of the game there was, quite naturally, from a near 38,000 crowd, a large-scale gathering of very disgruntled supporters congregating outside the director's main entrance seeking explanations. I was inside completing some post-match formalities when one of the directors approached the chairman to advise him of the trouble. Immediately it was perceived as being my idea alone, so with a police guard I went to the main entrance and tried to explain. The response was, quite understandably, quite abusive. I suggested that if the culprit wished to go around the corner to one of the club's toilet facilities, wash his mouth out and then return I would try and explain. Ultimately the crowd dispersed, clearly far from happy, leaving me to reflect on what was proving to be a very poor joint decision. One family who was in the front line, but not being at all abusive, were one of the last to leave and before doing so came up and apologised for the crowd's outburst, but equally reminded me that there had been an obvious under-estimation of the importance of such an event to the genuine fan. I did ask if they could leave me some contact details. I would consider their plight in the event of any non-take up by either shareholders or season ticket holders.

As luck would have it tickets were returned to satisfy the needs of that dad, mum and daughter. My secretary duly made contact and, without giving them any idea, asked if they could call in to my office to discuss the matter once again. The family duly came down, sat in my office and when asked if they would accept three returned ticket,s which I had in my possession, the office was virtually flooded with tears. My feelings at the time were full of remorse for the supporters and to this day I consider it one of the biggest customer relationship errors I made. However, given all of the factors before us and trying to take everyone's circumstances into account we were never going to come up with the right options.

The story doesn't end there, though. At the Annual General Meeting held in the Cutlers' Hall the chairman told me to prepare for an onslaught in "any other business" about the FA Cup Semi-Final ticket distribution arrangements, as he was sure it would crop up. Sure enough, a shareholder asked if he could address a question to the company secretary about that particular issue. No sooner was he on his feet than a gentleman, who was in attendance as a proxy member, jumped to his feet and said, 'before anyone lends any criticism at either the club or the secretary let me remind them of the good word and delivery of deed offered by the secretary and enjoyed by my family.' It was the same man who I had helped alongside his wife and daughter. There was no question therefore to answer on the night of the AGM. Matter closed I suppose, but certainly not forgotten, and I still offer my sincerest apologies to all those who missed out.

I thoroughly enjoyed my time at Hillsborough. So why move on relatively quickly you may ask? Whilst based in the Sheffield area I had always maintained contact with the director at Lincoln City, Dennis Bocock. He was the first chairman I had worked with, and during a particular telephone call he asked if I was settled in football or would I like to come back to Lincoln and work for him. At that time I said I was more than happy at Hillsborough and was working for the best club I had worked with to date. 'Anyway the next time you are across visiting the family, let me know. I would be interested in a catch up and a drink.' Time passed by until late one night the phone rang whilst I was in bed and slightly intoxicated. Dennis asked if I was about to visit Lincoln any time soon, which I was that weekend. 'Done deal then, we'll meet up,' he told me. We duly met and the outcome was the offer of the position of managing director for DWL Bocock Ltd and, after a satisfactory probation period, the transfer of all shares for sole ownership.

I did ask for time to consider, and I needed to speak to Bert McGee. I was conscious of the confidences Sheffield Wednesday had placed in me and did not want to let them down. It was made clear that the club didn't want to lose my services but as the chairman he was not going to stand in the way of me accepting such a potentially life-changing opportunity. Before finally leaving he hosted me for an evening meal during which he said, 'Remember this, if things don't work out you have the ability to turn your hands to almost anything in management, and I would, if possible, find a place for you to come back here.' Bert asked if there was anything he could do for me. I said, 'Yes, when the vote comes up at the next Football League meeting please vote against the awarding of the new TV contract to Sky.'

'Why's that? For, as I see it, we would have extra monies to enhance the facilities at Hillsborough, way above what you have already achieved.

'Chairman, I don't think that will happen, for, deep down, I am sure you know as well as I do that all the new money will find its way into the players' and agents' pockets.'

'I don't think that will happen here as long as I have any say,' being the reply. All makes interesting reading in today's marketplace.

Sheffield Wednesday had been completely different to either the Imps or the Blades in that, through the good management of the board of directors, they had passed their days of financial difficulties. There were other similarities, in terms of their recognition of the value of their supporters, excellent in every sense of the word, and the decline in the facilities directly connected to their main asset, that being the ground. Under previous excellent management and direction, Hillsborough had become a place of some standing within the football world – none more so than the 1966 World Cup, but in recent years there was an impression of resting on laurels, with no drive or direction towards keeping up with the times and the ever-growing demands of sponsors in return for what were then significant investments and commercial support. A later chapter covers the developments which were delivered during my watch and, whilst I know some have been engulfed in later developments, I was able to leave Hillsborough feeling very comfortable about my time and achievements, all of which were unhesitatingly supported by the board of directors with each of whom I enjoyed superb relationships and respect.

The decision was taken to return back to my native Lincoln and embark on a new career path at 46 years of age and, above all, to be closer to my family which was now growing up, forever expanding and where I had missed out a lot in those early informative years of family development.

Before the spring of 1987 things were to change again. Whilst the business side of things was going well, with enhanced profitability and identified future growth, I was ordered by the chairman, not just once but several times, to stop what work I was doing, to go to the village shop, to collect and deliver fish and chip teas for himself and wife, to which I objected quite explicitly. I had been brought into the business as managing director to assume responsibility for its future development and not to be treated as a lackey. There came a point of no return when I handed in my office keys and company car and left with no immediate job offer to hand.

I do believe, to this day, that the standards instilled in me by my parents carried me through the years in football, particularly in terms of honesty, integrity, and respect for others, particularly those your senior. I do believe that there is a need to work for respect and in my mind this can only be achieved by being in command of your work and responsibilities. I believe you should show initiative wherever possible, as this enhances your staff's trust in you, show respect for others' superior knowledge and learn from them, don't be afraid to say a simple, but meaningful thank-you for help and assistance and above all be honest and straightforward. All of these, I think, served me well and I can truthfully say that each club I have served have been in a better place when I left than when I joined. In the terms of this chapter, the clubs I worked for were closer to their communities when I left than when I started. My work made a difference that in some cases remains to this day. I had the help and support of many people with Graham Taylor, Bert McGee, Howard Wilkinson and others making a real difference. It may appear somewhat conceited but, with quite a bit of soul searching, I do think it is right to say that my work made a real positive difference.

andy daykin associates

TO WHOM IT MAY CONCERN

Re – Richard Chester, Business Consultant

I have known Richard for over 35 years and would consider him to be an ideal aid to any business as a non-executive director, especially within the sporting or charitable trust arenas.

We have both worked within the football industry for a lengthy time and I joined Richard's team at Sheffield United FC back in 1982 where he was the Company Secretary and which is where we first met, although Richard has also had considerable experience working with governing bodies and charitable trusts such as the Football Foundation.

A great planner and organiser, Richard is tenacious personally but an excellent leader, motivator and mentor.

Should you require any further information, please do not hesitate to contact me.

Yours faithfully

Andy R Daykin
Director

The Loose Box, Hathersage Hall Business Centre, Main Road, Hathersage, S32 1BB
Tel: 01433 695150 Mob: 07771 551155
Registered in England No 7391828 Registered Office: 51 Clarkgrove Road, Sheffield S70 2XH

Chapter Four: Managing to Succeed

"Money makes the world go round" goes the old saying. It certainly helps to oil the wheels of the footballing globe, to mix a few metaphors. The modern world of television deals, sponsorship and multi million pounds transfer deals may seem a world away from my time in the 1970s and 1980s. In some ways, that is true – the world was a simpler place and the amount of cash swilling around the game was much lower. However, there are themes and stories that may well ring true to today's football follower. In this chapter I'll discuss what I know of payments in brown envelopes (sometimes referred to as "bungs") and I'll show how different clubs and different people had varying approaches to dealing with this. "Filthy lucre" is another description of money. I'll aim to show here how money in football could be dirty or clean depending on the time, people and clubs involved. I will also try to relay how each manager used transfer funds available to them and what degree of success was delivered.

I'll begin with my days at Lincoln where Graham Taylor and I worked very closely together. We considered how the club could develop and move away from the dismal days of relegation, average results and lack of anything likely to bring about any material benefit to the City of Lincoln. During the time Graham spent at Lilleshall undertaking his various coaching qualifications he made a personal contact with Bobby Robson, as he then was before his knighthood. Bobby, as manager of Ipswich Town, had seen his club emerge and succeed at the top level. The outcome of one such chat was an invite for both Graham and I to visit Ipswich and enjoy the benefits of their much-publicised hospitality, generally hosted by club owners the Cobbold brothers. We saw a distinct likeness in the stature of Ipswich Town FC in the County of Suffolk to that of Lincoln City in the County of Lincolnshire. We felt that Lincoln had the possibility of becoming a similar-sized club, disregarding our county rivals Grimsby town and Scunthorpe United. These visits often took place when their reserves were playing their midweek evening fixtures. This meant many hours were spent in the car allowing plenty of uninterrupted hours of talking and deciding on the campaigns to enhance the profile of the Imps. To say we had to curtail the hospitality afforded to us would be an understatement, but the lessons learnt from a club who had risen from the lower divisions but were held in the highest esteem was one which was of immense benefit to both of us.

No single person can take the credit for the all-round success of a club. The board of directors play an important role, the results on the field under the management of a committed manager are an obvious necessity, and the senior administrator has to be on top of his job at all times. When the team enjoyed success on the field, the role I played became very demanding. When the results on the field of play were, to coin a phrase, dismal, then the work becomes even more demanding. It required more than a 100% input as the consolidation of the business rests on your shoulders when the main sales product is failing.

During the mid to late 1970s, Sincil Bank was the place to be, and credit is due to all. For my part there had been many hurdles to overcome, many challenges to face up to and many successes to learn from. I am pleased to say that I consider that I departed from the club with them in a much better financial state of affairs. All creditors were enjoying a normal business relationship, there were no demanding calls from the bank and the club were in the fortunate position where they had a sum of money invested on the London open money market. In addition, and much more importantly from a supporters point of view, the combination of the superb 1975/76 season and the marketing of the club saw an increase in average attendances from 5,808 (two seasons prior to my taking over) to 6,298 (the average home attendance from 1971/72 through to 1976/77). The club had succeeded with their on and off the field activities.

THE LINCOLN CITY FIRST TEAM SQUAD FOR THE 1975-76 SEASON

Promotion season 1975/76 really brought about some extreme pleasures for both the club and their supporters. It would be remiss of me not to highlight the depth of work injected by Graham. Many many hours – not forgetting the miles – were spent. Particular emphasis was placed on watching either the opposition or potential new players. On a number of occasions it was a twin approach, with me accompanying him, spending the travelling time to formulate future plans or keeping an amateur view on the game as well. On one such occasion at the end of March 1976 we trekked down the A46 Fosseway to finish up at Reading where they were playing Tranmere Rovers in an evening fixture. Graham had previously asked me not to bother to arrange hospitality tickets for the game: he wanted to stand on the terraces. Upon arrival Graham dug out of the back of the car some dressing-up gear including false moustache, false beard, dark rimmed glasses and a flat cap. In fact he looked like a right daft bugger! We duly paid to go through the turnstiles, and took our position on the terraces opposite the main stand. His target was Mark Palios, playing for the visitors.

As the game unfolded the home side's left winger was turning in a performance, creating a comment from Graham to a local fan standing at the side of us, 'God, he's some player. Is he like that every game?'

The reply swiftly came back: 'No, mate, you should see him on a Saturday after his session in the night clubs, he plays as if half-cut.'

Quite a bit of banter was taking place when Graham said to the lad, 'Who's the best team in the league then?'

'I suppose you would have to say Lincoln City they're top of the league. We play them next week here.'

Graham, still looking very serious then asked, 'Well who's their manager?'

The guy promptly replied, 'He's a gobshite called Graham Taylor, but we'll stuff it up him, you'll see!'

For a moment or two the banter was put on the back burner and as the game was within ten minutes of the final whistle Graham said to me, 'Shall we make an early get away we don't want to be stuck in traffic we've a long journey home.'

'Fine by me,' I said and as we were walking away Graham said to the guy.

'Cheers mate, thanks for the chat I'll see you at the Lincoln game.'

'Why mate, are you a Royals fan then?'

Reply swiftly came back, 'No, I'm Graham Taylor, the gobshite you have been talking about. When I take my place on the bench I'll give you a wave!' The look on his face was worth the trip down to Elm Park, the whole incident lightening the task of the miles ahead of us. The game against Reading in actual fact finished up as a 1-1 draw.

Graham, as readers will be well aware, enjoyed a successful, respected career taking in almost 1,400 games. In terms of his overall career statistics he achieved an excellent win ratio of 43.06%. In terms of his service to Lincoln City this was slightly better with a recorded win ratio of 44.06%. The 1% increase may appear a minimal improvement, but in terms of that achievement it represented considerably more to the Sincil Bank faithful who had taken him to their hearts. As a club Lincoln City had been present in the Football League since 1892/93 and from that date through to 2020/21 they had participated in 4,030 games giving an historical win ratio of 37.0%. Graham's record is comfortably in excess of that to which the fans were accustomed. Unlike his predecessors he was blessed with a generous cheque book to help revamp the squad before achieving that promotion from Division Four. All in all his nett spend was in the region of £50,000 with spending on players' wages going up from £57,116 at the end of the 1971/72 financial year to £67,516 at the end of 1975/76.

It is an interesting fact that in those heady days of success, both on and off the field, there were seasons where the total aggregate attendance at all home games was in line with the club's most recent successful season. The best year in the 70s saw only 62 fewer fans per game than in 2018/19. Compared to the relevant staffing levels for both of those seasons I would strongly suggest that what was achieved in the mid-1970s compares very favourably – if not better. As a further indication, the highest league attendance during my period of office was 16,498 compared to 9,005 in 2018/19. This was in a period where attendances nationally were falling dramatically. A total of 2,926,729 people attended Division Four games in 1969/70. This fell to a low of 1,992,684 in 1974/75 and only just broke the two million barrier the following campaign. Lincoln City bucked this trend. (Statistics from Richard Crooks: *Grandad, What was Football like in the 1970s*).

The exceptionally high attendance referred to at Sincil Bank was soon to be the norm for me at the Lane. Gates hovering in the 15-20,000 range were what was to be expected with local derbies and games against bigger clubs attracting many more. Welcome to life with the 'bigger boys.'

I'll begin my story at The Lane with a story related to me by Harry Haslam himself. It happened before I started working there. This is the story related to me by Harry, on more than one occasion, I must say, but it should be noted that other versions exist, containing differing interpretations. I can only leave it to the reader's judgement as to which one to run with.

During the July prior to my engagement Harry had the opportunity to travel to Argentina in the hope of signing Diego Maradona. On the trip he was accompanied by one of his footballing staff, Oscar Arce, himself fluent in the Spanish tongue. How the opportunity came about to secure such a trip I am not at all sure but at the time the player was commanding world-wide interest. He was, I was told, a bit of a gem within the Argentinian community and was highly valued. As discussions and preliminary negotiations unfolded it became apparent that Harry had the chance to secure a deal and bring him to The Lane – what a coup that would have been! There were two obstacles to overcome. One was the ability for Sheffield United to find the £400,000 asking price, and secondly persuading the player that it would be a good move for him at this stage in his career. After some exchanging of phone calls between Sheffield and Buenos Aires along with frantic discussions between directors in Sheffield, the outcome was a call to Harry confirming that no such sum could be raised. Apparently that was a relief to Harry who, whilst occupying his hotel room, had a knock on the door only to find their chief of police standing there wielding his gun and simply saying, in very broken English, 'Maradona – No.' A quick knock on the next hotel room door brought Oscar into the frame when it was quickly agreed that all negotiations would be terminated, but not saying that the club could not afford the transfer fee. Listening to this story it was immediately clear to me that this could be a very murky world indeed.

Harry Haslam

Not wanting the trip to be a wasted journey Harry was briefed on the talents and capabilities of another young Argentinian player who had been described as a talent for the future. The availability of Alex Sabella was made known. A considerably reduced fee of £160,000 was agreed with Boca Juniors and following further telephone calls with the United board funds were confirmed and agreement reached. This would seem to allow his presence in a Blades shirt, but I found that some further stringent processes were to be completed before ultimate clearance. I think it would be fair to say that his acquisition was, in the main, very well received by Blades supporters and at the same time created a much-needed boost to the club's overall profile.

Whilst all this was going on, the opportunity was presented to Harry regarding the availability of Ossie Ardiles and Ricky Villa, both Argentinian internationals. How this came about I was not told, and to this day have no proof. The first of those was Ardiles. An extract from Nick Harris's *Foreign Revolution* reveals the calls which took place between

Harry Haslam and Bill Nicholson, the recent manager of Tottenham Hotspur. Nicholson had just handed over the reins to Keith Burkinshaw but was still involved in player acquisition. Harry, Bill, and Keith had enjoyed a good friendship over the years and when Harry said to Bill, 'Would Keith be interested in signing Osvaldo Ardiles?' The response from Keith was, 'Is Harry pulling your leg or what – of course I would!' The outcome was that Harry completed all negotiations and the deal was done. A couple of days later Ricky Villa agreed an identical move and a combined fee of £750,000 was agreed and formalities completed.

Why do I include this when I wasn't even at the club? I can say that during my time working with Harry Haslam we had a very open relationship during which he told me a lot about his reputation as a wheeler dealer. He enjoyed that description, I felt. As a result of his dealings in Argentina on behalf of Tottenham Hotspur he told me that whilst he wouldn't give precise details of money paid as a back-hander it was sufficient to comfortably set him up. 'This is the sort of industry you are in, mate. If you keep your nose clean you can make a small fortune which you wouldn't be able to achieve in a normal business,' he said. 'And if you want, you can work with me, and we can laugh all the way home' – an offer I didn't take up, as I had legal responsibilities to comply with. It brought me to the conclusion that in any other transfers he may bring to the table, my involvement would be to deal with the formalities once the transactions were between the two clubs concerned. I needed to ensure my position would not be compromised or regulations breached. It was not always possible, but generally my role in transfers from then on was to leave player discussions to the manager. Prior to that, my role would be to liaise with the selling club via my opposing colleague and/or their chairman. It was eye-opening to me though that the murkiness of this type of business conducted overseas was stated to me to be "their culture."

Before I move on to foreign player deals done during my time at the Lane, I take you back to the Alex Sabella signing. One day I was in the general office where the clerk was busy calculating the wages and looking over her shoulder. I noticed that against Alex's gross earnings was a very sizeable deduction for tax. I discovered that since his arrival no one had bothered to help him settle into life in the UK or help him register with the relevant National Insurance or Inland Revenue processes. This meant he had been on an emergency coding since his start date. Not being in any sort of full command of the English language I arranged through Oscar Arce to call in at his home one evening armed with all the necessary forms for his completion. The outcome was a notification received confirming the correct code number had been issued by the Inland Revenue so when applied in the next payroll process he received a major tax rebate. After that I was his friend forever!

His lack of understanding of the English language was egg and milk to his dressing room mates. They taught him all the words the referees wouldn't appreciate if they were penalised. On one such occasion a game at Bramall Lane was being refereed by Pat Partridge, an accomplished north-eastern based referee who I had met during my days at Sincil Bank and established a good rapport with. Before the game I visited his dressing room to make sure everything was OK and he was comfortable, and also warned him of what to expect if he blew up against Alex. After the game I again visited to make sure we had looked after him and his colleagues, and during this chat he said, 'Dick. Thank God you warned me what I might encounter, as without that I could have sent him off on at least six occasions!'

One abortive transfer was the collapse of a deal which would have taken Sabella to Roker Park, Sunderland in a £800,000 deal. Accompanied by Harry Haslam and me, he returned home feeling less than comfortable about the presentation made to him by their hierarchy and did not want to move from Sheffield. Later on a deal was struck for him to complete a transfer to Leeds United FC for £400,000 which was finalised with little or no problem. Following the completion of transfer the chairman, John Hassall, came into my office to thank me for the efficiency shown, saying, 'As long as you are in football you will never do a better deal.' To which I replied, 'Thanks for the recognition. No need really, it is part of the job, but remember your words when you are sat in John Street Stand in the middle of winter with your nuts virtually frozen off and no one on the pitch to excite you like Alex has done.' I don't consider myself a footballing expert but I doubt there were many hardened supporters who wouldn't agree with me when I say he was an exciting player, always liable to do the unexpected and very often make opposition players look like they were chasing shadows. When the possible transfer was announced in the *Sheffield Star* Alex and his wife were in the city doing some shopping and on their way back they called into my office. On their way in they were covered, literally from head to toe, with spit from supporters. An utter disgraceful act by supposed fans! I can only say that it showed their frustrations at the loss of such a character and talent.

During the 1978/79 close season, the Blades put their foot in the water with the acquisition of further foreign players – namely Pedro Verde and Len de Goey. To do so they called upon the services of a Monte Carlo based agent, Burt Carlier. How these players landed on the club's radar system I do not know. To the best of my knowledge and belief neither had been watched and the club had no substantial information about them whatsoever, other than several phone calls between the agent and Oscar Arce, again because of his ability to speak fluently in several languages. Many calls took place, some of which were in my office, but what precisely was said was unknown other than the interpretation given to Harry and myself at the end of the calls. On the morning of Friday 5th May 1978, John Hassall came into my office enquiring if I was going to the FA Cup final the following day, for which I had no plans whatsoever. He said, 'Right then, the club will pay for you to have a weekend away. I will come back in later and confirm the arrangements, but I want you to go to Monte Carlo and complete the Pedro Verde deal.'

A trip to Monte Carlo seemed a very good option to me. During that lunchtime Hassall came back armed with flight tickets from Manchester to Nice – Friday evening departure, Sunday morning return – along with reservation details at Hotel Columbus, confirmation of the agent meeting me to transport me to the hotel and a bankers' draft for depositing at their chosen bank. His words were very clear, in as much as I was to deposit it personally and, once done, the chairman didn't want to know anything else whatsoever. The deal had been agreed but there was an element of discomfort about it all by the board as a whole. Nipping home to grab a weekend bag I tripped off to the airport for an onward journey to Nice. I arrived there at around 19.00 hours, looked out for someone holding a Mr Chester plaque and proceeded to the hotel. Whilst booking in, the agent asked if we were going to the bank that evening, an invitation I declined, preferring to get something to eat after a somewhat unusual day. Arrangements were made for a 9.00 a.m. bank visit the following day and, sure enough, the agent was on time to pick me up and get me there bang on the dot. On entering the bank we were greeted by the bank manager himself and six other persons. Who they were was still a mystery to me as introductions were off the agenda.

Once the bankers' draft had been lodged, the agent thanked me and promptly said the taxi rank was just outside the bank on the main street and when you get back to the hotel the reception desk will arrange a taxi to take you to catch your plane on Sunday morning. Quite a clear and definitive meaning behind those words, which I will leave to your imagination. No sooner had I arrived back home when, whilst enjoying a Sunday meal, the phone rang with Harry Haslam wanting to know if everything had gone according to plan. Again you need to use your imagination, as the following weekend Harry Haslam had made plans for a family short-break to Monte Carlo. Shortly after this there was the additional acquisition of Len de Goey, arranged through the same agent but this time there were no overseas visits arranged, just simply the usual essential documentation to complete a foreign transfer and completion via the banking system. Collectively transfer fees payable of circa £250,000 were involved. Who, how, where and when this was distributed will undoubtedly never be known. Lessons learned again by me – a somewhat murky, murky business!

Bringing the whole scenario of the transfer up to date, there could be some very interesting questions asked about the ever-growing number of agents and sums of money being expended by English clubs, particularly within the Premier League. The total spend on agency fees across the 92 teams in the English leagues was £317,126,972 for season 2020/21 with a similar sum of £311,797,860 for season 2019/20. In respect of season 2020/21, £272,220,223 (85.84%) of the total was spent by Premier League clubs, and for season 2019/20, £263,368,860 (84.47%). Breaking those sums down further it is interesting to note that the spending of the six clubs involved in the proposed midweek Super League breakaway accounted for £133,339,061 – or 48.98% – and for season 2019/20 the spending by those clubs was £126,634,437 – or 48.08%.

Whilst coming to the final stages of putting this story together, various members of the press reported on agents fees for season 2021/22. It would be remiss of me not to include these; though these statistics will instantly out of date. Trends of heavy spending continued with the total spending on agents fees continuing to rise. They have been recorded at £322,650,661 split as follows across the four divisions: Premier League £272,559,227; EFL Championship £44,378,940; EFL League One £4,426,888 and EFL League Two £1,285,606. What is particularly interesting is that when you analyse the top four spenders in each of the divisions it reveals that 75% of those clubs have foreign ownership. Would the reader consider that to be purely coincidental or would they feel that it highlighted the way that business is now being conducted? The sums of money going out of our game are considerable and it should not be overlooked that this large-scale involvement of agents has mainly come about since the significant increase in foreign investors. This may of course not be correlated (the two things going together but one not causing the other). To me though, it begs question.

Further transfer dealings at The Lane failed to deliver the intended improvement in results, with the team suffering a steady decline, ultimately getting to the position where, with the club sliding towards potential relegation, illness forced the resignation of Harry and the handover of team management affairs to Martin Peters in January 1981. Despite this change, virtually nothing seemed to happen in terms of securing better results or maintaining the credibility of this once highly respected club. The final match of the season against Walsall confirmed the club's relegation to Division Four. It also brought about the resignation of John Hassall, a true Unitedite in every sense of the word, and the appointment of Reg Brealey as Chairman.

I mentioned earlier the reputation Harry Haslam enjoyed as the "wheeler-dealer" but when I looked back on his days at Bramall Lane his so called wheeling dealing, allowing for the very lucrative deals involving the sales of Imre Varadi and Alex Sabella, there was a nett deficit of transfer fees of £349,000 with a further increase in players' wages of £145,094 – showing an accumulated deficit of almost half a million pounds. Combined with relegation to Division Four this dispels any belief that he was a successful wheeler-dealer. During his stay at Bramall Lane Harry secured an overall win ratio of 32.58% and during the time from me joining to Harry leaving in 1980/81, his win ratio was 33.84%. Regretfully these statistics show precisely why the club suffered a decline. The Blades have been members of the Football League since 1892/93 and through to the end of 2020/21 have played 4,890 games with an average win ratio of 40.24%. This only reinforces my view of Harry's unfortunate statistics and results. It is clear that with results like that the pathway led only one way – down to Division Four.

I enjoyed a good working relationship with Harry Haslam with several daily meetings – including his customary cuppa. I scripted his programme notes for him to approve before going to print – having been given the gist of the content; I enjoyed the process. I could, though, never accept that the work undertaken before any new signings was so lacking. I cannot recall any conversations where he gave any indication that he had been to watch a game the previous evening. John Harris, a real toff, and former manager, was employed as chief scout but there seemed little or no closeness or reliability on any of his recommendations. The real jewel in the crown for Harry was the availability of the annual Rothman's book within which he seemingly secured his information as well as by chatting to some of his pals in football.

In those days what the manager did was of no concern to the company secretary. The manager had a direct relationship with the chairman, on behalf of the board of directors. The duties of the company secretary could have an effect on working relationships. One example in Harry's case followed the need to advise him in writing that his company car was for his own personal use and was not there for his son to drive. His son was making regular use of the vehicle. The company motor vehicle policy did not include for such cover so Harry was advised that in the event of an accident or damage he would be personally responsible for the full settlement of any claim. That instruction had little or no effect on future usage of the car or driver. The board of directors had approved the internal communication but seemed reluctant to take the issue any further. Harry never once took offence at my insistence on complying with the rules and our relationship continued in the same vein thereafter, but it goes to show just how isolated you could become just simply doing your job.

Done properly the role of a company secretary can be a lonely existence, for it was, then, and I suppose still is, a position where it would be dangerous to form close relationships with any leading executive – other than a solid meaningful relationship with the chairman. I experienced that positive relationship beyond my wildest dreams only in my days at Hillsborough.

In the case of Martin Peters, the relationship, whilst not strained, was very much distant. Martin seemed aloof, indecisive, and displayed the air of someone who deep down felt his professional qualities were above the level he was currently working at. Unfortunately, his statistics reveal only an 18.75 win percentage – an achievement somewhat below the standards he had set himself as a player.

From the depths of despair came a return to some glories. In the summer of 1981, new chairman Reg Brealey was fully ensconced in his new role. Work was completed to transfer Bramall Lane from a shell into a meaningful, presentable complex. The club could never get full benefit from those areas until the fortunes of the team could be turned around. This began with the appointment of a new manager. An early June meeting at the Grosvenor Hotel was held at which Ian Porterfield was invited to meet the chairman, Derek Dooley, and myself with a view to assuming that role. The club had made the required approach to his former employees, Rotherham United, to discuss such a move. The thinking behind a sort of delegation from our side was that if Ian had any specific views on any element of the club's workings then they could be answered on the spot by whoever was responsible. Ian would then hopefully be able to make an instant decision, as he was the only one in the frame.

The outcome is etched in Lane history leading to a transformation in terms of transfer policies, player acquisition and success. His first season 1981/82 culminated in a return to Division Three after only one campaign at basement level. In some respects he was a very lucky manager indeed ,for I cannot recall one occasion in my time where he wanted to sign a player and was refused by the chairman. I say chairman, and not the board of directors, for at this time Reg was a controlling shareholder of the company. In essence what Reg wanted to do he did with the directors supporting him. Often Reg personally made the funds available.

With money seemingly no problem, Ian Porterfield was a very lucky, but, yes, successful, manager with deals involving Keith Edwards, Colin Morris, Keith Waugh, Alan Young, John McAlle, Terry Curran, and Paul Richardson, all of which proved valuable acquisitions, accounting for just short of £700,000. Not the sort of money one was accustomed to in Division Four. The contributions both individually and collectively brought about a real change in fortunes. They also brought into play an expectation from such players of being looked after.

There was an occasion during the period following Ian Porterfield's appointment, when it was necessary for me to advise the chairman in writing, if only to protect my delegated responsibilities, of the rigorous provisions of the Football League regulations re payments outside of the applicable contract. This was brought about by two players knocking on my office door, having been sent directly by the manager, to collect envelopes promised to them. Confirming no knowledge of any such arrangements the players left. Following which I had an immediate knock on my door and John McSeveney – assistant to Ian – came in enquiring what the players wanted and asking if I had approval to talk to them without specific approval from Ian. Once the circumstances were clarified John went on to say that they were two of many who had their demands settled outside their contracts – never disclosing who – but also confirming that it met with the manager's approval as he too had been 'looked after.'

It must be said that I never witnessed any such transactions, but it would also be fair to say that there was plenty of internal gossip going around. Following my note to the chairman, and for the first time in my football career, all future transfer dealings were dealt with on a completely different basis. My services were no longer required except to prepare and/or provide a completed contract with predetermined contractual provisions contained therein, together with the provision of registration forms. These were then handed over to Ian Porterfield, very often in the presence of the chairman, for pre-contract signing discussions. It is therefore difficult for me to be specific or assured that any malpractices were in fact happening. The autobiography of one of the players involved includes a reference to being in receipt of such a payment, giving some credence to my concerns. Again I'll leave the reader to draw his or her own conclusions. This was the only time in my career when my direct involvement in transfer dealings was overlooked in preference to that of a manager and chairman, both lacking in the detailed knowledge of the relevant regulations and transfer processes.

Ian Porterfield, whilst not diminishing his championship achievements, was lucky in terms of full backing and support from all around him. I am sure those who worked around him would concur that he was not the easiest to work with. I would describe him as being quite volatile at times. The players he signed came from two sources. Firstly, those recommended by his able assistant, John McSeveney, who he relied on hugely. Secondly, players who had caused his team some difficulties on the opposing side.

There are a couple of signings which particularly stand out for me in terms of circumstances, not in any way to do with a player's abilities. The first was the return to Bramall Lane of a former favourite goal scorer Keith Edwards. Keith at that time was plying his trade with Hull City. He had been on Ian's wanted list for a short time but in my discussions with Hull City was deemed to be not available for transfer. Early in the season – 19 September to be precise – the fixture list brought us together for a game at Boothferry Park – and lo and behold we came away with a 2–1 defeat with Keith scoring their winning goal late in the second half.

First thing on the following Monday morning an irate Ian came into my office with a demand for me to tell the chairman that he wanted us to increase the transfer price to £100k and get him signed. My response was just as clear, 'Before you start training, you speak to the chairman yourself as I am not going to get involved in player valuations. That is something I am not qualified in.' Ian exited, fuming and red-faced with anger; a trait which showed itself several times when not getting his own way. The next step was inevitable, with the chairman asking me to re-arrange my work schedules, contact Hull City, confirm the offer and, if acceptable, get into my car and travel over to Hull to complete. The outcome? Welcome back to the Lane, Keith Edwards.

A similar situation arose with the signing of Colin Morris. Although the result of our home game against Blackpool ended with a positive 3–1 result Colin had proved himself to be somewhat of a handful. He gave a bit of a skinning to Paul Garner and our left-sided defence. Again Monday morning discussions with Ian included his need to sign Colin Morris, but apart from an FA Cup exit at the hands of Altrincham, the league performances had been quite satisfactory, with Stevie Neville filling the right-wing berth. Ian's persistence paid off and, with the team playing away to Colchester United, I made the journey north to the sunny climes of Blackpool in February. I carried with me a completed contract with all agreed terms and conditions contained therein. Along with this I held partly completed registration and transfer forms so that in meeting with their secretary and completing formal signing procedures we could ensure registration compliance with the Football League to allow for his selection in the following midweek game. In both instances, and certainly unusual for Division Four transfer dealings, the fee was paid in full without any need for the negotiation of staged payments. Our fellow league clubs certainly enjoyed that side of things.

Whilst I was in Blackpool completing the transfer business, the team had an away game at Colchester United resulting in a nightmare 2–5 defeat. The travelling distance involved necessitated an overnight stay in a 4 star rated hotel. It was the best in the hotel group's ownership in that particular part of the country. Come Monday morning an irate Ian came into my office fuming about the "crap" hotel. He told me that it had caused the club to lose the game and instructed me that all other bookings with the hotel group should be cancelled. I responded, 'Until I get such instructions from the board, all arrangements will remain in place as I don't have the authority to overrule a board decision.' On a bit of a roll, I continued, 'Come back to me when you have confirmation from the players that when they go away on their holidays they all use hotels with a rating in excess of the one just used. It's no good whatsoever blowing your top and looking to move the blame off your own doorstep when the team may have just had an off day.'

Matter closed but it highlighted the depth of feeling that Ian had and the importance he put on gaining a result in every game. Clutching at straws some may say – the answer really lies in the hands of proper opposition information, management planning and team performance. Every team wants to win every game and that also applies to the management structure but that can't always be the case and it sometimes means going back to the drawing board whether it is a football match, a business or life in general. Certainly Ian went on to achieve greater things for the Lane fans

One game which highlighted the feelings and frustrations of football came in an evening game against Wigan in March 1982. In front of a 22,000 plus attendance the atmosphere was buoyant. With the away team being in contention with ourselves for both promotion and championship honours the result was important to both sides. Edging towards the final minutes of the game the directors sat in the away section of the directors' box were looking quite smug with the prospect of holding us at home. But, all was not done. An attack down the right wing in front of the Kop saw Colin Morris deliver a telling pass right into the path of Keith Edwards who was adept at putting the ball away in such a position. Sure enough it banged into the back of the net, the crowd went wild and following a re-start the referee blew for the final whistle. The atmosphere in the directors' room was quite amazing. Their chairman, Mr Freddy Pye and fellow director, the legendary, and now Sir, Bobby Charlton were so vociferous with their comments and views that it was difficult to detect any sentence which didn't contain a volume of words not generally found in the English dictionaries! The opposing views were all that you would expect with the result re-enforcing the quest for the championship. Would it be fair to say that there were a few smug faces? Of course it would and of course there were!

One player who had caused us earlier difficulties was a member of the Owls team in what Wednesdayites like to call the Boxing Day massacre. Yes! That's right – Terry Curran. Terry, along with other Owls players were involved in some less than friendly scenes in the tunnel before the players had taken to the pitch for the kick-off. Scoring one of the goals in front of the Blades fans he didn't do himself any favours in the eyes of Unitedites by throwing himself on his knees heading towards the Leppings Lane terraces. He was pelted with coins and verbal abuse which was never to be forgotten. That was 1979. Fast forward to 1982 and at the end of his contract negotiations with the Owls came to an impasse. This opened the door for Ian Porterfield to make a phone call to his fellow ex-pro saying that he would like him to sign for the Blades and that his chairman would like to speak with him. Terry had asked Jack Charlton for a two-year contract at Hillsborough, paid at £25,000 per year, plus a tax-free sum of £11,000 to settle his mortgage. The latter part Jack would not agree to. The meeting took place between Terry and Reg Brealey and the path was set for the Football League Tribunal meeting at the Royal Victoria Hotel in Sheffield.

Guess what? Neither Ian nor Reg were available to represent the Club, the dubious honour falling into my lap. Prior to the actual meeting I met Jack and their company secretary, Eric England in the hotel lobby and was faced with an opening greeting of, 'Hi, Dick. Where the f..k is

Porterfield and Slippery Arse Brealey – you're wasting your f...ing time, you've only offered him the same as us and he won't sign for that and play in your mickey mouse league.' Inside the meeting room I presented our case on the basis that the player felt he was not being recognised by his club for the valuable service and consistent performances he had given and that a change of clubs for the fee offered (£50,000) was both in the best interest of the player and more reflective of the fact that his existing club did not believe he was worth a better deal. Having not been involved in any of the preliminary discussions it was a precarious position to find myself in, but in presenting this sort of a case for his transfer to The Lane I was thanked by members of the tribunal for a frank and realistic presentation.

The outcome was two-fold. Firstly, A fee of £100,000 was the decision of the tribunal. Secondly, a further outburst from Jack Charlton who made his feelings – in his own words – about the "under the counter" dealings of manager and chairman clear. He felt that they showed their guilt by their non-presence at the tribunal for a player deemed to be so important for their squad. Whilst making our presentation I was dreading any questions coming my way about his inclusion in our squad as, whilst his talents were unquestionable, I could never see him being accepted by our supporters who I thought would still be harbouring ill feelings for his "taunting" on that never to be forgotten Boxing Day. I felt we had a manager and a chairman completely at odds with supporters. At the tribunal, I later learned, Jack offered him the tax-free sum only to be declined by Terry, as an offer far too late. Using one's imagination once more, it would not be unreasonable to assume that what Jack wouldn't offer, Sheffield United did. Either way, it never came to light during my days at the Lane. Terry went on to play 33 games and score three goals for the Blades. Whether all the fuss was worth it, I leave to more expert eyes than mine!

Brown envelopes here, "bungs" involved in the completion of transfers elsewhere. A murky world that I did not want to be involved with. The change in procedures meant that my hands remained clean. It does not take too much research into the footballing world of the time to find rumours of such happenings, though. Those rumours, were supposedly, proved as fact in the case of George Graham who was banned from the game for a year and made to repay Arsenal £425,000 plus interest in the early 1990s – according to official reports, that was. In terms of George Graham's point of view, that can only be left to the man himself to be open and honest. Players being "looked after" with these extra brown envelope payments is more difficult to prove as fact. I'll leave it to the reader to decide exactly what was happening at Bramall Lane.

What I do know, and what I can categorically state, is that I was never ever involved in any such deals. The rules and regulations make it very clear, with the responsibility of ensuring compliance resting firmly on the shoulders of the company secretary. If he cares, which he should do by accepting such a position, for his career then there can be no grey areas in the management of the club. It is simply black or white. It should also be stated that those that seek to administer such murky dealings should take a serious look at themselves. In my mind they should ask if they do, or do not, respect the position and careers of those administering the rules and regulations, or whether they feel their own financial discretions are more important to their egos than other people's livelihoods.

The game has had a long and infamous history of scandal. Examples date back at least as far as 1960 which accusations of a Southampton player deliberately giving away a penalty against Don Revie's Leeds United. The incident ultimately gained headlines in *The Sun* - 30 January 1982 – "The Day Don Revie Fixed a Game." In 1964 Wednesday players Tony Kay, Peter Swan and David Bronco Layne saw press headlines in *The Sunday People* accusing them of betting against their own team when playing Ipswich Town in 1962. These offences were proven with the players in receipt of prison sentences and life-time bans. Just a couple of cases but a review of earlier years in football will show that there were far more and not just confined to one particular era.

The Blades supporters, like any other club supporters, will have opinions as to good or bad but whatever their mixed views may well be they should not undervalue the time spent at The Lane by Ian Porterfield. During my time, whilst having a nett outlay on transfers of £600,000 he delivered a very creditable 50% win ratio. His overall win percentage during his stay at The Lane was 42.75%.

There is an old saying of "when one door closes another door opens." This was certainly the case with me when the disappointment of a broken promise at The Lane was put to bed for the time being, with the opportunity to join the Owls. More elsewhere on the circumstances of my departure. Reflecting back now though, I wonder if I fully realised the implications of that move at the time. I'm not sure if I did. I was aware that it would have consequences amongst supporters but not necessarily with the loss of friendships with many who cut me stone dead when the news leaked out.

It has to be said that any successful football club has to have good professional working relationships at the highest level and during my time at Hillsborough this was certainly the case. Confidence was the order of the day between the chairman, Bert McGee, and manager, Howard Wilkinson, and I. With regards to Howard, the template was put in place on day one when we met in his office to talk about our way forward. As it quickly became clear Howard was not interested in treading into my territory and neither was I intending to tread on his toes. It was readily understood that if either of us picked up any Chinese whispers from any quarter whatsoever about each other's performances then it would be the case of each one informing the other. With regards to team performances it was exactly the same. Howard was only too well aware that almost everyone had an opinion about results and performances. He asked if I wanted to pass any comments, to do so in his office and not join in the crossfire which very often stems from the directors' room after-match chats.

With regards to the transfer of players – both in and out – he made it quite clear that although he would be the "guvnor" in this area, once he had identified a potential move, he would confirm asking prices having spoken with his opposing counterpart and then step away from the financial implications and leave that to be determined by the chairman and myself. The whole visionary, working relationship was new to me, for, although enjoying a good relationship with Graham Taylor, he was always intent on being the "top dog" and involved in everything, although not always crystal clear of all the financial regulations. Also in the case of Ian Porterfield, manager at The Lane for the majority of my time, he would go out of his way to keep things to himself and when necessary deal only directly with the chairman. The money invested by Howard in the team was minimal compared to his competitors but the output in terms of commitment, fitness and organisation saw the registering of points when realistically odds were stacked against them.

Howard, in my opinion, was the best manager I had the pleasure of working with. It was the best relationship I enjoyed in that respect. He also had a thoroughly professional staff supporting him from grass roots development to the first team. In terms of treatment of injuries he worked with one of the best club physiotherapists in the game in the form of Alan Smith. Howard also had an excellent coaching and scouting network incorporating the services of two true Wednesdayites – Peter Eustace and Micky Hennigan.

In the case of Micky Hennigan, I was called into Howard's office for a meeting. The board of directors had given Howard the approval to appoint a suitable person to handle the grass roots development and the management of the Northern Intermediate League Youth team. Hennigan was known to Howard from their playing days together at Hillsborough. The story goes that Mick took a phone call from Howard – it must have been one of the very early mobile phones – whilst an employee of the local electricity board. At that moment he was somewhere atop a pylon!

Howard explained the nature of the call to him whereupon there was an instant acceptance to the extent that he came down the pylon, gathered himself together and within an hour was sat in Howard's office. The negotiation that followed must rate as one of the easiest and quickest signings I was ever involved in. Explaining the intended role Howard said, 'There you are, mate: that's the job. What do you think?' 'Fine, said Mick . When do I start.' We didn't discuss money, it was whatever was the offer and when a start date was mentioned the response was, 'I'll start in the morning.' Whatever happened to his severance processes from his previous employers I don't know but sure enough he was there. He began immediately with the youth development squad and never ever looked back, always putting his complete heart and soul into the job allocated to him. And what a fine job he did too. One player who springs to mind in breaking through into the first team squad was Carl Bradshaw. There were others including Kevin Pressman, Wayne Jacobs, and Tony Gregory. It was almost a production line through to the first team. I know that Howard thought very highly of Mick, taking him with him as his assistant when he moved to Leeds United a few years later.

Alan Smith went on in later years to be appointed physio for the full England squad but during his time at Hillsborough he was approached by the Sheffield Hospitals Trust to consider an application to become a late entrant for a consultant orthopaedic role, such was his capabilities. Currently he operates his own physiotherapy practice in neighbouring Rotherham. He was an excellent physio as proved by his work rehabilitating Ian Knight from one of the worst injuries ever seen on a football pitch at that time. I know that Knight and many other players of the era cannot speak highly enough of Alan. I was present many times in Howard's office with Alan and listened to what were in those days revolutionary discussions relating to correct intake of food, calories, their benefits both in terms of health, training and playing, the constant need to control those correct levels to enhance bodily strengths and shape, speed of movement and how those could overcome that of opposing teams. I was left spell-bound and grateful I wasn't on the receiving end of those disciplines but, more to the point, very impressed with the thought and application. Nowadays clubs engage specialist staff covering virtually every individual discipline you can imagine. In those days at Hillsborough it was down to the forward thinking of both Howard and Alan combined. Apart from being the ultimate professional Alan was also a thoroughly nice man.

As anticipated at the time of my engagement Howard delivered on the objective of returning to the top by finishing as runners up to Chelsea and securing the Owls' place in Division One. Whilst credit has to be given to the players for their successful delivery, recognition should also be given to the chairman and board of directors, Howard, his professional and astute backroom staff and their ability, along with those operating behind the scenes and not overlooking the supporters and their fanatical support. Objective delivered!

What a season!

Not unlike supporters, there are games which become etched in your memory. In my case it was two games in the 1984/85 season which really stand out and, funny enough, they were both against clubs regarded as being top guns. At the end of September we were drawn to play Liverpool at Anfield. Sat in the directors' box I was on the next row to Kenny Dalglish's wife and children, all bubbly and buoyant that they would be leaving the game with daddy and the customary three points. In the first half it was all Liverpool, although somehow or other we managed to go in at half time one goal to the good. The second half was even more demanding on our defence as the home side continued to totally dominate the match but on the break we managed to secure another goal. When the final whistle blew the Dalglish family were in tears with the children saying to Mum, 'We are going to have a miserable night with Dad tonight – he won't want to play with us or talk to us.' In Howard's programme notes for the following home game against Sunderland he was quoted as saying, 'Our victory at Anfield last Saturday was perhaps our best result since I arrived at Sheffield Wednesday last season.' Further testimony to this result was reflected when being awarded "The Fiat Performance of the Week Award."

Amongst the customary Christmas festival of football was a daunting visit to Old Trafford on New Year's Day 1985. Howard had decided that this would be a day trip allowing the players to have time with their families but to be prepared for a reasonably early departure. The coach journey across the Pennines was interrupted when Howard asked the driver to stop the coach whilst right on top of hills and ordered his players to get out and go for a walk across the cold and bleak terrain. They eventually returned to the coach with me wondering what the hell was going on! The players were talking about their walk all the way into Old Trafford with no mention of the game whatsoever. Maybe a spot of psychology from Howard. I have no idea what the team-talk consisted of but not unlike the earlier Liverpool game we spent much of our time in our own half. There were times when Mark Hughes lazily came out of our half for our attacks to be broken down and the ball lifted up front only to find himself in an offside position. Home supporters around the directors' box gave us visiting officials some right flack accusing us of only knowing how to play the offside, big kicking game. Imre Varadi virtually delivered an action replay to the earlier Liverpool game scoring in both the 45th and 90th minute. There was quite a celebration on the way home with a 2-1 win under our belts. The real lesson to be learned from these two games was that under Howard Wilkinson, Peter Eustace and Alan Smith the Owls were probably the fittest team in the then Division One and opposition should not rest on their laurels until the final whistle was blown.

Howard was very much under the cosh when it came to convincing the chairman for incoming player transfers. Bert McGee in true Yorkshire fashion always wanted a pound and a penny for any pound spent. His usual response was along the lines of, 'Ah well, Howard, we'll give this one the green light if you must have him, but you know you will always do better growing your own cucumbers.' I'm not even sure that Bert grew any of his own cucumbers! Howard, during my time working alongside of him, never once appeared to be at all reckless in either his signings or his spending and I think it would be fair to say that if you look at the player structure at the club it would, on paper, be considered to be inferior to those clubs we met in the then First Division. His nett spend during my time was a paltry sum really, at £250,000. An investment which took the club from Division Two and more obviously limited, when you consider a virtual 25% increase in attendances.

During my time with him at Hillsborough Howard secured a more than impressive win ratio of 46.18% and in 71.37% of his games he was not on the losing side. The Owls have been members of the Football League since 1893/94 and up to the end of Season 2020/21 had played 4,879 league games during which they accumulated a win percentage of 38.0% One does not need to be Einstein to see that Howard's achievements were way above the historical average – surprising as it may seem the average for the number of games when not losing of 63.6% is still well below that registered by Howard and his teams. Throughout his entire professional management career his teams competed in 69.7% of their games without being on the losing side.

Not being directly involved in the football management side of things I can only look at the managers I worked with, and, like supporters, draw personal conclusions. As a senior executive though I did have the advantage of an "in-house view." Howard, Graham and Ian were always committed to their objective of securing success and trying to be the best team in whatever division they were participating. Howard, in particular, had a very professional support team whose opinions were valued, and many times acted upon. Ian and Graham were similar in as much as, whilst they had good support from their back-up team, I can't recall that any one of those would ever prove to be a threat to "the boss." The boss was a good description, as their work was full and final and not up for discussion, backroom staff not being any sort of a threat to their supremacy – unless things went wrong when it was invariably someone else's fault. With regards to Harry Haslam and Martin Peters, unfortunately, there was not the same level of positive day to day planning and management, which, one could say, showed itself in their results, or lack of them. I consider myself fortunate to have worked in the same business as several managers. In differing circumstances, I learned a little about how they earned their success. A ring-side seat that money could not buy.

In terms of the cash floating around, I am reasonably convinced that there was "dirty money" in the game during my period. Transfers involving overseas players involved some murky dealings. Keeping players happy seemingly involved some being "looked after" outside of their contracts. The huge amounts of money in the modern game makes me worry about how it is all allocated and to what effect. I believe that, if I had wished, I could have done very well out of the money in the game, even in my time. Certainly I had conversations to that effect with one or two key individuals. However, I am convinced that my hands remained clean at all times – a lesson about honesty – from my childhood, and that I did what I could to ensure that all my clubs played within the rules, particularly when aware of the full happenings. In my next chapter I'll consider the rules of the game more broadly, how I kept to them, and how I tried to influence change for the better.

Howard Wilkinson

I first worked with Dick Chester when he moved to Hillsborough in 1983/84. He had of course worked with the Owls' rivals across the city in the years beforehand and I knew he had a reputation as a well-organised and efficient operator and administrator. He had some big shoes to fill at Sheffield Wednesday. His immediate predecessor as club secretary was Eric England who was approaching retirement. Prior to Eric England was his namesake Eric Taylor, often nicknamed "Mr Sheffield Wednesday." The two Erics had accumulated decades of service to the Owls.

By the time of Dick's arrival, we were well on the way to a return to Division One for the first time in fourteen years. The job of club secretary is a huge one; in modern day terms it is akin to a chief executive officer. So, Dick had a new job, taking over from a hugely experienced predecessor, at a club that was on the verge of promotion. On top of all that, he joined the Owls after previously serving our fiercest local rivals! In lesser hands, it could have proved a tricky job.

Dick, though, was just the man in these new circumstances. We immediately established an excellent working relationship based on trust and mutual understanding. The club secretary may sometimes feel like the centre of a whirlwind. He must deal with responsibilities from the league, the directors, the manager, players and their contracts, financial reporting, the media, fans, and ticket sales, and what may feel like a million and one other areas. Dick dealt with all this with aplomb. His administrative and managerial skills meant that all the important tasks were completed effectively and accurately. Importantly, he did this and developed a positive relationship with the staff at the club. I know that many people who worked for the club at the time consider it to be one of the favourite times of their careers. This is in no small measure due to Dick's work. Dick's success in all these areas helped ensure that my thoughts and efforts could focus on the success of the team.

Not only was Dick an excellent manager and administrator, but he also helped lead the club forward. Dick's drive and zeal helped ensure that the club came on leaps and bounds off the pitch. Dick's work helped develop facilities at Hillsborough that were worthy of a top Division One club. Facilities for supporters, for club management and for sponsors and executives all improved remarkably. Dick's work helped move all this forward and ensure that work was completed on time and on budget. The largest project of the time was the roofing of the Kop. Dick not only helped with ensuring that the project was successful, but he also managed to persuade the Queen to come to Hillsborough to officially open it.

Dick is a man of the highest standards, of impeccable character, and with an eye for detail that misses nothing. He is also a thoroughly nice man who was a pleasure to work with and to know. I am proud of what we achieved at Hillsborough in the 1980s. Dick helped ensure that success. I am more than happy to write these notes for his autobiography and wish him every success with it.

- Howard Wilkinson, January 2022

Chapter Five: Playing by and Making the Rules

In this chapter I'll look at how important rules and regulations are to football. I'll consider how I tried to keep to the rules, and how I aimed to influence them. I always tried to work for the benefit of the club, fans and the wider game. I'll reflect here on how far I kept to those principles.

Little did I realise when I first joined the football business just how much the game was controlled by, not only the numerous rules and regulations, but also by the differing organisations. Each club was accountable to a variety of institutions for the proper and efficient presentation of the game. Firstly I'll consider run of the mill league games. They were played in those days, in the main, on a Saturday afternoon and covered by BBC Television and Radio. Each club and therefore fixture was affiliated to its respective professionally operated league – the Football League Limited. The national game of football in the UK is subject to the overall control of the Football Association and that takes in also the Football League. In addition each county has a County Football Association – themselves also accountable to the governing body – to which all registered clubs, including those professional clubs within each county jurisdiction, have to be affiliated. The County Associations are then accountable for the control and proper management of all other levels of football within their boundaries. In my days all of the professional clubs within each county were required to participate in a County Cup competition. This, in essence, had no real feeling of priority in the club's calendar but with rules requiring their entry the main outcome of this competition was to provide the County Football Association with added funding to aid their coffers. During my time it was always expected that clubs would turn out their recognised first team players to give credibility to the competition. In many instances this proved to be difficult for managers to accept, as on many occasions, with limited squads and injuries it was not always as simple as the rules required. Maybe the reader can see already that the structure of the game had some potential conflicts of interest.

Every area of the game had a set of governing regulations all designed to ensure that each and every club worked to a required standard. Needless to say breaches of these would occur at some time or another. The club would then receive due notification of such breach and be given a period of time to respond before the relevant governing body made their decision. This inevitably resulted in a fine, or warning. Before the advent of the new television and media deals the income being derived from these infringements were very often significant – for the governing bodies. The reader can be excused for drawing the conclusion that the running of the entire English game is a bit complicated.

To secure any amendment to any of the regulations needed agreement at the Annual Meeting. To be even discussed, agreement had to be reached to place an item on the agenda. Often these agenda items were considered by their appointed management committees in advance of the meeting. Only if approved would such items be considered by all members. I believed that amendments would either be approved or rejected depending upon the view of the clubs on the committee, not with a view of the game as a whole. Maybe a proverbial Catch-22 situation.

As we've seen elsewhere, finances in football could be tight at best in the lower leagues. I was of the opinion that where Division Three and Four Clubs were desperate for money, then there should have been an option to act as a nursery club for one of the larger teams. The bigger clubs were financially stable and both teams would have benefited from the option to use the services of surplus squad players. This, in my opinion, would have had two significant benefits. The lower-level clubs could have access to players they otherwise couldn't afford and wouldn't have to pay for. The other benefit would give players from the higher clubs the opportunity to gain much needed match play time. They would not be kicking around in reserve team games which do not have the same competitive spirit as is required for first team action. This never saw the light of day due predominantly to the worries of the governing bodies that such an arrangement could lend itself open to abuse by any unscrupulous operator. I am still of the opinion that such an amendment to the rules would be of benefit to the game. One only has to look at the present-day constitution of the current Papa Johns Trophy to witness that u21 squads involved do not attract crowds of any distinction. The academy players from the top teams are devoid of real time competitive experience and as such have failed to win anything. The trophy has been won by the first team of a lower league club every year since it began.

Each of the governing bodies has management committees made up of nominated representatives. As mentioned earlier Bert McGee, Chairman, Sheffield Wednesday, held one such position but openly admitted he did not profess to understand in detail all of the rules and regulations and their implications. As a consequence he invariably involved me in dissecting the contents of both the minutes of previous meetings and the agenda for any forthcoming meeting. He used to openly confess that he, along with many of his counterparts, had the best interests of the game in heart but was reliant upon the guidance given by the appointed secretary or delegated officers. He always used to say that whilst he voted for any specific proposal he was somewhat in the dark as to any implications and thought that there must be a better way to administer the game than what was currently on offer. He felt there was a void between those employed by the respective bodies and those involved in the game at club level but did not know what that was or how it could be achieved. Currently there are rumours circulating that the Government have given thought to a root and branch review of the game and that makes me wonder whether or not there has been any whispers in the corridors of power. I helped with the governance of the game as far as I was able, through Bert in this case, but found dealing with the structures and bureaucracy somewhat frustrating at best.

With governance matters put to bed there were direct issues relating to the many elements of match day arrangements. This was my day job and vital to get it right. It was so important as it covered the running of the game that all supporters see. A smooth running match day doesn't happen by magic. It may be less stringent than governance matters but there were many areas of organisation, controls and rules to follow correctly. In the first instance the club received draft fixtures from the Football League and was allowed a period of time to consider and make any adjustments. Thereafter the fixtures were deemed final. When the season opened the club were advised a month in advance of their appointed referees and linesmen and it fell upon the home club to notify each appointed official and confirm match details. Prior to match days, particularly in my days, with hooliganism at the fore, the liaison with the Police Authorities was essential in terms of crowd management.

On the match day itself, I needed to be ready for the police reporting at the ground some two and a half hours before kick off. The senior officer would make his address to all officers and on many occasions I was in attendance to both listen to the instructions and advise of any particular issue relevant to the club's own findings. Match day staff were also down at the ground in readiness for the opening of the turnstiles – opening times variable according to opposition. Each operator would be allocated a different stile than their previous match in order to counteract any abuse on entry and they would remain in situ until after the game had started. It was the role of the senior steward to take gate counter readings and close the stile down. A stile for each section of the ground was allocated to remain open into the second half of the game to allow for later arrivals. Stewards for both crowd and car park controls would be given their instructions and allocated positions. Commissionaires for the main directors' entrances would be provided with guest tickets, given details of any VIPs and be in position in plenty of time to ensure careful controls. Match officials reported to the secretary's office, were escorted to their dressing room and catered for as guests of the club. Catering arrangements for both spectator and hospitality areas would be checked in readiness for delivering the right level of service with members of the press being extended a warm welcome and allocated a press box seat. Guests attending the boardroom and supporting areas would upon arrival also be warmly welcomed and escorted through to their designated areas. In essence, everything which happens prior to, during and after the 90 minutes playing was prepared, checked and hopefully efficiently delivered.

As the game ended, the senior steward had the responsibility to ensure that all turnstile readings were verified for actual cash taken. The operators were then discharged from their duties and monies collected for banking. At this point the attendance for the day was established and announced. Attendances and gate income were then subjected to cross-checking in the days following the game. The required submission of the match gate summary was completed for both the levy due to the Football League (league games) and the cheque for the opposing team within the statutory time frame as required by authority rules. Some of that may now not apply as things seem to have changed a lot and in fact when you review the results pages in the national press, there are, on many occasions, instances where the day's attendance figures are not confirmed. That is beyond my expectations and in my opinion reflects on present day standards. Similar reporting and marking of the referees' performance also had to be submitted to the Football League or to other governing bodies responsible for the staging of FA Cup or ancillary competitions.

Other responsibilities were less regular but also of major importance. Legislative standards as required by the Local Authority in accordance with the provisions of the Safety at Sports Ground Act brought into play yet another set of rules. These were all designed to ensure the safety of supporters. This, in general terms, resulted in at least one annual visit by the appointed working party, viewing all parts of the ground and discussing any essential works to ensure full compliance. In the interim stages the Local Authority had the overall authority to intervene, inspect and require any works to be undertaken to ensure full compliance and customer safety.

The end of the season might be thought of as time for a break. Not in my life as club secretary. With governance and match day rules and regulations attended to, further attention was needed to cater for all club administrative issues. As one season was coming to an end, decisions needed to be taken in terms of which players were available for transfer, and who was to be retained. Related to this was the agreement of new contracts and their formal lodging with the Football League. From the club's angle there are further rules and policies to adhere to with an essential requirement for them to present to their playing squad an incentive scheme for negotiation and agreement. This formed part and parcel of their terms and conditions of employment and was a constituent part of their contracts. Generally speaking these were designed to offer some form of encouragement to perform better on the pitch. In turn, to deliver the results likely to give the club possible promotion opportunities. There were also enhanced payments for results and increased attendances. I am not at all sure whether all this still exists today. I suspect that with the level of remuneration being received by modern footballers clubs probably can avoid the need to pay a striker additional money to score goals or for the defence to keep clean sheets.

Away travel is yet another fundamental part of the operation which needs close attention and arrangements. Prior to season starting consideration would be given to the fixture list to agree those fixtures requiring an overnight stay. Negotiations would be completed with both the coach company awarded the season's contract and with recognised hotel groups. I aimed to establish the best possible facilities and pricing structure for both overnight and pre-match meal costs and pre-match meals for day travel. As with all other arrangements telephone calls would be made to confirm all the arrangements and that there were no likely hitches, to ensure player comfort.

A fundamental part of the administrative processes of a football club is no different to other companies operating under the watchful eye of Companies House and other statutory bodies where again full compliance is the order of the day. In terms of the football club, share issues and transfers seemed to attract greater attention than one would expect under a general limited company. Shares owned by the fan base gives them the opportunity to attend any general meeting convened by the club. General items on the agenda such as approval of annual accounts go by uncontested almost every time. However, when it comes to opening the meeting up for general comment then the shareholders very often had a field day. Nowadays, with many clubs under singular control, fans lose out badly. The maintenance of the statutory share register was always one where meticulous management was essential. Upon the death of a shareholder proof of transfer entitlement and formal probate had to be lodged before any approval to issue a new certificate. More often than not the nature of supporting a team the ownership was transferred to a family member.

Having managed all of the above, essential compliance responsibilities to the many and various regulations then switches to normal business processes, the likes of which includes Inland Revenue, VAT, HR, Companies House filing processes and other areas of a general nature, not forgetting of course the management of board meetings – very often interesting, to say the least. Managed properly these paled somewhat into insignificance compared to the rigorous rules and regulations of the industry. All of this opened the door for me to meet many high profile interesting characters of the game. More of that later.

With all that under the belt, the attention and management turned to the renewal of all marketing, sponsorship and commercial elements. When the players and staff were enjoying the summer breaks, my time and attention was tuned to all of the above. Satisfactory conclusions to all of those relevant issues ensured the smooth running of the club and finally provided me with the opportunity of my annual vacation once the season was underway and running smoothly. At each of my clubs there were pre-season tours to various venues. Apart from one at Lincoln City I opted not to be a member of the official touring party, as it was the only time to effectively close down the previous season So, a busy job with rules, regulations and organisation to follow, manage and complete. A job though like no other, and I am grateful for the experiences it gave me and for the opportunities it brought.

I am sure everyone grows up with likes and dislikes both in terms of life, hobbies and interests and certainly I was no exception. As a young boy, playing football or cricket with my pals was an ideal pastime for me and one where there never seemed to be enough time. Travelling from home to Sincil Bank on a Saturday was a real family treat and if I played my cards right I could enjoy a trip to the café opposite the bus station in town. Following the death of my father that sort of activity went out of the window but playing for the school's U14, U15 and first team naturally took over. Playing or spectating, sport was hugely important to me as a youngster.

Moving on a few years, I was back to spectating. Along with a gang of mates, in particular one long-standing pal from primary years, Tony Cant, trips to both Sincil Bank and Old Trafford became the order of the day. Visits to Old Trafford, with six of us in a small Austin A35 car, driven by Tony over the Woodhead Pass in the Pennines were nothing short of an experience. It did, however, bring into the equation an alternative to the Imps and a leaning towards the Busby Babes and the then manager Matt Busby, later Sir Matt. I enjoyed watching players such as George Best, Dennis Law, Bobby Charlton, Harry Gregg and the like. An over-populated Austin A35 saloon car rocking and rolling all over the road and over the Pennine hills was worth it to see the quality of the club and its players. It would be fair to say that I began to admire the qualities of Sir Matt. At a time when I knew nothing about the inner workings of football he became something of an idol.

Joining Lincoln City when I did, I was able to talk to David Herd. He was a former Manchester United player who I had watched many times. We were able to reminisce about games and I learned a bit more about Sir Matt from an insider's point of view. The fixtures were released for Season 1971/72, initially giving us two away games on the trot, one at Stockport County and the other at Crewe Alexandra. When David viewed the fixtures he spoke to the chairman and asked if the club could afford overnight stays so that the two games could be combined into one journey. Following their approval, I contacted Stockport County and gained approval to change, meaning we would play Crewe Alexandra on 1st September and, with accommodation booked at the Alma Lodge Hotel, play Stockport County on 3rd September.

On this occasion I travelled on the team coach. It was the first time I would see the reaction of the players to a 3–1 defeat on the short journey back to Alma Lodge. I spoke to David and asked how I could get from Stockport to Lytham St Anne's for a Football league meeting on the morning of the Stockport game. 'Don't worry leave it with me I'll get you a lift.' Breakfast finished, I was waiting in reception not exactly knowing what the arrangements were, other than David saying on the Sunday evening to be in reception and someone will call for you. Patiently sitting there, the girl from reception came over and said there is someone waiting for me at the main entrance. I made my way and this gentleman introduced himself as Les Olive, secretary of Manchester United. 'Follow me to the car, I have another passenger.' Imagine my face when I got to the car and the passenger was none other than Sir Matt Busby, my idol. He was a gentleman out of the top drawer, immediately putting me at ease, talking as if he had known me for years and asking about my joining Lincoln City and relationship with David Herd.

The journey seemed to be over before we had left – it went so quickly. We arrived at Football League HQ and made our way inside. No sooner had we stepped over the threshold than it seemed like the space was being invaded by officials and fellow chairmen all wanting to shake the hands of Sir Matt. The first person to greet him was Alan Hardaker, the then secretary of the Football League. On approaching, Sir Matt stepped to one side and said to Alan Hardaker, 'Please welcome Dick Chester the newly appointed secretary of Lincoln City and please ensure he is properly looked after by yourself and staff to ensure he settles in to his new job properly.' I just couldn't believe how someone so well-known and professional could step aside for a total newcomer. People in the room gravitated towards Sir Matt, a bit like bees round the honey pot, with every single step he took and on each and every occasion he made sure I was introduced to them first – many of whom I would come across later in my career, but all of them remembering that occasion.

Buoyed by my encounter with Sir Matt, I returned to Lincoln determined to do the best job I could for the club, the team and its fans. An opportunity to change the rules for what I saw as a benefit of the club, fans, and the overall game soon presented itself. The *Lincolnshire Echo* reported that on 15 April 1972 that I had taken a telephone call from a commercial operator asking if he could submit a form for my signature to lodge with the Football League permitting them to use our fixture list for their own commercial gain. I was advised that they had previously produced large wall charts with the fixtures set in the centre with supporting advertising around the outside edges. The fixtures were used in fold up pocket size cards. All of these were distributed within the city: to pubs, clubs, shops, and businesses, following which the club was given a supply for their own purposes. I immediately declined. Having dealt with the programme editing and the selling of advertising within, I believed that it could be done more in the financial favour of the club than just a few for distribution. I was promptly advised how disloyal I was being towards a business which had supported the club for several years. Immediately after the call ended I called the Football league offices and, with an earlier introduction to Alan Hardaker, was instantly put through to him. After outlining the purpose, he immediately confirmed that he would decline any application for use of Lincoln City's fixtures but asked to be kept informed of the outcomes. These were significant in terms of better financial returns to the club and with very positive responses from the local advertisers who were more than pleased that it was the club who were going to be the main beneficiary. I provided Alan with a financial summary, following which I was asked to address the next regional meeting of the local clubs. That meeting took place where I explained my reasoning and the financial gains made by Lincoln City. Following this all the regional clubs followed the same processes. Thereafter the Football League included this information in their monthly league review for all clubs to be made aware. Lincoln City could quite reasonably be credited with a fundamental change in a new and better way of protecting the licensing rights of clubs. The current system of club control over official crests, fixtures and licensing rights stemmed from that early initiative. Certainly the current substantial financial benefit to clubs bears no recognition to the early days of fixture control but they always say "from little acorns big oak trees grow."

Around the same time it had become quite obvious that the financial difficulties at Sincil Bank were far from unique within the football world. The bigger clubs were generally rich and comfortable and the smaller clubs pretty much destitute and in a poor state of affairs. Many times the lower division clubs were saved by the bigger clubs coming along, snapping up budding young players, paying healthy transfer fees and then hiding those players in their reserve teams until it suited them. That would be a nice feature in today's market. It seemed to me, with ongoing reviews and negotiations with the banks, that the Football League could consider an amendment to their rules and constitution. They could have formed a dedicated bank under their own direct control and require all clubs to use this central bank. In that way the bigger clubs with healthy credit balances could aid those clubs in trouble. The central bank could have only charged borrowing clubs on a nett monthly basis, or alternatively soak up the interest element within their own in-house transactions and where necessary pay out the annual levy to all clubs on a reduced annual basis. I again met up with Alan Hardaker who certainly didn't throw cold water on the concept which I thought was an ideal arrangement. Following his further considerations and some delicate enquiries within higher circles he came back to me saying that it was doubtful that the "big 6" would flex their muscles to gather support. He felt that it would be declined at any annual general meeting whilst at the same time it could derail current delicate discussions. What they were I had no idea. No telling, therefore, if it would have worked or not, but at least it did show that clubs in the lower departments of the football scene did have a part to play.

Despite the failure of the above plan, it seemed I had begun to develop a very close relationship and understanding with Alan Hardaker. This was quite unique really, for in general he was regarded as an unpopular tough nut who took no prisoners and didn't suffer fools gladly. I always found him to be straight, someone who would listen to your point of view and, if at the end of a conversation he didn't like what was on the table, he would say so. At the same time he would always offer an alternative to work on. In my time at Lincoln City, considering we were a lower tier club, he couldn't do enough and soon developed a close affinity towards the club with a definite bond with myself and the chairman, Dennis Bocock. It was interesting that, when one of his proposed visits to the ground was being discussed around the boardroom, two directors, George Cook and Heneage Dove, wanted to know exactly who he was.

A separate chapter outlines details of the planning application for a major stadium development with the incorporation of commercial operations to help stabilise the finances of the club. This stemmed from an agreement with the club's then chairman, his own employed architect and another meeting with Alan Hardaker.

Alan quickly recognised the purpose of the scheme and allocated an associate, Eric Francis, Managing Director of Football Business Services Ltd, to work with us and to use his business contacts to ensure finance was in place for us. Eric went on to say that if he failed to deliver he had been told he would lose his job. This was an opportunity to stabilise the industry not to be missed. The concept got an exceptionally good hearing with Alan Hardaker, to the extent that in January 1973 he attended, along with Eric Francis, a meeting that me, the chairman, and fellow directors Sid Haigh and George Cook, held with Lincoln City Council Director of Planning, Percy Jackson and City Surveyor, W Struthers, Chief Supt G Parker and Supt W Carey of the Police Authority and Deputy Chief Fire Officers, P Crout and B Simons. This was to consider in full both the details of the planning application and the fundamental benefits to the city as a whole. Both Alan Hardaker and Eric Francis made valued contributions. They recognised that this was an initiative of the club but also saw the likelihood that this could be a route forward for other clubs. They also understood, as I did, the immense publicity benefit to Lincoln City Council and the city as a whole.

Alan Hardaker, Secretary of the Football League – a real taskmaster

Further communication with the Football League, and again Alan Hardaker, came as a result of me wanting to include an article in the club programme based on head-to-head results between our club and that game's opposition. To do this, though, I needed some back copy material. In those, pre-internet days, this was far from easy to find. I started by asking our groundsman, Ned Pinkstone, if I could view the club's old records stored in his cubby hole underneath the main stand.

'I've bont (his version of burnt) 'em. When I put this years in, I bon last years.'

'You can't do that mate, you have to keep records for at least seven years for revenue purposes,' I said.

'Too bloody late then cos they've gone'.

My only option was to seek help from the Football League as, with regulations necessitating each club to return match and finance details after each home game, they must hold them. Alan Hardaker instantly offered the services of four members of his staff (Graham Kelly, Mike Foster, Andy Williamson and Lee Walker) to assist me, although nothing was available prior to the 1920s, for those records had been lost in a fire at a previous base. However, after several visits trawling through their archives I gathered sufficient to be able to produce meaningful programme material. This did not stop there, for as you will read in a later chapter further developments were to follow. My work with Alan Hardaker taught me the importance of developing the best possible relationships with those in positions of power and authority. In Alan's case, that good relationship meant that the club and league worked together on several projects which proved beneficial for both, and the wider game.

Some of the rules governing the game altered as the 1970s, progressed and moved on further into the 1980s. Some of these changes affected on-field matters, and others the commercial side of things. 1973 saw the rules relating to promotion and relegation changed to allow for three teams to be promoted and three relegated. 1974 saw the first ever league game take place on a Sunday when Millwall played Fulham at the Den, Millwall. This brought about all sorts of issues with objectors voicing their views that football broke into the Sabbath day and each club having to allocate one turnstile to allow objectors free access. This was introduced but many clubs would move that free turnstile around each area of the ground every so often causing great distress to those wishing to take advantage and club's protecting their revenue streams as much as possible.

Season 1976/77 saw yet another change, where promotion, relegation or league positions were concerned: any clubs finishing the season on the same number of points were separated by goal difference and not by the previous method of goal average. In the event that the new formula showed clubs to have an equal goal difference then the team scoring the most goals was awarded the highest placing.

The following season saw the Football League permit the use of advertising on the front of shirts – referred to as shirt sponsorship. However, initially this was restricted to an area not exceeding 32 square inches, so referred to in the game at that time as 8 inches deep and "tit to tit." Nowadays that has long passed by, as sponsorship covers all sorts of areas of a player's kit from the front, to the number on the back, to the sleeve. During my days at Bramall Lane several attempts were made to secure a suitable sponsor but unfortunately due, both to possible conflict of interest with existing commercial partners and their status in Division Three it proved too difficult to land. At Hillsborough, however, whilst consideration had to be given to current commercial partners and the success of the team, a deal was landed with Finlux TV appearing on the shirts.

Season 1979 saw the very first £1million transfer when Brian Clough secured the services of Trevor Francis for his Nottingham Forest squad, completing his transfer from Birmingham City. This set alarm bells ringing throughout the game with many of the big clubs, including both of the Sheffield clubs, coming to a gentleman's understanding that they would not enter into any future negotiations where such a fee was involved. I am not at all sure exactly how long that remained, and if one was to review the current market trends, I feel that many would question any such arrangement,

The Football League Cup had been in existence for a number of seasons without incorporating any element of sponsorship. An announcement was made confirming that from 1982 the Football League Cup would be rebranded as the Milk Cup, marking the first sponsors of any major cup competition in English football. In advance of the 1983/84 campaign, Canon announced their sponsorship agreement with the Football League. The leagues carried their company title and logo, triggering a string of future sponsors through to the present day.

The early 1980s also saw change on the pitch. Season 1981/82 saw points for a win being changed from two points to three. The English League was the first in world football to adopt this. Sheffield Wednesday were left cursing its introduction, as with two points for a win they would have accumulated enough points for promotion rather than agonisingly falling one point short.

In conclusion, therefore, rules and regulations have a huge effect on the game of football. They had a large impact on my day-to-day working life as a club secretary. There were times that I felt that if I breathed there was a rule telling me how to do so! I did my very best to ensure that all my clubs played within the rules. Hand on heart, I believe that each club did exactly that. As well as working within the rules, I attempted to change some regulations for the benefit of my clubs and the wider game.

The success I had with gaining control of fixture lists may seem a minor matter, but, from there, a system in which clubs now hold much more commercial control over their crests and image grew. I also learned how important it was to nurture good relationships with people at all levels. Working effectively with those at the top level of the game, even when I was a "young pup" at Lincoln, allowed me to have influence on how the sport was organised. An understanding of the mechanics of committees, agendas, and decision-making helped, even when I was once removed from power – with Bert McGee trusting me to help him in his role in the governance of the wider game. The next chapter considers how some of the top teams in the 1980s tried to change the game for their own benefit, before the advent of the Premier League.

Chapter Six: Stuff Yer Super League

In April 2021 the press was alive with reports of the formation of a new Super League. An article appearing on the BBC webpage on the 19th of that month covered the proposed formation of that mid-week super league which was seen as an alternative to the existing Champions League. The new structure was to include six leading Premier League clubs: Arsenal, Chelsea, Liverpool, Manchester City, Manchester United and Tottenham Hotspur, whilst the European contingent would be three teams from Italy: AC Milan, Inter Milan and Juventus, and three teams from Spain: Atletico Madrid, Real Madrid and Barcelona. It would not be an understatement to say that this announcement brought widespread criticism from all quarters. There was particular emphasis in much commentary that those clubs had put greed before all other aspects of football. Not being privy to the full coverage given in either the Italian or Spanish media, I can only reflect upon that which would have impacted on English football and the Premier League in particular. It certainly provoked strong reactions. It also provoked me, in a way, into writing this book. It sent my thoughts spiralling back to events of the mid-1980s.

Whilst not applauding any such move, I can in some way understand the position each of our Premier League clubs were in, particularly if the initial proposal for such a newly constituted league had come to them from their European counterparts. Back in the mid-1980s, I was involved in many meetings amongst the leading Division One clubs to establish a not too dissimilar structure. I received a telephone call from my chairman, Bert McGee, asking if I could make myself available one Sunday to transport and accompany him to an important meeting. He was clear that this meeting would be totally confidential. At the time he was a member of the Football League Management Committee and, as he had always trusted me with any confidential papers he received – mainly because he didn't rightly understand all the ramifications of the rules and regulations and was looking for some guidance, I believed it to be something along those lines. There was no way he was going to inform me of any matter pertaining to the meeting I was driving him to, but once arriving at Villa Park and noticing others, not members of the Management Committee, he disclosed that the meeting was with a select band of Division One clubs and, once the meeting got underway, it would become crystal clear. The attendees made up an impressive array of then leading figures in football with the following clubs in attendance: Arsenal (David Dein and Ken Friar), Aston Villa (Doug Ellis and Stephen Stride), Chelsea (Ken Bates and Sheila Marston), Everton (Phillip Carter and Jimmy Greenwood), Liverpool (John Smith and Peter Robinson), Manchester

City (Peter Swales and Bernard Halford), Manchester United (Martin Edwards and Les Olive), Newcastle United (Stan Seymour and Russell Cushing), Tottenham Hotspur (Irvine Scholar and Peter Day) and Sheffield Wednesday.

The conversation around the room confirmed that the gathering had been created with a view to considering a potential opportunity to form what would then have been the "Super League" and, subject to all of the formalities being in place, the clubs would tender their resignations from the Football League and become affiliated directly to the Football Association of which Ted Croker, their then secretary had confirmed the backing of the governing body. How that ever came about, or who in actual fact was involved in those discussions, I had no idea and to this date still haven't. The initial meeting was designed to explore the possibilities and level of support and to formulate a plan of action including the next meeting again at Villa Park.

During the journey back to Sheffield, the topic of the conversation in the car was very mixed indeed. In the first instance the chairman was very concerned about the clandestine element of the meeting, realising of course that it had to be. He was at the same time worried about his personal position and future conduct on the Football League Management Committee. The chairman was, during all my dealings and associations with him, a man with very strong principles, extremely fair and honest, whilst not suffering fools gladly. Considering his responsibilities to the governing body, he also, above everything else, didn't want to see the Owls miss out on what might be a real opening to establishing the club as a lead club, both inside English football but also expanding its reputation and standing into Europe. He kept repeating that Sheffield Wednesday must come first and if things were to get a bit uncomfortable for him around the committee table then he would have to put his loyalty and commitment to the club before anything else. For my part I had real mixed feelings. I had travelled up the pathway from the very lowest positions in Division Four into the First Division with an opportunity to compete with what one could only describe as the elite, and yet I felt guilty that I could be part of an organisation which would be seen as turning its back on the lower levels of football. I think it would be fair to say that anyone finding themselves in that sort of position would have mixed feelings as well. The opportunity of being able to present top quality opposition week in and week out could only be seen by our supporters as a good move – after all they pay their money and expect the best, whilst the feeling of stepping away from the rank and file of the industry I had developed didn't sit well at all.

What was to follow was a series of the same sort of clandestine meetings with the sole purpose of formulating the broad-based criteria and operations of the new league. In principle it was agreed that membership to the newly formed league would be on the basis that all clubs had a ground capacity for a minimum of 30,000 fans and that each club had a strong balance sheet. Relegation and promotion would be subject to clubs meeting these criteria with a not dissimilar system for clubs in the non-league climbing the pyramid system. There would be a strong emphasis on the clubs remaining an integral part of the English scene but with a determined approach to achieve a greater share of both the pools, television rights and annual league levy share. This was recognised as having a detrimental effect upon smaller member clubs, but was an area not up for negotiation in any future discussions. This latter issue was one which, with my previous development in football, struck a real chord, as I knew only too well that in many instances this was their real lifeblood. The consensus of opinion amongst the clubs around the table was that whilst they were working to become bigger they would have their own obstacles to overcome. There was a genuine recognition that such a move would create further difficulties for the lower clubs who would have to address the management and control of their own affairs. Easier said than done – I had been there!

From a personal point of view, my specific task was to formulate a paper based on the proposed engagement, promotion, and development of referees, bearing in mind my previous involvement as an active referee, albeit not at the level intended with the proposed new league. I undertook a full analysis of all of their previous appointments, highlighting the deployment of the then current senior officials controlling games in lower than Division One games. The purpose of this new league structure was to see the best teams performing against the best opposition week on week, and with that went the same level of requirement from the referees' panel. One of the underlying thoughts was age against experience, with the then system requiring referees to retire upon reaching a mandatory age limit. In my view, providing the level of fitness could be retained, there seemed to be a constructive argument in keeping their experience. This could only be achieved by creating a properly constructed fitness and psychological programme, thereby endeavouring to ensure the best level of performances possible. Recognising that my experience as a referee was far below that required to get the right balance, I invited Sheffield-based referee, Keith Hackett – one of the best referees on the circuit at that particular time – to meet me in my Hillsborough office to review and comment, which, after some time met his full approval.

Whilst all of the deliberations were going on in terms of the proposed format it was evident that somewhere along the line European Clubs had become aware of the potential formation and expressed an interest in their involvement. This was quickly seized upon and deemed an appropriate development at the end of the first season, thereby showing a major development. There were of course clubs participating within European competitions and whether anything had been mentioned I have no idea. The thought of the Owls all of a sudden spreading their wings across the seas into Europe did seem at the time to be a good deal for the fans.

Throughout all of the meetings there was always the reminder of confidentiality, but somewhere along the line there had been some sort of a breach, for, before the convening of the Annual General Meeting of the Football League, Graham Kelly, their then secretary, came out expressing his concerns for such a proposal, as potentially detrimental to both the Football League and the general footballing public as a whole. Nevertheless there was still a determination of all member clubs to continue with their resignations, but at the actual meeting there was no movement whatsoever and the status quo was maintained. It was, however, interesting to note that some years later, following a switch from the Football League to the Football Association, Graham Kelly picked up the threads, ran with them and in a short space of time the Premier League had received the blessing of the Football Association and launched itself in 1992. Would it be fair to say that the work done in the mid 1980s was an initiative with some substance after all?

When the Premier League was launched in 1992 there was some jubilation at the secured £191 million pound five-year television deal. With the combined involvement of Sky and Setanta this had risen to £1.7 billion by 2021. On a similar basis, Barclays Bank paid £48 million for their naming rights in 2001, but for their renewal in 2007 this had risen to £65.8 million.

Throughout all of these seriously enhanced revenue streams I cannot recall reading about any, or many, clubs where their leaders have sat down and said, 'You know what this is the time when we can reward our fans by either holding down match day prices, or even offering some form of reduction.' The supporter does really get a raw deal. In fact, this was often true in my time. As the new season comes along the usual message of optimism is pushed by the clubs, designed to encourage the supporter to put his hands in his pockets and invest early. Considering that in the Football League system of twenty-four clubs per division there can only be two success stories in any one league – that is only an 8.33% rate of celebration. What is the supporter then faced with?

Let's just have a bit of a closer look at the outcomes of these lucrative deals and ask ourselves if this was the point in football when "the Golden

Rule" came into play. This rule is simply that those who own the gold control the rules. The current media coverage of games which imposes variable times and days for matches to kick off cannot really be seen as being in the best interests of the fan but more to meet the demands of the broadcasters maximisation of advertising revenue streams. To compensate the fan for any inconvenience caused over kick off details, are variable packages all seemingly designed to settle any discontent but in reality maximising income streams still further. Since the formation of the Premier League the scope of coverage across the globe has grown immensely, certainly giving the game more exposure than ever before, whilst at the same time extolling the virtues of the English game, but no doubt whetting the appetite of foreign investors even more so.

There can be no doubt that the emergence of the Premier League has attracted significant foreign player involvement. Moving on from such an inequality on the player front, a closer review of the clubs in general reveals more concerning data to swallow for our customary traditions. Of those 20 Premier League clubs, 70% are owned by non-British investors, 65% of the managers and 25% of the chief executive officers also reflect the ever-increasing influences of foreign involvement. It doesn't actually stop there, as a review of the current EFL clubs also shows an increase in non-UK controls with 52% owners, 35% managers and 9% CEOs. The above does not in any way whatsoever suggest that the interests, control, and management of these clubs are inferior to what they could have been had they remained in British ownership, as has been the tradition throughout the history of the game.

Is the Golden Rule restricted to those companies providing the media deals? It doesn't seem so from recent industry comments. The Premier League themselves seem, from the outside looking in, to feel that it is their prerogative to apply that rule also, pretty much deciding how much they want to give away. At the time of compiling this autobiography there are moves afoot for the EFL to make a representation for a greater share as being one example. At the same time it seems that the Premier League exercise that Golden Rule within their own operations if the article released by *The Guardian* on 12 May 2014 is to be believed. The article referenced a leak of Richard Scudamore's email exchange to the *Sunday Mirror* in which he referred to women as "gash," "big-titted broads" and irrational when they have children. Breach of any discrimination policy one would ask?

Subject to much publicity and supposed in-depth consideration, no disciplinary action was taken, presumably this being considered by those in judgement as not in the best interests of the commercial operations of the league and therefore risking the absence of their main negotiator. I do wonder if this was more due to the Premier League applying the Golden Rule. *The Guardian* press release does also confirm the said negotiator being awarded lucrative terms of engagement with reported salaries in 2012-13 of £1.9m with further bonuses from that date of £2.8m and £2.5m. So when it came to his departure date, each Premier League club was requested to make individual contributions of £250k to allow him to leave with a £5m award. One would instantly recognise his immense contributions in the level of his contractual negotiations whilst at the same time begging the question: 'Would a player within the game making the same discriminatory remarks, or a fan making a similar comment to a non-UK player be granted the same outcome?' Many of you would, I suggest, come up with a not too dissimilar response to mine.

Now where else can you see the Golden Rule seemingly applied? A lot of exposure has also been devoted to the Professional Footballers Association. It appears that over the last two years alone the PFA have received £14m from the TV contract from which a lucrative golden handshake was awarded to their CEO of many years standing, Gordon Taylor. With players' contributions being at a level well below their earnings: a seasonal contribution of £150 per professional and £20 per scholar it does indicate again that the Golden Rule also applies in this part of the industry as well.

Move the issue forward and what do you get? Yes, not everything can be right in the Premier League as was portrayed in April 2021 when an announcement was made that the so-called big six in the Premier League plus three Italian and three Spanish clubs had developed plans to create a new midweek super league to run alongside the UEFA-controlled Champions League. It was interesting to note that whilst all of the English Clubs were involved back in the mid-1980s, they still appear to be dissatisfied with their lot 35 years down the line. One interesting further point should be noted: five of those six are now owned by foreign investors. Does it really mean that their own personal interests have now totally surpassed the value of their fans or are they in fact still looking at a desire to provide quality opposition without the need to qualify for European Cup competitions? The outbursts which followed from their fan bases quickly answered any lingering thoughts, and, such was the ferocity of fan reactions, that they had to quickly climb down from their position of supremacy and succumb to fan power. At the same time it left their European counterparts in a state of limbo, which one imagines will not evaporate overnight and will leave some semblance of distrust for a while.

The reasoning for the proposed launch of a new midweek Super League can only be answered by those sitting within, or privy to, the initiatives and desires of those parties directly involved. I think it is fair to say that at this point in time no one person has the answers to this but, putting some sort of a slant on the proposal, could it be argued that there must be some sort of foreign influence brought to bear? A quick glance at the squads for the clubs involved shows that 63.69% of the nominated 2020/21 first team squads of the six English teams were of foreign nationality. In the case of the European clubs they too showed 56.28% of foreign nationals. The one English club within the so-called big six not directly owned by foreign nationals had a lower ratio of 45.16% .

Will the possibility of any sort of breakaway now simply pass away? In my opinion: not a chance. The big clubs will always be looking to better themselves. In fairness, no different than leading commercial brands, and the more foreign ownership continues to bare its teeth in our national game the more such a possibility grows. Will the owners take heed of the public outburst they endured and wrap their ambitions in cotton wool and carry on forever with the status quo? I don't think so, for as long as they keep pumping money into the playing squads and appease the supporters with "big name signings" they will feel they always have a chance. Personally, I concur with the views of leading commentators and reporters who feel that this influx of foreign ownership is not at this stage good for the game. Of course not every foreign-owned club is tarred with the same brush. Leicester City FC is one who appear to have gone closest to recognising the true value of their place in the community with numerous gestures of support and goodwill.

"Stuff Yer Super League" was a statement seen in fan magazines and in letters to the papers in the 80s. It certainly reflected some fans' negative opinions of plans to change the league's structure. Quite what those fans would have made of the wider European plans that Sheffield Wednesday were privy to, I am not sure. Those plans were partly driven by money, and partly by a genuine desire for excellence. As I look at the modern game and am reminded of those plans, I am convinced that more recent proposals are driven by the opportunity for financial gain. Football has changed, and many clubs are now in the hands of foreign owners. If still recognising the importance of the club to the fans, this is not necessarily a bad thing as the Premier League winning supporters of Thai owned Leicester City may well testify. With the ever-growing influx of international players into the game, I become more convinced that the 2021 plans may not be the last supporters hear of plans for a "super league." Given the situation of the game in the 21st century, I fear it might not be easy for fans to suggest that the authorities "stuff it" – after all they have their positions to consider and it is difficult to bite the hand that feeds you.

If you look back into the days prior to the Premier League, English clubs, with home grown talent, won the European Cup every season from 1977-1984 and in fact in the 32 seasons from inception of the European Cup to the first season of the Premier League, English clubs registered a 25% win ratio of the European Cup. That record alone seems to suggest that our game was in pretty good shape, whilst I am sure there would have been criticism from certain media arms. In the period from inception of the Premier League to season 2020/21 that win ratio had reduced to 20.69%. From those days of pure English talent and, using Arsenal as an example, they went from season 1989/90, when amongst the 19 registered players only two were foreign nationals, to Season 2009/10 when, amongst their 27 registered players, 23 were foreign nationals. Other teams, no doubt, would have seen similar patterns. A further review of lead football personnel within the current structure of the Premier League clubs reveals a foreign influence of 61.66%.

Going back into my time in the game, again it was not unusual for long-serving club players to be granted a testimonial game after ten years' loyal service. To me that is something which we will see repeated less and less. The loyalty shown by the players has seemingly disappeared in favour of their agents working their magic to arrange moves bringing about greater earnings for themselves. A recent article appearing in the *Mail on Sunday* written by Nick Harris highlighted the sum of £1.181 billion being paid by Premier League Clubs to agents from year ending Jan 31 2017 to Jan 31 2021. In anybody's mind that is a staggering amount of spending, and whilst it is suggested that FIFA, the game's ultimate governing body, are seeking to re-visit legislation appertaining to agent's fees and services, it would seem pertinent to commission a full auditing programme on what happens to the money once invested in agents' bank accounts, ensuring that none finds its way back in any way shape or form for the benefit of third parties. The article goes on to highlight a transfer, but not I may add involving English Clubs, where the agent secured a £16million pound commission from a transfer fee of £20million. That is probably one in the far extreme, but it does beg the question as to how club officials can approve such dealings and where can they show, or prove, that such a deal was in the best interests of either the club itself or their dedicated fans. The article reveals that FIFA have already passed a number of amendments which in essence are designed to curb such exorbitant fees. Believe it or not but such amendments have met with fierce opposition from the agent network. Shall we just say it is a culture in need of being addressed?

What then about the Governing Bodies, the English Football League Limited and The Football Association? All of these major governing bodies have seemingly benefited from this newfound pot of gold. In the first instance the Football League took a nasty knock when it lost members in 1992 to the Premier League and continued governing the remaining seventy-two clubs. Clearly it is an onerous task to fulfil those functions but according to LinkedIn they have 151 staff members plus their governing body. For my part it seems an awful lot of staff when their membership declined almost 22%. I may be proved wrong but during this time I cannot recall any revolutionary new initiative being developed by this governing body which would serve to seriously benefit its members. Yes of course there will be lots of deliberations, meetings and reimbursement of expenses coupled with top brass privileges, but nowhere have I seen any sort of positive outcome from this array of staff. I think it would do no harm to set the senior management the specific task of such a development in return for their lucrative pay packages and overall benefit to the league and it's members. Yes, of course they will be in place to charge any club of any wrongdoing and imposing fines where appropriate – quite in order – but instead of sitting in judgement of others why don't they put themselves in the frame for others to judge their initiatives and overall interest of their members.

The Football Association is a different kettle of fish. This is the organisation responsible for the control of all football played in the country and also the success and profile of our international team. Two very different but equally vital roles. This is also the organisation which, it has been reported, could well be the subject of a root and branch enquiry with its possible implementation, "kicked off" by the government. Will that happen? I'm not at all sure. Should it happen? I'm a bit more positive about that, as I feel our game, both nationally and regionally, needs some much-needed impetus. This may only be to see our national side as a power to be reckoned with, which I do believe has been taken out of the hands of the appointed team manager by circumstances beyond his control. The Football Association had 925 members of staff in 2019, although an article written by Sami Mokbel in *The Daily Mail* 19th October 2021 referred to there being 124 redundancies less than a year ago. Assuming that this was following the 2019 statistic it still leaves a staffing level of 700. Casting my mind back to my days in active service, you virtually got to know their employees on a day-to-day basis. I can't see that that would be the situation now, whilst at the same time it is difficult to see positive outcomes coming from such a task force. Of course they benefit from registration fees, television and media rights, fines, staging of major cup finals and international games and all similar income streams. In common with other organisations and, looking from the outside in, it seems to me that the FA may well be over-staffed and bureaucratic. Isn't it said that most people work hard enough not to get the sack but paid enough not to quit!

Working alongside the national organisation there are the local County Associations whose main aim is to encourage greater participation in the game at all levels and for all ages. But where, I must add, are there any established programmes producing additional income streams from new initiatives? I may have missed picking up any new initiative by either the national body and/or its county associates, designed to encourage greater participation in the game and which is now showing a positive return. I would strongly suggest that there hasn't been any – other than in the women's section, where the growth has been exceptional. This suggests to me that the members of the FA Board are quite happy with their little lot and, as long as their life is unaffected, then just sit back and enjoy.

What actions have been taken to specifically stop the decline of the amateur game? There are 51 affiliated County Associations. Without undertaking a full, detailed appraisal it appears that throughout the amateur 11-a-side game there has been a significant decline at all levels and leagues under their control. Another article this time reported in *The Independent* reveals that more than 1,600 sides have disappeared across the country in the last three years. In fact the Hampshire County FA site confirms that 15 years ago there were 182 affiliated teams playing in 13 affiliated leagues, whereas now they have 43 teams in 6 leagues – a serious decline. What do they say? "Nothing is more dangerous than an idea when you only have one idea." It appears to be more of a problem if you don't have any ideas at all, which from the outside looking in, seems to be the current position. A similar report emphasises the decline in people participating in football, confirming a reduction from 2016-2020 of 18.83% (433,000 in total)

Based entirely upon local knowledge, that sort of trend continues through to today, meaning in essence that since at least 2008 there has been a declining trend, which appears to have either escaped the attention of County Football Associations or there is a nationwide turn-off from football by the young and amateur fraternity. More interesting though is the growth in staff within the management of the game – thank you, Premier League! This seems to me to lead to an assumption that the game can rely on the Premier League to continue the funding and can sit back on its laurels for the time being.

Of course it's not all to do with the lack of initiatives coming out of the management of the game. The solving of this problem is not one with an overnight solution, but one has to raise the point as to why, with this national decline, it is necessary to retain all of the existing County

Associations. In business there are occasions when things are not going as planned. In that case there is a need to review and, if necessary, consolidate. It therefore follows that there has to be some root and branch investigation undertaken. A logical suggestion would be to amalgamate two or three geographically located associations into one, which alone would make a considerable saving to both County and national purse strings. County Associations are dependent upon the annual levies provided to them from their governing body and, again, there is nothing tangible to be seen by the County FAs to create any sort of commercialism to their operations. Each one of them has a well-paid county secretary, or whatever title is used, on top of a relatively permanent staff mainly commissioned with the task of developing the game in all forms and genders, which again is not happening. It really must have been a blessing to these organisations to witness the rise in girls and women's football, otherwise their real purpose of existence would have been put to the sword. Size is a handicap unless efficiency goes with it and it is difficult to see proof of real efficiency or development when the ground beneath them all is steadily collapsing.

The provision of grassroots football was, in my day, fundamental for the good of the professional game, as this is where the players of the future are both developed and supplied, generally to their local professional club. One of our key ingredients in community programmes was to portray the club as one where a good local lad would be looked after and become a player capable of first team duty and acceptance by the fans as a "local boy made good." The decline in grassroots interest and participation makes that even more difficult today, without even considering the impact of the influx of foreign nationals. A review of foreign players in the differing international associations does reveal that the Premier League has the highest proportion of nominated first team squad players of 63.8% with Serie A Italy coming second with 60.8%.

What does this tell you? In my mind some alarm bells are ringing. Looking back to the formation of the Premier League, Wikipedia confirms that there were no foreign managers and only 13 foreign national players, whereas in 2021 there were 14 foreign managers and 518 players. When you couple all of this with the increased level of foreign investors taking control of our clubs, then to me it seems to suggest that someone in the corridors of power will wake up one morning with an "electric light bulb" moment and come out with a revolutionary comment of, 'Do you know what! We have lost control of the English game!' I would say that that sort of time is very much upon us now.

Just ask yourselves a couple of questions. How can Gareth Southgate have an upper hand on the international scene when so many of the opposing players are treading their professions on our boards? Those players are privy to the detailed analysis which all managers will deliver in pre-match build up and talks – all of which will be carried back into their respective international training camps. Gareth is then expected to take a team weakened by a lack of quality to choose from when many English players are debarred from useful, top quality game time but still expected to deliver the goods. If the continued growth in both foreign ownership and players continues it will become increasingly difficult for anyone appointed to the role of England Team Manager to achieve any semblance of real success. It is also reported that the top three earners in the Premier League come from this elite band of overseas players. Transferring your attention to the grassroots side of the game and with diminishing opportunities for young players to be snapped up by professional clubs, why is it that the Football Association has failed to address the situation? Surely it must be evident to them they are the governing body, supposedly consisting of highly qualified knowledgeable personnel, and yet they seem to not address the question of, 'where oh where is the natural flow of young English talent coming from?' The members of the FA Council always used to be referred to as the "Blazer Brigade," turning up in their droves at major Wembley occasions and international trips, enjoying all of the hospitality on offer. It may be necessary for them to cast aside these benefits and consider whether personal perks are of more importance than the overall best interest of the English game.

Of course there are established academies at most, if not all, clubs. In comparison to previous eras, is it now a case that the quality of young players has gone backwards in terms of development and progress into our national game? Or, could it be that with foreign managerial influence within the Premier League that the interest in developing young English talent has been put on the back burner in favour of the injection of young foreign players? We are talking here about the future of the English game and establishing ourselves as a world power. This surely has to be addressed by all the powers that be? It's time to salvage our English game and put priorities before personal positions.

At the same time as looking at reduced opportunities for young emerging playing talent, let us not forget to take a serious, long look at the same limited market for the young emerging English bred managers. Compared to previous eras, this market has seemingly dried up. No English manager has ever won the Premier League. The last English manager to win the top division was Howard Wilkinson with Leeds United in 1992. Thirty years ago!

The whole idea within any business organisation is to maximise their strengths to the fullest degree possible and in the case of the Premier League that is exactly what they have achieved. Alongside that is the overbearing influence which money plays and where best for it to go. Not having the precise insider knowledge, it can only be left to formulate a view by being an observer looking in from the outside and expressing a simple opinion. As mentioned above, the actual objectives of the game have not changed in years and it seems to me to be incredibly difficult to justify that revised legislation and compliance requirements have caused such increases in salary structures, staffing and benefits.

Going back to my days in the late 1970s in Monte Carlo, it was suggested that this type of business was within the culture of overseas clubs and businesses in general; it does make me wonder whether similar issues exist today particularly with the ever-increasing number of foreign owners and influences. I wonder exactly where all of this money ends up. It can also be argued that this significant growth in spending has gone hand in hand with the ever-increasing media coverage of our game and the direct involvement of major television and media coverage – congratulations to football's negotiators! Indirectly, though, much of it is paid for by the subscribers to the various packages. If they were to stop would you see a more fundamental return to the traditional trends of "yesteryear?" Is that something the paying supporter would want to see? I'm not sure, but I suspect some homes where it is wall-to-wall football every day may have their own views.

Prior to my leaving Hillsborough, the chairman offered his good wishes saying I would always be welcomed back and if there was anything he could do for me all I had to do was ask. At the time of my departure there was a new proposal on the table for the television contract award and I asked if he would use the Club's vote against the deal and the emergence of the "Murdoch Empire." I remember the look on his face and words saying it would be good for football, with an opportunity to significantly enhance the supporter facilities at Hillsborough. I did respond saying, 'No chance, Chairman. You know as well as I do that it will only go one way and that will be into the player's pockets.' I rest my case and without being smug in any way, just look at what has happened in the escalation of players' earnings – not forgetting of course that the chief executive of their union – the Professional Footballers' Association – has been able to walk away with bonuses of several million pounds. For what, I ask? The responsibilities associated with that position have not materially changed and whilst doing that, it appears from press coverage at least, the self-same union who are meant to represent the best interests of their members find it not in their interests to support the current research programme into dementia. Persistent heading of the ball by their members seemingly being a major contributory factor to ex-players suffering from that dreadful condition.

I find myself in 2022 in agreement with the views of a former Prime Minister, Gordon Brown, himself an avid follower of football through his own Scottish based club Raith Rovers. A lead article appeared in *The Mail on Sunday*, 2 January 2022, by Robert Dineen, headlined "Greed is Ruining The Game," saying 'We must stop being held to ransom by the profiteer owners and return football to the people." One of Gordon Brown's key concerns was related to the negative views of several Premier League clubs, and indeed the Premier League's chief executive, to the proposals contained within Tracey Crouch's fan-led review. He also commented that, 'Runaway greed, made possible by what often seems like a free-for-all in club ownership and poor overall supervision, is in danger of destroying the best football league in the world and all that is good about the game.' It really does beggar belief that so many elements have found their way into the administration of the game that leading renowned figures in society can express so many concerns. It all takes me back to my earlier comments that those in ultimate control should be strong enough to put the good of the game before personal positions. Outside of the game there is also another activity which appears to have grown and grown and that is the betting industry. Currently they are subject to a tax levy of 15% which Gordon Brown suggests should be raised to 20%. I am not sure that that is the only imposition to be placed on the many companies in that particular marketplace. The promotion of betting via national media channels is ever-growing with many forms of gambling being promoted, some of which are devoid of football involvement. One of the earliest companies to seriously expand their profile in football being Bet365, who, when launched, was owned by an actual sitting member of the FA's Management Committee. They, along with other leading companies, can be seen on clubs' ground advertising boards, Wembley and other main stadia boards and various media channels. Part of Tracey Crouch's proposals suggests the introduction of an independent regulator, and one has to ask the question if the awarding of contracts would see a clear and definitive impartiality in the future, thereby steering away from any potential conflict of interests. For the benefit of society as a whole a curb on betting profile via national media needs to be addressed overall and not just confined to the game of football.

The Premier League has brought huge sums of money into English football. It would be remiss of me to say that this has not seen any benefits. There are new stadiums and facilities. Some of the world's finest players have plied their trade on English grounds. Equally, so have some of the world's greatest managers. To me though, this has come at a heavy cost. The cost is both at grassroots level and at the very top. The amateur game is in decline and it seems that the organisation of the Football Association has not been up to the job of stopping that or making life easier for the England team to compete at the very highest level, with such a glut of foreign players and managers within our game. I worry that footballing associations are seemingly incapable of driving the improvements needed. In conclusion, I worry that extra money in football, particularly since the launch of the Premier League, may end up in the hands of agents, in excessive player pay, and among the top brass employed within the game.

Chapter Seven: The Nights of the Long Knives

Football can be a brutal business. In this chapter I recall some of the behind the scenes machinations at the clubs I worked for. People gained and lost positions in murky circumstances. I'll describe and explain what I know and leave the reader to judge what kind of business football could be.

I'll start at Lincoln. You may remember the issues surrounding the Supporters' Club. Heneage Dove, Supporters' Club Liaison Officer was smarting with his wounds after seeing the group treated so badly, in his opinion. Behind the scenes he was plotting changes and was preparing the ground to step in with a proposition to sack the manager David Herd. He had spent time in advance of this talking things through with Graham Taylor, who was on the injured list but undertaking coaching duties. Heneage persuaded Graham to seek support from some senior players to write letters to the board complaining about the training methods and team management in general. Coupled with a poor run of results he felt this would be enough to secure the sacking. At the same time those senior players, if they so desired could apply for the vacancy.

All letters had to be processed via myself and through to the Chairman for the appropriate meeting of the directors. They were not to be shared with individual directors or anyone else. Despite this, Heneage regularly approached me asking if any applications had been received. In one telephone call he told me that they had all been received and he was coming to my office to read them! My reply was courteous, but firm, in saying, 'You can come in if you wish, but you will only have access to them at the same time as other directors at the forthcoming meeting, excluding the chairman to whom I am accountable.'

Heneage needed to wait for confirmation that Graham Taylor, Derek Trevis, and Terry Branston were three of the four who wrote to the board and who would ultimately be encouraged to apply for the vacancy. Those combined factors saw the decision by the board of directors to sack David Herd on 7th December 1972. Whilst the directors were left to consider options I was instructed to go down to Graham Taylor's home and bring him to the ground for an interview. I advised him to be sensible over asking for improved terms of employment and to wait for the time when success was seen. Before leaving the ground, Heneage came running out to my car asking me to assure Graham that all would be OK and that things were going the way of his plans for the future. It was quite a surprising read, therefore, when within his own autobiography Graham stated that he didn't know the full circumstances that led to them sacking David Herd and giving him the job. Could have been a lapse of memory! I can't be sure you'll need to use your own imagination.

At this particular point in time David Herd had formed quite a personal relationship with the then chairman, Dennis Bocock, and this was seen as part of the mystery and intrigue around Heneage Dove's thinking and plotting. I know from comments made to me that if he could secure the appointment of Graham and at the same time push Dennis Bocock into a corner he could secure the title of chairman. I was asked if I would be prepared to become involved. Delivering a strong rebuke I advised that he was tangling with danger for not only was my position deemed to be fully compliant, but Dennis Bocock had provided substantial financial support and if he were to depart the state of affairs from a finance point of view were precarious to say the least.

This was the first time in my working life that I had really been privy to such manoeuvrings but, with Heneage around, it wasn't going to be the last. The role of the senior administrator is to be completely neutral. You must observe the commitment to be answerable to each member of the board of directors and whilst you may have views, those have to remain confidential unless specifically asked with your answer being specific to fact.

Later on, the time arrived for Heneage to assume the mantle of chairman. It would be fair to say that he too always supported the club financially and there was never an occasion when funds were required that he declined. Although, I don't think his pockets were as deep as some on the board during his time at the club. He seemed to me to regard his position to be untouchable with no one daring to offer any sort of a challenge.

Not long after the appointment of Reg Brealey as vice-chairman, all members of the staff were handed gift vouchers to exchange for goods in his deli shop in Sleaford so all could enjoy a festive Christmas season. A gesture greatly appreciated by all staff, but not entirely so by the chairman who interpreted it as a move to gain popularity. Not for the first time was I asked to speak on Heneage's behalf to try and establish Reg's motives. I had to remind him that if he required an answer to that he should seek a private meeting during which the two could thrash out both his concerns and the way forward. I had recommended Reg for nomination to the board at the time it was re-constructed. I had not become involved in the fine-tuning of any such appointment that was entirely outside of my responsibilities. It is interesting to note that within a reasonably short period of time Reg Brealey resigned both as vice-chairman and director due to the development of his own business empire. His priority, as reported in the press, and in reality, was to develop his company into one listed on the Stock Exchange. Although my career took me down the Reg

Brealey route I never enquired any further into the circumstances in which he left Lincoln. I would say that what he was to achieve later on in his Sheffield United days he could have done at Lincoln City. With a link-up between Dennis Bocock, always a willing financial supporter, and Reg Brealey, the new entrepreneur on the block, I can only leave it to your own imagination to guess as to what the future of the club could have been!

It was a pity that there had emerged yet another undercurrent in what was at that time a very good and well-balanced board of directors. It also delivered a clear message to any employee (myself included) not to become embroiled in internal politics!

I thoroughly enjoyed working at Lincoln City at this time. Graham was a joy to work alongside, as long as you recognised that he didn't want anyone to threaten his supremacy, being equally committed to his responsibilities and targets as I was. We both looked forward to continued success, inevitable promotions and club development. We wanted to create a positive future for both the supporter base and the city at large. Graham had put together a very good team on the field and equally as good with his backroom staff. Within the dressing room he had the ears and eyes of his team captain keeping him fully apprised of any goings on. He could stamp out anything almost as soon as it occurred!

Ideally Graham would have liked to have had complete control over all aspects of the club and in fact made many overtures to the chairman, Heneage Dove, for this to be done. To be fair it was not something that the chairman, or board of directors, wanted, as they recognised that things were going well in all quarters with individual, dedicated staff in situ. Another late-night foray took us to the far reaches of Cheshire when I accompanied Graham to watch Chester FC play Portsmouth on a Monday evening in April 1977. His purpose was threefold. One: to run the rule over Chester who we had to face before the season ended. Two: to watch two of the Portsmouth players, Chris Kamara, and Paul Gilchrist who Graham had on his potential shopping list for next season. Three: to give both of us the opportunity to consider our marketing campaign for the following season. I don't think he was too impressed by what he saw on the pitch, as I never heard the names mentioned again. On our way home, long before the motorway networks had been developed, we took a turn in Manchester which Graham said he had used before as a shortcut only to find ourselves literally up the back streets and alleyways. That detour resulted in our early morning arrival back into Lincoln leaving little sleep before opening hours the following morning.

Graham was in my office collecting his post that following morning when Heneage Dove called in to let us know he was meeting some people at the ground. He passed comment on us looking somewhat tired. We related the escapades of the evening before. He looked meaningfully at us both before passing the soul-destroying comment, 'Whilst you are both here let me just make my position clear. As long as I am chairman I don't want Second Division football here at Sincil Bank.' Heneage left the room almost as soon as those words passed his lips.

Graham and I sat and looked at one another, initially numbed. After a minute or two of stunned silence Graham spoke first. 'What the hell are we supposed to do?' My reply was, 'It's OK for you, mate. You only have to go back to Elton John, I'm sure you can renew your interest there. He wanted you the first time and I'm sure he will want you again. Apart from that, doesn't that statement from the chairman disappoint you. All of our time has been spent trying to reach the top knowing only too well that if we had failed we would have achieved some level of success. Now Heneage wants to aim for mediocrity and if he doesn't achieve that he has got failure. As for me I've no idea, mate.'

It seemed to me then, and now, that the moment was a turning point. Heneage's words came home to bite him on the bum later on when a decline set in and the ball started rolling downhill until it embedded itself in the Conference League. The proof of the pudding is in the eating, for, when Elton came back knocking on the door, Graham accepted an offer far above his initial expectations and went on to great success. Heneage secured the compensation sum of £20,000 for Graham's services from Watford. He firmly believed that he had pulled off a good deal for the club. It is of course a rhetorical question, but what would have happened if the management structure had remained in place for years after? Would there have been more than £20,000 in the coffers and what enjoyment could have been delivered for the punters? That is really unanswerable but would be a good topic of conversation over a pint or two in the local pubs and social clubs.

I signed a three-year contract on 19th June 1975 at a princely salary of four thousand pounds per annum with an additional incentive bonus payment. The bonus was based upon exceeding pre-determined commercial income targets with the assumption that any such deals had been fully paid for. I am able to say that those targets were achieved annually. I decided, on Graham's departure, that I would carry on for another year. I fervently believed (maybe hoped!) that the undertaking given by the then chairman, Heneage Dove, to improve my terms would at least be honoured.

The managerial responsibilities were handed to George Kerr, who in my opinion had been a true stalwart to Graham Taylor. Rather than move to Watford, George decided that his ambitions could be best served remaining at Sincil Bank. During this managerial spell the club lost the valued contributions of Reg Brealey who resigned from his position as vice chairman – to my mind seriously disrupting the strength and visions from within the Board. Dennis Bocock, former chairman, publicly expressed his views in the *Lincolnshire Echo* that the board should have made £100,000 available to enable the then manager to sign much needed additions. This statement attracted the support of the recent vice chairman. At the same time Mr Bocock went on to add that the manager was only under a one-year agreement and that the secretary (me!) was working without any term contract and that the club could be in danger of losing a lead administrator. The outcome was that Heneage decided that no money was to be made available and following a meeting of the directors on 13th January 1977 George Kerr was sacked.

The meeting was interesting as virtually no other director spoke to the manager other than the chairman, although he did say several times that he had the authority of all members of the board. The room in which the board meetings were held was the one used for match day hospitality and had a large oak table capable of seating a dozen people in the centre of the room. Sat on the tabletop at all times was a large and heavy ashtray. For board meetings it was placed at the opposite end to where the chairman occupied his place. In this instance it was very close to where George was sitting. As the decision to confirm his sacking was made the ashtray, carefully aimed by George, flew down the table and landed in the chairman's lap whereupon George left the meeting. Obviously this time – no smoke but plenty of fire!

The board soon approved the placing of national adverts to secure a replacement manager. Following due consideration of applicants and the necessary interviewing processes the appointment of Willie Bell was confirmed. A fresh face into the Sincil Bank scene did not have any major impact in terms of on-the-field results. From my point of view, virtually no interest was shown in terms of the previously adopted community programme or indeed the importance of the supporter. The only exception was a few comments in the press when he was seeking their added support when things weren't going particularly well. Unfortunately for the club, there were quite a few of those times!

At the end of the season, my contract situation still was not clear. Working through the close season, getting all the necessary arrangements in place, there was no positive approach from the chairman to consider my contractual position until one day he sat down and said, 'Well then, let's have a look at where we stand in terms of your contract.' Following which he made me an offer which was on terms far less favourable than the existing ones. My response was quite blunt saying, 'Heneage, one of us is not very good at maths and that sure ain't me. You need to go back to the drawing board.' 'Right, we had better leave it to the board to decide. Put it on the agenda for the next meeting.' Come the night of the meeting, and very much in line with the George Kerr sacking, Heneage did all the talking and confirmed that his previous offer was final. That evening in May 1978, I confirmed my decision to resign and when leaving the meeting one of the directors, Alan Davey, a pig farmer, said, ' If you don't find anything else, I'll give you a job.' Was this as much how much he valued me or a simple goodwill gesture? I will never know – nor do I want to. I had learned plenty at Lincoln about the workings of a football club at board level, but it was time for me to move on.

In my time at Bramall Lane there were certainly plenty of movements in the constitution of the board of directors. They were brought about by circumstances both on the field, following relegation to Division Four, and off the field following the announcement of a major share capital increase. Between these two happenings the board witnessed the resignation of Mike Watterson, Prof F O'Gorman, Ken Lee and Bert Jackson, who were not prepared to honour the joint and several guarantee promised in the prospectus to shareholders. More about that elsewhere in the book. Albert Bramall who unfortunately died, but who had previously tendered continuous support. Finally John Hassall, who within a few days of relegation to Division Four inflicted under the Harry Haslam and Martin Peters' tenure as manager, instantly resigned as both chairman and director. John was a person totally committed to the Blades' cause and, as well as financial support to the club, he gave his managers full support, only to be badly let down. A cruel game this football business! Change at board level was something that I was beginning to get used to.

The 12th June 1982 will forever be a day etched in my memory. I had had a visit earlier in the week from Dick Wragg, both a Sheffield United director and also member of the Football Association Management Board – in fact at the time he was chairman of the International Select Committee, asking what I was up to at the weekend. Quite puzzling at the time for, whilst he was quite a regular visitor to my office, he was not always the chattiest of people. He was usually much more interested in what had been happening at the club during his absences in London.

'I've nothing planned, hopefully a day tidying up the garden and pottering around doing the usual things one does at the weekend,' I said.

There was a facial change and leaning out of his chair on the opposite side of my desk he was almost lying on the desktop when he said, 'If I ask you something, will you promise me it will go no further, not even to your wife and certainly not to the chairman?'

'Of course, you have my word. I'm not in the habit of breaching confidences but it would be nice to know a bit more about your enquiries,' I replied. What followed was, to say the least, somewhat unexpected and quite flattering.

'Could you be at the Royal Lancaster Hotel' – a hotel, I knew, used for various football meetings – 'in London Saturday morning? I want to introduce you to some members of the Football Association's Senior Management Board, I think you will find it interesting.'

'Can you give me any further detail, as it can't just be for me to meet up for a friendly chat on a Saturday morning.'

'Look Dick, I am under the strictest possible degree of confidentiality and if I breach that you must show total surprise on the day, but I recognise that you need a bit more information before giving up some of your weekend. They want you to replace Ted Croker.' He was the then secretary of the Football Association, who basically was regarded as the top man in football.

'My god are you being serious?'

'These are the arrangements for you: travel down to London to arrive at the hotel by 11.15am for a meeting to start at 11.30am, report to the upper-level car park and I will be waiting for you to arrive and take you into the meeting room. Telephone when close so I know your arrival time but please not a word to anyone.'

I was awake early, in fact I hardly slept at all, mulling over my thoughts and feelings, but duly arrived at the hotel on time and, as soon as I had parked my car, there was Dick Wragg waiting. I was taken through what appeared to be an exit door, down a corridor and into the meeting room. To my astonishment, excluding Dick Wragg, there were eight other members of the Management Board: Jack Wiseman, Bert Millichip, Lord Westwood, Len Shipman, Peter Swales, Jack Dunnett, Len Cearns, and Lionel Smart, all of whom were introduced to me by Lord Westwood, who seemed to be in charge of the gathering. Formalities out of the way Bert Millichip opened proceedings by immediately asking if I knew the purpose of the meeting. I replied saying, 'I was asked by Mr Wragg if I could make myself available to meet you all for a meeting which could be in my best interests.' Being relatively new to this football game I was feeling somewhat overwhelmed and, to this day, I cannot be certain who actually said, 'We want you to replace Mr Croker as secretary of the Football Association.' I had met Mr Croker at various football meetings in the past, had never really made acquaintances, but believed he was a respected member of the Association. So, with some hesitancy in my voice I asked, 'Whilst I appreciate the confidence you have shown in me why do you find it necessary to consider such a replacement, and why pick me when there are far more administrators in football with a much greater pedigree of football management?' Mr Millichip came back with a response, 'Mr Croker has been with the FA for a number of years now, but we are finding that his commitment to his family business is taking precedence over his responsibilities here and his performance of duties is of a standard not acceptable to members round this table, and your name has been repeatedly mentioned. We are finding that his financial package is both, not justified, and subject to abuse. We will not confront him with our concerns until we have reached an agreement for his replacement.'

'The first part of your reply, Sir, is of interest to me and somewhat flattering, as I have only been in this business for less than ten years, seven of those being in the bottom tier of the Football League, only spending a short period at Bramall Lane. The second part is of an internal issue to yourselves, which I would not wish to comment upon, not knowing the inner workings of the Association. Can you explain the responsibilities and expectations of the new appointee?'

Quite lengthy discussions took place with many of the members in the meeting, all responsible for differing working committees of the association, making their own contributions. Several issues and questions were submitted and answered by all concerned, following which it would be fair to say that things seemed to have gone quite well. The meeting concluded without there being any final decision, with Bert Millichip saying that once those present have had the opportunity to discuss in private, he would be telephoning me with their decision, but in the meantime total confidentiality was paramount.

Sat in my Bramall Lane office the following, Tuesday the door opened and in walked Dick Wragg, still concerned about the confidentiality of the whole affair, to which I offered total assurances.

'Well then, how did you feel the meeting went?' was his first question.

'I thought I had addressed all of the issues presented, but I do have concerns about the precise job,' being my reply. Asked what I meant I went on to say that unlike a club where you have an end product and a specific job to do and deliver for your employers, I am not sure how I would cope with having to attend committee meetings over and over again. I explained that I would not have the sort of individual responsibility I had in football to get things done. I was also concerned about needing to go through a drawn-out process of getting things approved, which would invariably involve people who would not be as committed to the task as me. In essence part-timers.

At the same time I was thinking of the promise and undertaking given to me by Reg Brealey when assuming his role as chairman. He told me that in recognition of all of the advice and help I had given him, the delivery of projects and general managerial skills, that when the Football

League approved the appointment of paid directors then that position would go to me at Bramall Lane. Day to day committee attendance and nothing more to aim for, was not totally appealing to me. I was then told that Lord Westwood would be telephoning shortly, with the approval of members, to confirm their positive decision, but again I was sworn to secrecy for the meeting decreed that it was Lord Westwood who should deliver their decision. Quite late on in the afternoon, reception put a call through to me saying that a Mr Millichip was calling from Birmingham. Accepting the call I recall the conversation being of a very friendly tone with the caller seemingly anxious to get to the real reason for the call.

In short, Mr Millichip offered me the post. It was a verbal undertaking, which, subject to my agreement, would be handed over to solicitors to complete all necessary contractual formalities to effect the appointment. The terms offered were quite unreal in comparison with my existing terms of employment. A salary more than three times what I was then paid, self-contained, free accommodation above the Lancaster Gate office premises, a fully expensed car of my own choosing, a fully funded lucrative personal pension scheme and reimbursement of expenses wholly and necessarily incurred, inclusive of first-class travel. Trying to gather my breath, I asked for time to consider, which was readily agreed, but again emphasising the confidentiality until matters satisfactorily concluded.

I said before I went down to the original meeting that I had had a restless night. I can now tell you that I had many, many more, trying to weigh up the family benefits that such an acceptance would deliver, whilst at the same time not forgetting that I did not really see myself tracking around the corridors of power from one meeting to another. Yes, football always attracts many paper inches of coverage, investigation and opinions and I couldn't get out of my mind my lack of top-flight experience, trying to pre-empt how this would be received with major players in the field of news and television. Did I really want to be thrown to the wolves when in essence my work would be governed by votes in a committee room and not necessarily personal? I also had a promise from Reg Brealey to be elevated at Bramall Lane to a more influential board position. There was much more that I wanted to achieve at Sheffield United having seen through some major changes and enhancement of their financial standing. How could I be employed within the governing body, equally accountable to all, and yet maintain a leaning to any one club? I believed I needed an end product to aim for and to be able to quietly work behind the scenes without the necessity to explain to the press or media. If I stayed with the Blades, I could sit back whilst the press drew their own conclusions and say what they wanted to say. If I moved the FA, I worried that I would be in the firing line. It was a tough decision.

The outcome was a call to Mr Millichip in the presence of Dick Wragg to advise that I didn't feel the time was right for me. I went on to say how grateful I was that senior members of the management committee had the confidence in me to offer such a prestigious position. I apologised for any inconvenience caused and assured him of total confidence. At the end of the call Dick Wragg tried to convince me I had the qualities and abilities to deliver at the highest level but wearing his other hat was also pleased that I was prepared to commit myself to the Blades. There was also a combined agreement that this event would not be released to the club chairman, as Dick wished to see out his days at the Lane. Those undertakings, up until the last twelve months, have been honoured in full.

Never at any time thereafter did I allow the event to disrupt my commitment to the Blades and at all times I felt I did my utmost to work in the best interests of the club. I settled myself down in the knowledge that there was a promise from the chairman to enjoy a future promotion as the first paid director of the club as permitted by revised Football League regulations.

On the Friday afternoon prior to the board meeting scheduled for the first Monday in April 1983, the chairman was at the club. His duties that day included a meeting with the manager and also a call into my office to approve the draft agenda for the board meeting. Prior to leaving he called back into my office saying that he had a very difficult weekend in front of him. He had invited Derek Dooley and his wife for a meal during which he was to advise Derek that he was to be relieved of his duties. My first thoughts were if you are going to tell Derek that sort of news then be prepared for an outburst, because that was his style when things were going wrong. I should of course also have listened to comments passed on to me by members of his own company staff when they said that any sackings in the business were done by brother Len. Afterwards Reg would always meet up with the outgoing staff member and present them with a sweetener.

Come the day of the board meeting, work was undertaken as normal with the boardroom prepared for the lunchtime meeting. Following the arrival of all of those attending, the chairman asked if he could present an item outside of the agenda for which there were no objections. To my utter surprise he went on to say that he was nominating Derek, who he had previously stated privately as being not up to the standard he required to be appointed as the first paid director of the club. The motion was carried, and the appointment confirmed. Many years later I had the opportunity to read Derek's life-story, within which he related the offer from Reg shortly after his appointment as chairman, to make him the first paid director. To me that smacks of duplicity!

I finished my tasks, cleared the boardroom, returned to my office, collected personal belongings, and left for home knowing that was going to be my last day at the Lane. During the evening I made a call to the chairman and asked for a meeting in his Sleaford offices the following day, which was agreed. During that meeting I expressed my utter surprise, disappointment, and annoyance that he never at any time had the decency to be truthful about his intentions. It was not until many years later when reading Derek's autobiography I learnt that following his appointment as Chairman, Reg had offered the same undertaking to Derek as he had to me.

If ever there was a case of making use of someone, particularly one who seemed to be just as much a friend as a colleague, then I had yet to find anything to compare. I advised Reg that I had taken all personal possessions from my office and that I would not be returning at all, and my employment had now ceased. Not a flicker of disappointment appeared on his face. I think to this day that it was what he was expecting. As a person of honour I did not feel I could work alongside someone with unequal values. Please bear in mind, though, that I regarded Reg as a friend. In my hour of need in the past he was the only one there to help me and I did not want to lose that friendship. It was several years before the relationship was renewed.

Almost three weeks later I received a telephone call on the 11th August 1983 from Dick Wragg asking if I would meet with him, Alan Laver, a fellow director at the Lane, and a previous heavy investor in the club, as they would like to talk to me. I accepted and attended at the stated time and was instantly greeted with a request to reconsider my decision and allow them to take the matter back to the board. They knew it would get majority support as they had already canvassed support from other members, excluding the chairman. The decision would be reversed. Both went on to say that they recognised Derek's high profile in the City of Sheffield, which I agreed with, but was less convinced about his abilities to grasp all the business elements associated with a directorship. It was said that they would seek to transfer his duties to that of a club ambassador, thereby retaining his extensive reputation in the City. During my time at The Lane I spent many hours with Derek and Sylvia, his wife, and regarded them both as close friends in football. I hadn't spoken to Derek at all about his new position and was not about to become embroiled in a cloak and dagger situation which could scupper all of the good memories I had during our relationship. The outcome was that I would pursue the chosen path of football consultancy work, leave well alone and let them all get on with it, knowing that I would not have been able to trust anything said to me by the chairman. I was a bitterly disappointed ex-employee of the Blades.

The close working relationship between the chairman and *Sheffield Star's* Tony Pritchett ensured that the real reasons for my departure have never been aired until now. But then again, football is renowned for undercover moves and manoeuvres with supporters left to draw their own conclusions.

The rivalries I came across in the game could have darkly comic undertones. Very early on in my career it became apparent that there was both friction and split in the boardroom at Sincil Bank. In essence there were six directors and when it came to discussions and votes it was apparent that on one side of the fence sat Charles Warner, Roy Chapman and George Cook and the other side there was a definite affinity shown between Heneage Dove and Sid Haigh, with Dennis Bocock, tending, but not always going, their way. During Charles Warner's reign as chairman the club were unfortunate to lose the services of Sid Haigh when he unfortunately passed away. The family made an approach to the club to seek permission for his ashes to be spread on the Sincil Bank pitch, which was unanimously approved. At the same time, unaware of the friction and differences of opinion with the then chairman, Charles Warner, the family asked if the chairman could undertake the formal duties of spreading the ashes. The occasion was a private family affair and on the day it was my duty to ensure no-one encroached. The spreading of the ashes was confined to the Railway End – now known as Stacey West end – but on the day the weather decided to blow a right howler and as the chairman was spreading the ashes many were blowing back on to the black overcoat he was wearing. After the event he came back into my office and asked if I had a brush so he could brush himself down. To which I replied, 'Unfortunately, Mr Chairman, I do not possess one but it looks to me as though you still can't get rid of him he's stuck to you like glue.' A few laughs before a clothes brush from the directors' room salvaged the day.

So, what did I learn from my time in football? I titled this chapter 'Night of the Long Knives.' In history that title relates to two events. Firstly, Hitler brutally executing people he felt were his rivals in the Nazi party in a successful attempt to consolidate his power in 1934. Less violently, it refers to Harold Macmillan sacking a third of his cabinet in a failed attempt to shore up his position as Prime Minister in 1962. I learned that football can also be a ruthless business. It is a results-based game both on and off the pitch. It is also one that in many cases is controlled and run by people with big personalities. Mixing the need for results, large characters, and organisations that only have space for a handful of people at the top, leads in my experience to some manoeuvring and to high-level politics. These movements can override friendships and long-lasting work relationships. I learned that people in top positions even in a national organisation such as the FA can plot and plan, as can those in our league clubs. My friendships and closest working relationships were put at risk at times. I describe the business as brutal and ruthless here. I'll leave it to the reader to decide if my choice of words is correct!

Chapter Eight: Eaves to Ashes – Building Projects

Football stadia of the 1970s and 1980s were different in many ways to those common today. Almost all grounds had a standing section – Coventry City's Highfield Road becoming the country's first all-seater stadium in 1981. Many grounds dated from the late 19th or early 20th Century, and some were showing their age. There were examples of architectural merit – modern supporters would still recognise the cottage at Fulham, or the Archibald Leitch designed stands at Everton, Liverpool, Aston Villa and elsewhere. Some supporters though suffered in what Simon Inglis described in his classic 1983 book *The Football Grounds of England and Wales* as "poor design, outdated facilities and extremes of discomfort." One of my driving aims, having been on that side of the fence far too often, was to improve the lot of the match-going fan. This chapter discusses the successes and failures that I, and the clubs I worked for, had in improving facilities. I also consider the lessons I learned and look to apply them to today's game.

Reg Brealey asked me, before he accepted the invitation to join the board, to prepare a paper for him highlighting my personal assessments of the essential requirements to turn things around at Bramall Lane. In the paper I mentioned the need for greater use of the ground, similar to my advice to the chairman at Lincoln City, and I came up with a phrase "Maximisation of the utilisation of Assets." I think it must have been one of those light bulb moments. Even as a relatively inexperienced club secretary it appeared inconceivable that a major company could afford to run or exist when their main assets were in the shop window to earn money, probably no more than 50 – 60 hours per year. If you compare that to commercial or industrial outlets they will be looking for each of their main assets – manpower or machinery and equipment – each to be working 40 hours per employee per week, with the assembly lines or in-house equipment doing likewise. There is no real comparison, and neither is there any other alternative other than for a football club to think outside the box and create that opportunity.

The very first development that was undertaken and completed under my wing was at Lincoln City. It involved the revamping of the social club. Sincil Bank had been home to the social club for many years. It had the flavour of a working man's club. Their regular Friday night event was an open house disco aimed at attracting the younger element of the community. These proved to be very successful with significant numbers in attendance. Society in the early 1970s was beginning to alter. After each Friday night event, and before a home game the following day, it was necessary for volunteers to clean and sweep up bags of broken glass, used condoms and debris. As efforts were being made to transform the standing of the club within the community, things needed to change. During one of the regular monthly meetings I had with the brewery representative I broached the question of a possible loan in order to undertake major changes and enhance the overall presentation.

Approval was given, pending a good business plan and building proposal. I quickly constructed that meaningful business plan with complete costings for the renovation and fixtures. At that time there was an exhibition being held in Manchester displaying all aspects of the hospitality trade including furniture and bar fittings. I spent a full day there and, when at the end, I came away with virtually all the internal fixtures required, having persuaded them to provide the same on a free gratis basis in return for advertising or sponsorship deals at the club. Amazing what a link with a football club could do even then! With confidence now growing I telephoned the area brewery representative asking him to call in to consider progress to date. The business plan showed that there was provision for the buildings to continue as a normal social club with enhanced facilities and extended programmes available to members. At the same time it would become a facility with an area available for outside organisations with seating numbers of up to a maximum of 350. This would make it the largest facility for such events in the city whilst at the same time giving the punter a much-respected opportunity to enjoy all their drinks at social club members' prices. These prices were significantly lower than city competitors. The brewery came good with a loan of £35,000 with no interest payable, subject to the barrellage turnover exceeding a declared minimum level. The only outstanding work to tie up was the internal decorating, the kitchen provisions and the appointed caterer. This turned out to be quite easy as the decorating was undertaken by a firm already registered with our Executive Club – zero cost again with sponsorship deals taken in lieu. The caterer, Starbuck & Son of Market Rasen, had picked up the possibility via the local bush telegraph. The outcome was job settled and work soon underway. The transformation was immense and following a hard telephone sell the first year exceeded all expectations. Those users re-booked for the following year and, with ongoing marketing, the facility very shortly reached a total sell out. In fact when I left in the summer of 1978 most of the bookings for the next two years had been taken. Whilst I had moved on to pastures new, future management policies decreed that this was a facility either not paying its way or surplus to requirements. I clearly was not part of that decision-making process but such a decision has to be debatable at least. This was a facility enjoyed by many social and sporting groups from within the city and could ill afford to be taken out of the social scene.

Running alongside the completed social club development was a major ground redevelopment programme. My original discussion with the chairman, Dennis Bocock, and his associate was based on what I saw as a need to make better use of the ground, after all the ground was the most valuable asset on the balance sheet which was failing to operate to maximum potential. Every time discussions took place in the board meetings it was the same old case. What can we put out to the supporters to raise extra revenue or where can we increase our charges? Could we increase season tickets, gate prices, programme prices, catering charges? And on and on it went. My thoughts were: why not make better use of the ground and introduce commercial operations each day of the week and each week of the year. Combined with the newfound commercial and marketing programmes this could generate a flow of revenue not likely to be equalled by extra charges to supporters. The basic plan consisted of commercial letting to a national supermarket chain, a crèche to accommodate children whilst parents enjoy their chosen leisure pursuits, a new stand incorporating gymnasium for both club and community and an increase in capacity from 24,000 to 32,000 – including a new 6,000 seater main stand. The combined effect of all these areas would have provided a nett return to the club of circa £50-£60,000 for the initial ten-year period and thereafter one hundred percent of all rental income. In that way everyone would benefit. More revenue to the club, more people visiting Sincil Bank, with the hope of them being converted to support the club through the turnstiles, and no need to keep on relying on the supporter to keep putting his hand in his pocket.

The magnetism of a Football League club in each and every town or city where the game is played should never be under-estimated. The true value of that public asset can only be fully judged if the club loses its league status. A sad example was Barrow-in-Furness whose shipyard business went into rapid decline and was largely transferred to another port town following the football team's demotion from the league. The team was lost, and the town suffered from a major decline in publicity which they could ill afford.

I felt that the plans for Sincil Bank would benefit the club and the city. I was frustrated, therefore, to see the plans turned down by the local planning authority. It is true to say the main reason given by Lincoln City Council – that of suitable access and egress arrangements – was valid, but for whatever reason no opportunity was given to consider alternative options. Just a bland NO, thank you very much for trying but hard luck, mate! I felt that a little more vision could have been deployed and seen the application over the line. At the same time Lincoln City would have been at the forefront of such a development, but following the negative view and ultimate decision of the council that honour fell to Crystal Palace. The failure of the application did not in any way deter me from the possibility that at some time in the future a similar opportunity may present itself. I had learnt lots that would stand me in good stead for the future. It does beg the question of what if? Would it have been possible that this would have given Graham a real bargaining tool when talking to players – seeing that the club were not just a seemingly downtrodden Division Four club but one of some potential if its surrounds were anything to go by.

The wisdom of that planning decision was, many years later, to throw itself back into the frame when the Lincoln City Council agreed, in times of further difficult financial circumstances, to an approach from the then chairman, Gilbert Blades, to offer a mortgage package to save the club from administration. A positive decision to the earlier submitted planning application would have provided the club with significant commercial revenue streams to have avoided any future plea for help. What do they say – things have a habit of coming back and biting you on the bum! The vision at the time was innovative and commercially strong and came from a business who had to work hard for their income streams and who weren't in the privileged position of having it handed over to them on a plate.

Season 1975/76 saw the club come out of the hat in the Football League Cup with a home tie against Stoke City, then a respectable First Division side. When the Imps winning goal in a 2-1 scoreline went in, the perimeter wall behind the South Park goal collapsed. The game was stopped, those injured speedily attended to, and, when deemed safe, the referee continued and the game finished. The outcome was the immediate intervention of the City of Lincoln Engineers' Department who were looking to a replacement wall and influencing the design. What they suggested was deemed by our professional advisors to be extreme, and we quickly told them! The result was a visit from their senior engineer, Joe Stead, who, without any authorisation whatsoever waltzed straight on to the ground to view the relevant problem. I had to remind him that this was private property, and would I be allowed to walk through the corridors of City Hall without any authorisation? A few words were exchanged, following which I advised him that the wall was not being replaced. The area would be cleared and, with more people wanting to advertise on the ground than we previously had capacity for, we would be erecting advertising boards. That was completed and expenditure not needed but additional revenue achieved. A fairly positive outcome all round.

If this was a victory for the club, it was a short-lived one. The backlash came the following summer when, following the annual safety inspection, the club were presented with a lengthy list of works, deemed to be essential to support the relevant certification. There was no way such work could be avoided as any omissions would leave the club without any valid safety certificate. I am to this day convinced it was a case of the council licking their wounds and wanting to prove who was in charge. That view was not shared by our appointed professional advisor. The club fully complied with the schedule of work which was completed in time for the season's kick-off.

Moving to Bramall Lane saw me working for a club where there had already been developments at the stadium. During the Blades earlier and headier days, under the reign of John Harris in the top echelons of the football world, the board of directors approved the development of the New South Stand. As a result, the final Yorkshire County Cricket match was played on 7 August 1973 and a new stand replaced what was previously part of the outfield of the cricket ground. It also covered the pathway from pavilion to wicket on which many world class cricketers had walked.

That decision significantly contributed to the club's overall financial borrowings. Unfortunately, as the costly investment occurred so did the demise of the football club on the pitch with relegation being the ultimate "smack in the face." The decision was then taken to make use of a re-designed layout of the old cricket pavilion to accommodate the administrative functions of the football club. Within this building was my first working office at the Lane. Part of the report I had provided to Reg Brealey before his director appointment was the need to have the underneath of the partly built South Stand completed and the area immediately behind re-configured with a suitable frontage and enhanced profile. Plans were drawn up, and approved, to complete the entire project. This consisted of: new dressing rooms for home and away teams, referees' room, physio and treatment room, an executive suite, accommodating banqueting facilities for potential use by local functions, a social club, club shop, new administration unit, new directors' hospitality area, with both a "ladies' room" and private chairman's room, including a bed built into the wall for the chairman's overnight stays, a dedicated room for executive club members, demolition of the old cricket pavilion and extensive car parking facilities.

All of this work was completed with some urgency, with much of it being overseen personally by the chairman. For a Division Four club these facilities were the envy of many visiting clubs, and I can say that I have been in the official's corridors when visiting teams have arrived and quite openly stated that this was the nearest they would get to a Wembley set up. Unfortunately for the Blades, that view very often showed up on the pitch when the opposition raised their game for the occasion! It was another case of a hard-sell to secure those bookings from outside functions, but the size and quality of the venue became a major attraction in the City of Sheffield.

The club decided to throw open the facilities for supporters to view during a club open day, with staff and players acting as tour guides. It turned out to be a huge success and instead of finishing at the intended time, such were the queues that the whole event had to be extended. The new Executive and Banqueting Suite was formally opened by the Lord Mayor of Sheffield, Councillor Enid Hattersley – mother of the Right Honourable Roy Hattersley MP. The Executive Suite was full of club directors, invited guests, staff and players. When I was advised that the mayoral car had arrived the chairman and directors were at the far end of the room leaving me to extend the initial greetings. On entry into the building I asked, 'Could I arrange a drink for you madam?' and chancing my luck, 'Or would you like a cuppa instead, duck – whichever you prefer?' 'I would love a cuppa, as you so nicely put it,' she replied, beautifully! The arrangements were being made whilst I escorted the Lord Mayor through the throng of guests to make the formal introductions to the chairman.

I mentioned Roy Hattersley in this story for, when I'd moved on to Hillsborough, he was a regular guest in the directors' room, as well as a regular for away games, when I usually was the one to make all the formal arrangements. No sooner had I made his acquaintance than he said to me: 'I have to relay my mother's thanks to you for when officially opening the Blades Executive Suite she received the warmest of welcomes of her entire period of office as Lord Mayor when you addressed her as "duck" and arranged a cuppa for her!' I was on the receiving end of an annual bottle of House of Commons whisky from Roy Hattersley for the time I had taken to make sure he was catered for when he wished to watch his beloved Owls.

I enjoyed a good relationship with the then publicity officer for the City of Sheffield, Peter Wigley. Much later he became a member of the staff at The Lane – but on this occasion I liaised with him closely on the desire for Sheffield United Football Club to become a valuable cog in the publicity wheel of the city as a whole. In one of these discussions I briefed him on my views relating to the better utilisation of the ground making it a 24/7 business, which he quickly keyed into. At that time there was talk of limitations in the facilities afforded to athletes outside of London. Gateshead was seen as the only alternative, which had been subject to some negative press reports. Arrangements were made for me to visit Peter at the town hall when he would introduce me to the then leader, Councillor David Blunkett and provide the opportunity for an open discussion. At the end of that initial meeting I left fully in the knowledge that, when I had a working committee assembled, he would make available both staff and councillor colleagues to work with us to ensure that all eventualities were covered prior to submission of formal planning application processes. The one stipulation made was an undertaking that I would ensure on my part that all discussions and proposals were kept in total confidence with leaks to no one until the day that the relevant application was lodged. The principal City of Sheffield representatives were Roland Adamson, Planning, and Councillors Richard Caborn, Clive Betts, and Bill Michie. The regular members of the working group on behalf of the club were made up of Richard Costall – a Lincoln-based Architect – and differing members of his staff, plus Dr Bill Eastwood, Design and Constructional Engineers, with Roland Adamson, representing Sheffield City Council Planning Department. A powerful and influential group of people.

All terms, conditions and restrictions were both honoured and obeyed from day one by all serving members, with progress steadily developed and achieved. The overall development at The Lane was to see the introduction of an integral world class athletics provision, an on-site hotel facility, and the conversion of the John Street Stand to incorporate newly designed business office facilities. These would double up as match day executive facilities, ideally attracting users from within the city centre. There would also be provision for "bachelor pad" type buildings at corners of the ground. The only remaining need for the city would be a space for the staging of field events. This issue was to be overcome and provided for on land registered to Hadfield & Sons, City Engineering Company. It was to be located at the city end of the Parkway having attained the agreement of their then Managing Director, Dan Norton. It would be fair to say that all of the elements presented a real opportunity for both the club and the city to enhance their profile.

I cannot say that the vision to deliver such a far-reaching development was equally shared amongst some staff engaged within the club. During one such conversation with Derek Dooley, in the presence of Andy Dakin, I was reminded by Derek that "this was a football club and not a f-----g building site." A not unexpected view of a football person, other than to say that, at a much later day during Derek's tenure as a board member under the then chairman, Kevin McCabe, his view was that a hotel development – complete with proposed drawings – might be worthy of his considerations. Was I to assume that the opening of a building site had now all of a sudden become top drawer?

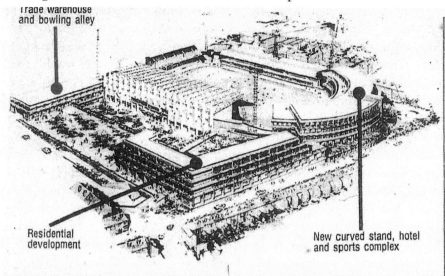

Trade warehouse and bowling alley

Residential development

New curved stand, hotel and sports complex

Sheffield United's plea for a Bramall Centre plan . . .

LIVE OR LET DIE

SHEFFIELD United this afternoon unvelled the dream for the future of Bramall Lane — the fourth major plan for the ground and surroundings.

THE STAR'S chief sports writer TONY PRITCHETT describes the club's vision . . .

THE BRAMALL Lane dream, the vision of turning Sheffield United's headquarters into something more than a football ground, has been kept alive for almost 20 years.

Now, the most ambitious scheme of all has gone to the planners; a £10 million brain-child of the club's Board headed by chairman Reg Brealey.

"And," says Brealey, "now is the time to kill it, perhaps for ever, or let it go ahead . . ."

Successive Boards of Directors have nurtured the hope that one day Bramall Lane would become one of the

Three plans .. three turned down

SHEFFIELD United has had an abrasive relationship with the local planning authority with three major schemes rejected in the last nine years.

In September 1973, a planning application was lodged for club social amenities, a squash club, an office block, an hotel and a

So what went wrong? To try and keep up with the happenings in the football world I used to have all the daily newspapers delivered to my home. The tabloid papers were the ones who were particularly pro-active in stories and gossip, thereby allowing you to keep up to speed with current matters. On this particular Saturday match-day morning I went downstairs for my breakfast and then retired to the lounge to review the morning's press coverage. To my utter surprise, disappointment, and frustration I opened up *The Sun* to see a lead article from their sports reporter, John Sadler, relating a story given to him by chairman, Reg

Brealey, blowing wide open all the details of the proposed development. Travelling to the ground I tried to work out in my own mind all of the ramifications. At work, I took a very early phone call from David Blunkett when with a very annoyed tone he asked: 'Will Brealey be at the game this afternoon? If so tell him to be in your office Monday afternoon for a meeting.' Upon the chairman's arrival I promptly advised him of the nature of the call and requested we adhere to the Leader's demands. Come Monday early afternoon the chairman and I awaited the leader's arrival, with us both discussing the potential outcomes. That was soon made clear for, when entering my office, the Leader addressed the chairman quite specifically when he said. 'Sir, you're a Capitalist, I'm a Socialist. You have completely betrayed all the confidences that Dick has honoured throughout all of the time the development work has been progressing and as long as I am Leader of the Council you will never ever get planning approval – good afternoon and goodbye.'

Following this potential setback the chairman asked that work continued to process the plans for lodging of the formal planning application with Sheffield City Council. In early January 1982 came the expected refusal. Appearing not to be outdone, the club contested the decision to refuse the application and the inspector, appointed by the Department of the Environment was called in to adjudicate. The City Council arrived for the first morning of the hearing, complete with leading Counsel, whilst our chairman had decided not to expend any further substantial sums of money and allow Roland Adamson to handle our case. Without casting any aspersions on anyone's professional capabilities, I would go so far as to say that, at the end of the first day, we had been completely outgunned and a satisfactory outcome from our point of view was already lost. A view ultimately declared by the inspector.

Another development programme assigned to the bin. This time basically lost on the strength of breach of confidences and conflicting political views. Whether the club or the council were right or wrong is open for discussion. I believe that it could have stabilised the club beyond all recognition. At the same time it may have avoided many of the difficulties which came from Sheffield Council funding a new athletics facility to accommodate the 1991 World Student games. These facilities in the east end of the city incurred excessive long-term borrowings for which the local tax-payer picked up much of the tab. If press reports are correct, the bill still is not fully paid, even now the development is demolished. In everyone's interest, the burying of strong personal and political views all those years ago and the deployment of some basic common sense, together with egos being put on the back burners, could have had far better outcomes all round. Personally, with two projects gathering dust, I began to wonder if I was somewhat cursed! More to the point, maybe, I was lacking in the understanding of the workings of local authorities and the political overtones operating within the corridors of power.

Moving to the Owls was a bit of an action replay in terms of the facilities at Hillsborough. Whilst I was working in the shadows of Eric England I had the time and the opportunity to take myself around the differing match day operations, meet up with the sponsors for the day, and go up into the press box. All of which allowed me the time and opportunity to review and assess potential alterations. On one particular occasion I entered the general hospitality area where I found that sponsors, invited guests and general guests of the club were mingling. Nothing particularly wrong with that in terms of a general get together but when you saw the club's general guests helping themselves to the food provided and paid for by the sponsors it was a matter for concern. The other significant concern for me was that the person responsible for the selling of the specific sponsorship deal was not present to host the party and on most occasions never presented himself. It was not so dissimilar in my early days at Bramall Lane either. With some frank exchanges of opinion, that changed: to the extent that many of the sponsors and their guests departed showing visible signs of enjoyment regardless of the result on the pitch. From a sponsor's point of view having spent some serious money on a public relations exercise they found that their guests were in contact thanking them for an enjoyable day and maintaining whatever business connections existed between them. From the club's point of view, the following season, the person responsible for the marketing of sponsorship found that it was the client who was buying and not themselves selling.

I have never been one for possessions, although I enjoy standards befitting the circumstances. I do, however, recognise and respect honesty, integrity and being true to oneself. With this in mind a development plan was drawn up to create quality facilities for both sponsors and directors. There was to be the creation of a banqueting suite, catering for upwards of 200 persons, and kitchens to elevate the club to being one of the best equipped in the country. The existing reception lounge was to be extended but still remain as the reception area. The original directors' room was also to be extended but earmarked on match days as the dedicated sponsors' lounge. The private directors' room would be used for both match days and board meetings and there would be new offices for both Howard Wilkinson and me. All of these to be equipped with appropriate furnishings, but trying to maintain a warm and welcoming atmosphere, rather than opulence, and an air of sincerity and respect to all users. The contract was awarded to Sheffield based builders, Gleesons Limited, and completed in time for the 1984/85 season.

The laying of a new pitch does not particularly come within the terms of building projects, but it does come within the framework of developments and improvements. Following the final game of 1983/84 season, appointed contractors, John C Pullen, an Otley based landscape construction maintenance firm recommended by the Sports Turf Research Institute, moved in, and by the time staff reported for duty on the Monday following, the ground looked like a beach! All grass was removed, the ground rotovated and trenches were dug out for the under-soil heating and a new automatic watering system. Contracts of this nature and magnitude invariably run into problems once work is underway. Sure enough during the first week's work I took a phone call from their director, Dick Ranshaw, quickly followed by a visit to my office from David Barber, groundsman.

David suggested I go with him to view what appeared to be the old bed of the river, which now flows behind the South Stand. What I saw indicated that possibly a thousand years ago the river course was where the pitch now is. As a result they had to remove a lot of the boulders but had overcome the problem. At the same time they had put down 1,400 tons of sand, laid the new herringbone drains to aid better pitch drainage and were about to start the installation of 15 pop-up sprinklers.

Looking at it at that time you thought how on earth were we going to open up in less than three months with a pitch – let alone a superb surface.

David Barber with evidence of the River Don flowing under the pitch at Hillsborough

151

Contractors assured me there would be no problem and said to carry on with all our new season plans. How right they were, and to provide the team with a quality surface was a real relief. I may have lost some of my hair in that time but Eh! Oh! We finished with one of the best playing surfaces in the then Division One.

In this close season alone, the outcome from a spend of some £400,000, the club had secured for itself quite a significant upgrade. The new playing surface was a remarkable improvement and very much to the liking of Howard Wilkinson, whilst the transformation in terms of the directors' areas, the offices, improved press facilities and banqueting rooms with attached new kitchen facilities provided the right ingredients for the club to confidently move forward in its desire to be well equipped for life at the top. The new catering developments were ideal for use for Executive Club members and their pre-match meal requirements whilst also being used for evening functions, creating added income streams. There was one thing in common with the development I had done at the Lane, in as much as the board would not agree to the incorporation of a "Ladies Section" or "Ladies Luncheon Club" which I found strange to say the least. In my mind women are as integral to the fortunes of a football club as their male counterparts and in many cases it is Mum who has the task of bringing the family to the games and ensuring continuing support for the clubs. Whilst all this was going on, the club secured record season ticket sales of £500,000.

Another major expense was brought about following the horrendous Bradford City fire disaster, when all grounds, including Hillsborough, were subjected to in-depth inspections to substantiate their satisfactory structures and elements regarding fireproofing. 11th May 1985 in Bradford was to have been a day of celebrations starting with the presentation of the Third Division championship trophy and no doubt hoping that the day could be further enjoyed with a win over opponents Lincoln City. Just before half-time John Helm, Yorkshire TV reporter, commented about a small fire in the main wooden stand. Within four minutes, in windy conditions, the fire had more or less engulfed the main stand in smoke and fire, with John Helm describing the situation as "a burning hell." People ran on to the pitch with their clothing on fire whilst others were trapped at the back of the stand unable to escape due to the turnstiles being locked. In all there were 56 deaths recorded including a gentleman called Bill Stacey who I had had personal dealings with during my days at Sincil Bank when he was the organiser of home and away travel for supporters based in the Sleaford area.

The ensuing inquiry required the industry to be subjected to legislation governing improved safety at football grounds including the banning of new wooden grandstands at all sporting venues. The essential work, applicable to Hillsborough, included the covering of all wooden sections within the stands with suitable material to prevent any possible outbreak of fire, this involving the installation of 42 tons of two-millimetre-thick metal sheeting, suitably coated with a non-slip material held in place by 32,500 screws. It is beyond comprehension as to fixing a true value on this work but at all times during my time at Hillsborough the chairman was adamant that if any work involved safety issues then as long as satisfactory tendering processes had been deployed the work must be done.

With many improvements done it was time to turn attention to the supporter facilities. As mentioned earlier, each discipline within the club, excluding the training and playing elements, was down to me, but I had a director allocated to work alongside me for each. In the case of the building and development projects the allocated director was Keith Addy. To say I spent a fair amount of time with him would be something of an understatement! Alongside potential projects were the regular, but essential, meetings with the Local Authority in respect of the Safety at Sports Ground Act and provisions. Both of us expressed our satisfaction at the achievements to date, but were turning our attention to the main fabric of the ground. Initially work on the main North Stand roof was completed alongside the enhancement of the floodlights, and whilst this was all underway considerations were given to the extension of the Kop area. This saw designs drawn up by the club's appointed advisory consultants, Eastwood and Partners, and the preparation of tender documents. Whilst not necessarily restricted to solely Sheffield based contractors it was openly discussed that it would be only right and proper if the work could be completed by a firm from within the city boundaries. Ultimately two submissions were chosen for further discussions, during which it was emphasised that both needed to go away, have a revised look and come back with a firm and binding tender as it was stipulated that there would be no latitude for any additional charges. It was to be a firm and final tender.

After further due considerations, the contract was awarded to Akroyd & Abbott. The relationship between Contractor, Consultant Engineer, Keith Addy, and myself was excellent throughout. It has to be said that there were many confrontations where additional work was needed in previously unforeseen areas but with each request came the same response: 'Sorry you prepared your own bid document and accepted that it was for a fixed price so if you want extra then please find reductions in the original bid because at the end of the project the price paid will be the price quoted.' The Monday morning site meetings turned out to be very good practice, as by the end of the construction the cost had been controlled to budget – credit due to all involved.

Early stages of work going on to provide some excellent facilities

The outcome proved to be most valuable in terms of supporter facilities although it has to be said that supporters significantly contributed by supporting differing events to raise money including a fun-run, walk and an open day – attracting almost 15,000 – all of which were superbly successful. For season 1986/87, season ticket and day tickets were subject to an increase but these were restricted to a level not less than 5% and not more than 11% but hopefully counterbalanced by the introduction of a family season ticket incorporating some significant savings for those taking advantage of such an offer.

During the summer months of 1986 the *Sheffield Star* ran a lead story announcing that Her Majesty the Queen was visiting South Yorkshire and whilst a date had been set there was no indication of the nature of her duties for the royal visit. I deliberated long and hard before contacting the offices of the Lord Lieutenant of South Yorkshire, who were the commissioned authority for such a visit. I contacted his private secretary asking if an official opening of this new facility at Hillsborough would be considered appropriate for inclusion in the schedule being drawn up.

At this time the club chairman was on holiday in South Africa meaning that any contact had to be done via his own personal secretary and transmitted by telex. During one of our regular conversations I asked his secretary if she could advise him of the possibility of such a royal visit. Before his reply was to hand I had official confirmation from the Lord Lieutenant's office that the official opening of the Kop had been included in the royal schedule. I again spoke with the chairman's private secretary asking if she had received any sort of acknowledgement to which she instantly said, 'In actual fact one arrived this morning, but if you want to know what it says you'd better come down to my office to read it because I am not going to repeat his reply over the phone.' At her office I read his reply which said: 'Just tell Dick Chester to stop trying to take the piss out of me. I'm on holiday enjoying myself and I can well do without his sense of humour trying to ruin it.' Trying to hide her embarrassment she smiled and enquired if there was any further progress. I simply asked if she would send another reply to the chairman confirming that approval had been received and the visit was now official. I didn't get any apology for a misguided interpretation of my sense of humour although I must admit it's a wonder it didn't get me in any deeper water than it did! Arrangements were made for the Lord Lieutenant of South Yorkshire, J Hugh Neil CBE, Her Majesty's private secretary, Sir Phillip Moore GCB GCVO CMG, to meet at the ground to consider and finalise formal arrangements. During these discussions, Her Majesty's representative asked where the red carpet could be laid, and here, not forgetting the colour code which landed me in hot water whilst at Bramall Lane, I said 'Sir, unfortunately this ground is situated in the blue half of the City. Our neighbours are in the red half.'

'Very well,' was his reply. 'It will be nice for her to walk on a different coloured carpet.'

I understand that the Queen did walk on a blue carpet. Due to my then leaving Hillsborough I was not present on the day, much to my regret. It was, though, down to my then work commitments not by virtue of any non-invitation. We were advised of certain protocol that needed to be followed and that it would be necessary for the club to have someone to be nominated to formally represent the club on her arrival. This became a discussion between myself and the chairman on his arrival back from holiday, and he took time out to thank me for securing such a visit and then reminding me of my sense of humour and his misunderstandings. It was my fervent belief that this person should represent the heart and soul of the club and not just be a figurehead commanding the attention on the day. The club, I quickly found out during my very early days, had a wealth of staff who had given years and years of service with little or no recognition, so I received the approval of the chairman to come up with someone to fit that bill.

My office and that of Howard Wilkinson's were next door to each other and, on the occasions of visitors being in attendance, or indeed ourselves wanting a cuppa, a lady called Lily Shelton was our first port of call and never once did she fail us. Lily had worked as a laundry lady, cleaner and all round helper for almost fifty years and was a person of some character, disposition, and knowledge.

Lily Shelton: she deserved the honour

She came into my office this particular afternoon with my cuppa and as she was going out I stopped her and said, 'You've heard about the Queen's visit I suppose.' Her eyes lit up and she quietly said, 'I never ever thought in my time working here that I would ever see anything to measure up to that.'

'Well,' I said, 'will you do me a favour: come back tomorrow afternoon, and tell me if you can think of anyone, during all your years at the club, who you believe would be the right person to welcome the Queen to Hillsborough.'

'OK – I will think about it and see you tomorrow.' Next day, the next cuppa comes in, carefully handled by Lily. She started to deliver a few names only for me to interrupt and say, 'Sorry, Lily, I didn't mean to put you to all that trouble. A decision has already been made.'

'No problem, pleased to be asked.' As she was leaving I called her back to say, 'Lily, that decision was for you to perform the honours.'

'Bloody hell, me! I can't believe what you are saying, are you bloody winding me up again'

'No, not at all. Both the chairman and I would like you to perform that role.'

'Oh, thank you, thank you. I just can't take it all in.'

'That's OK, it's a pleasure for me. Now I want you to go home and practice the official curtsey and when you come in again tomorrow I want you to show me.'

True enough cuppa time arrived, and Lily came in full of smiles. I quickly stood up in the middle of the office and said, 'Right Lily. I'm the Queen let me see what you have mastered,' to which she presented herself twice. 'Sorry, Lily, you haven't got that quite right, try again tonight in front of your husband and we'll see again tomorrow.' Quite a story this. But in she came and again I stood in the middle of the office and she performed two more curtseys. 'Sorry, Lily, you still haven't got it quite right.'

'Bloody hell, I was at it all night last. My husband was sick and fed up with me standing in front of the telly ruining his night. What am I doing wrong?'

'Look, Lily, your curtsey is passable, but you must remember when you do curtsey you have to fart!' Laughingly, she said, 'You bugger! All bloody night I was at it and that's all it was. Well, I'll go home tonight and do it again in front of my husband and if I fart I will blame you.'

Come the day come the lady! Unfortunately whilst she was honoured to stand in the presentation party, changes in arrangement had been made. From day one of confirmation of the details surrounding the visit of Her Majesty the Queen I reached an agreement with the chairman that it would be right and fitting to bestow the honour of representing the club to someone who had given their life to the club. After I had left the Club in October 1986, and before the visit two months later, changes were made and on the honour of presenting the floral tributes was made by the daughter of the lady who had temporarily been filling my shoes. Opportunism you could say! Lily did however continue her work with the club and was given the opportunity to meet royalty when representing the club at the City Hall, Sheffield on the occasion of the visit of Prince Charles and Lady Diana.

With the development work completed, as had been identified by

Keith Addy and me, a future further development was to look into the question of ensuring all stands were of the same height and that a definitive cantilever profile could be established. At that time consideration was given to the filling in of all four corners of the ground. The idea was to incorporate, in a not dissimilar way to what had been identified in the abandoned Bramall Lane project, blocks of offices or accommodation units where a financial return could be achieved. Having left before any significant designs had been implemented, I can only assume they never saw the light of day.

My experience, therefore, ran from developing a social club, through the facilities for the sponsors directors and staff, to major ground developments for the match-going supporter. I'd like to reflect now on what I learned and how far those lessons can be adapted to the modern game. Far too often, in my humble opinion, are football grounds left undeveloped and thereby totally reliant upon limited opportunities for revenue generation. Even in today's world such opportunities exist and would, again in my humble opinion, nullify the need for such heavy investment by owners intent on the glory of the game but desirous of protecting their investment in which -ever way possible, very often via the security of the club's main asset – it's land and ground.

I have looked on with horror in recent years as football clubs around the country have separated the ownership of the stadium from that of the club. This seems to me to have been done as clubs chase the proverbial promised land of the Premier League and owners look to invest heavily in the team and circumvent the rules put in place by the Football League to ensure financial fair play and stability. I cannot think of one team where there has been a happy outcome for the fans. I can think of several where the outcome has been very difficult. I am concerned therefore about what I hear to be currently happening at Sheffield Wednesday.

To my mind, Hillsborough stadium has been taken out of the hands of the supporters seemingly without any attempts to seek their approval. I believe that emotionally and to an extent financially the ground belongs to the fans. It is somewhere that is precious to the fans and has been over a great number of years. You only need to look at the efforts that fans went to in fundraising for the Kop roof, and prior to that supporting the building of the North and West Stands – before my time I would add – to understand how important the stadium is to them. From the outside it seems as if the owner has come along in recent times and seemingly got the management of the club wrong with their own independent management techniques and spending. Transferring ownership of the stadium to a related company means that the owner has the comfort of knowing that if all goes wrong they can always have the legal title of the club's main asset neatly tucked under their sleeves. It could be used to protect not just their investment but their independent management. Of course it has to be said that if the club needed a bank loan they would need to provide suitable securities one of which could be a charge on the ground but in instances of that nature it would not be unreasonable to assume that the club were being managed by a shareholder elected board of directors. Once an investor is able to secure the controlling majority of shares in issue then all controls pass from a board of directors accountable and answerable to shareholders in general meeting to that of simply being at the whim of any such owner. As I sourced from the web it would appear Mr Chansiri has borrowed against Hillsborough Stadium, using his company Sheffield 3 Ltd. He borrowed the money from New Avenue Projects Ltd and secured it against the ground – probably at a higher rate of interest than would normally be paid. The deal has just 'rolled over' but with an extra £200,000 on top.8

The ownership and leadership of football clubs is clearly a 'hot issue' at the moment. One does not have to look too far to find examples of where seemingly poor ownership has led clubs into all sorts of problems. The government's ongoing fan-led review of the game describes owners as 'simply the current custodians of a community asset'. The interim findings of that review comment that 'the evidence has been clear that football clubs are not ordinary businesses. They play a critical social, civic, and cultural role in their local communities'.9 The findings are well worth a look for those interested in the future of the game.

The three clubs where I spent my career are all now led by foreign investors and, whilst I am not deeply involved in the inner workings of any, it does seem on the surface that only Lincoln City has maintained the true value of a family club and retained a positive belief that the supporters are to be recognised, valued, and respected. This is evident by an appointed representative of their Supporters Association having a presence around the boardroom table. I must add that I am not a lover of supporter run football clubs, suffice to say that that is only a personal point of view with no direct experience or involvement in such operations. I feel, particularly with today's game being so much more demanding in terms of success and treading the golden path towards the Premier League and the financial benefits flowing their way, that there is a fundamental need for a specific leader. Football is at all times a game of opinions and I am sure if you had a group of supporters gathered together enjoying a pint or two discussing the last game you would have all sorts of differing views. Yes it is necessary to have varied points of view and opinions and with football being such an emotive subject all too often there are differences and disagreements some of which have been known to break up friendships. I have seen in my time enough upheaval in the boardroom to last me a lifetime particularly when one director is not getting his own way and that can be quite disruptive. Someone does need to be at the helm who has an investment to protect and has a standard of business acumen behind him who can carry a motion with authority and respect. I may be wrong, but I don't envisage that to be the case with a fan-based arrangement. Of course, the counter side to that point of view is that there is a total lifelong commitment to their particular club which can't be measured in pound notes alone.

The fan-led review recognised the potential difficulties of fans involvement and ownership. There are no easy answers, but a solution which includes supporters, ensures effective intervention where ownership is poor or in difficulty and protects against the need for owners to keep throwing money at a club must be found. Strong, effective ownership, regulated well by the authorities is key.

In conclusion, I was involved in successful projects, projects that failed, and developments that should have got off the ground but for some reason or another did not. What did I learn? Firstly, a successful project needs support from lots of areas – from the football club, to architects, contractors and the local politicians and planners. Secondly the bigger projects need a vision, one that is bought into by all involved. Finally, I learned that football stadiums are under-utilised and that with a clear vision could be a valuable asset to the club, their fanbase and the wider community. I am convinced that further investment in stadia and their surrounding facilities brings financial gain to a club. One that may negate the need to play financial games such as selling the stadium to another company. That game is a dangerous one with few if any happy endings. Attempting to develop stadiums meant I was involved in some of the most difficult meetings of my career but also saw some of my treasured memories. I did my best to improve the lot of the match going fan and believe that aim should be at the front and centre of all that football clubs do.

Chapter Nine: I'm with the Club

Can you ever be yourself in football, or can the influences from above cloud your judgement? Do you ever really know just how people view you as either a colleague, customer or as someone in authority? After early day reservations the standards instilled in me from childhood bore fruit in management. Let's give some examples in collating my thoughts.

As a young secretary, starting off my career at Lincoln City, I was surprised at how some of the initial transfer negotiations were completed and what an impression they formed. Whilst there was never a formal rule within any of the clubs I served, it was an understanding of the board of directors that when a manager was looking to sign any new player, he and/or his staff would undertake all the necessary due diligence. This would be in terms of his current playing performances, character, and capability of slotting into the current team structure. All sounds very convincing. In reality there were a number of completed transfers during my tenure when signings too place without the player being watched.

The first such incident was very early on in my career when David Herd, in 1972, signed Colin Symm from Sunderland and also Brendan Bradley from Finn Harps, Northern Ireland. There are two stories surrounding these signings. Towards the end of the 1971-72 season I was on duty for a re-arranged reserve team fixture against Sunderland at Sincil Bank whilst the first team were playing away. I had been asked by David to let him know if I saw any player who I thought may be of interest to him. From the team originally announced, Sunderland made some changes, including the shirt numbers for Colin Symm from 8 to 4 and John Lathan from 4 to 8. I advised David that the number 8 had had a good game and was worth another look. David, picking up a spare team sheet where the changes had not been completed, made his own enquiries and following a call to Sunderland was advised that Colin Symm was available on a free transfer, with David arranging for him to visit the ground and complete a free transfer. On the day, David did not travel down from Manchester but confirmed the terms of the contract between himself and the player which I had already pre-prepared, just awaiting his signature for finalisation. To my utter amazement the No. 8 I had seen was a tall, well-built, dark-haired player whereas the player in front of me was a medium-build blond haired individual! To be fair to him he went on to notch up a respectable number of games.

The case of Brendan Bradley was similar, with a contract already prepared and ready for my meeting with the player at Manchester Airport. David asked me to take a sign saying that I was there to meet Mr Bradley and when I enquired about his description he quite obviously had never seen him in the flesh!

From those experiences I summoned up the wherewithal to make sure improved processes were followed. I never had authority over any manager – that I was quite happy to leave to the board. I realised that I had to set myself standards in the best interests of all concerned and ensure that my ongoing duties and responsibilities were in line with protocol. I must forget all about popularity and self-promotion. I've considered in later life what that did to me as a person. How did people see Dick Chester? The representative of a football club, or Dick Chester the man? A bit of a conundrum.

I have made several references to the influence of football in society and the magnetism of the game. I believe this could influence how people treated me. One of the first occasions I came across this was when seeking a new home during the autumn of 1983. Needing to make a purchase quite quickly I spent time viewing around the Lincoln area and eventually came across one which certainly took the eye and would meet my needs. I did not have an appointment to view but took it upon myself to knock on the door and ask if it was at all possible to view. The response was positive, the viewing confirmed my earlier hopes, but the downside was that there was another purchaser in the frame. On my way from viewing I called into my bank, Barclays, and asked if I could speak to the assistant manager, who also looked after the club's account. I explained the position and asked if he could arrange a quick mortgage. After exchanging all relevant details he agreed to speak to his area management team at Peterborough. He was asked if the applicant was the same Richard Chester who was handling Lincoln City's account, which was confirmed. Then came a surprising response. 'If he can get me four tickets for the forthcoming Peterborough United v Lincoln City game he can have his mortgage today.' Deal done, move completed within about 14 days, and a further excellent relationship developed. Was the deal done because of who I was as Richard Chester, or what I was as company secretary of Lincoln City Football Club? As many mortgage applicants would agree it would be very unlikely their application would be approved in such a simple way. Is it fair? No, of course it's not. Truly, to receive such favours, I found somewhat embarrassing. Nevertheless it was more than acceptable to me, enabling me to secure a property close to the ground which was a requirement within my terms of engagement. Proof here I think of the magnetism and popularity of football. Personal magnetism? Maybe not!

A later house move involving my change of residence to Sheffield United saw many many hours over a few weekends trekking around the area having no success at all. I quickly learned that the transfer of the

Manpower Services Commission and a major bank into Sheffield was causing available properties to be snapped up, whilst at the same time causing a lot of gazumping. With only a limited budget available, the task was becoming more and more difficult and I had reached the stage where if I didn't find anything over that weekend I would advise the chairman that I would not be staying and would remain in Lincoln. With a well-known estate agent on the club's board there had been a total lack of co-operation or help, which I found particularly disappointing.

I had earmarked the Dronfield area as a suitable option and had been looking around for most of the Sunday morning when at the top of a hill, Falkland Rise, I spotted a sale board. Driving up, I had decided that I would knock on the door and ask if I could view, bearing in mind I hadn't any appointment. The occupier granted me the opportunity but said it would have to be quick as he had a luncheon engagement. Whilst viewing I was asked why I was looking to live in the area and explained it was for my job. Following further questions, he learned I had been engaged at Sheffield United Football Club and he quickly put two and two together realising I was replacing Keith Walker. He said, 'Give me the asking price and it's yours.' Within my budget, I confirmed a deal, following which he agreed to instruct his solicitors on Monday morning and advise an earlier potential buyer that he was withdrawing his agreement to sell. Guess what? He was a staunch Blade who had previously done work for the club and was aware of the pending changes. His luncheon engagement was across at the adjoining sports ground to the local pub, the Hyde Park Inn. I gained was an invitation to join and the opportunity for him to introduce me to his friends as the new secretary at Bramall Lane. The magnetism of football again. I like to think there might be a little of the magnetism of Dick Chester as well, but I'm not so sure! Whichever way, my connection to the game had helped smooth over a potentially difficult situation in my life and career.

It's interesting to consider the role of the press. Individually, I got on very well with many of the reporters of the clubs I was involved with. They had their job to do, and I had mine. The press are an integral part of a football club, with both needing each other. This was particularly true in my era before the days of the internet. Their coverage of club affairs and match reports provided extensive column inches. These potentially could not be funded from club finances if they were costed out on the similar basis to general advertising rates! It was best of course if this reporting was positive.

With the likes of Maurice Burton at the *Lincolnshire Echo*, Tony Pritchett and Paul Thompson at the *Sheffield Star*, Harry Gration at BBC Look North, Alan Biggs at Radio Hallam, John Helm at Calendar and

Bob Jackson at Radio Sheffield, my aim was to be able to talk to them not just as the press but as people in the first instance. At the same time there needed to be a definitive line between the internal affairs of the club and what could be reported in the press. This at times seemed difficult to accept, as each person's job had differing objectives.

Harry Gration

When I first started broadcasting and covering football, my old mentor, John Helm, told me to make contact and have a good relationship with the club secretary. It was outstanding advice.

So from Dick's days at Lincoln and then the two Sheffield teams it was a path I was happy to follow. The main ingredient of this understanding was trust. When I asked for a steer I got one because of a mutual respect. A tip off you'd call it these days.

"You can use that, Harry, about the transfer, but only when I tell you." That's how it worked.

Dick's days at Hillsborough were vital for me. I had just started on Look North, and Howard Wilkinson was manager. I was lucky. My relationship with both was probably almost a daily one. An early call on early news often revealed nothing, but when something did occur they called me. I was on a par with all the journalists and rarely missed a thing.

Integrity, loyalty, and friendship made my time at Look North a bumper one for stories thanks to this understanding. They don't exist these days, I can tell you.

Thanks, Mr Chester.

I remember a meeting shortly after Reg Brealey's appointment as chairman when he gathered together Ian Porterfield, Derek Dooley, and me to say that he did not wish to have any dealings with the press. He wanted Ian to deal with all football matters, Derek to deal with commercial matters and me to deal with management and company matters. I intervened at this point and said, 'Chairman, I have never heard such a load of b....s in my life. You will absolutely be inundated for requests to speak with the press. You will get far more press coverage in your first two weeks as chairman as you have had throughout your entire working life.' He reminded me of my bluntness but still wanted to remain in the background. That lasted for probably no more than a couple of weeks, following which he established several close relationships with press representatives. His relationship with Tony Pritchett helped considerably in the promotion and marketing of the club as they were virtually in each other's pockets. I must confess that I too enjoyed excellent working relationships with both Tony and Paul Thompson at *Sheffield Star* and was able to confide in them and work closely to the benefit of both Sheffield clubs at any particular time.

There is, I recognise, a requirement on football clubs to be accountable for their actions to the paying public but there is also a time when the football club business should be treated the same as the majority of commercial businesses within any particular town or city and retain their dealings and discussions in-house. I cannot ever remember reading about the workings of the board of Sheffield Newspapers or *The Daily Mirror* or *The Sunday Times* – those seem to be exempt from the same level of exposure that they dictate should be forthcoming from the football industry. Equally, whilst the press imagine it to be their duty to report on any misdemeanours by players in the media spotlight – drinking, drink and driving, extra marital affairs, or the likes, I wonder, if ever one of the leading editors or sports editors was to be guilty of the same error of judgement, we would see major headlines and stories to the same extent or whether in fact there would be a closing of ranks and the matter swept under the carpet. This could all be very frustrating of course in my role.

The freedom of the press is a phrase widely exploited. The words of the club official making any press statement is dissected word for word and stored in the archives to be used at a later date should the right opportunity prevail. The words used by the pressman are in general covered by some stock phrases such as 'it is reported that' or 'I have it on good authority from within' or 'a confidential source has revealed' – all phrases with similar meanings. What I found in my dealings with the press during my days at Lincoln City, was that news, whilst important to the local community, had little or no meaning in the wider football world.

Moving to Sheffield it took on an all too different structure, for not only were you dealing with the local press, but the national papers invariably had regional reporters requiring the same level of respect and cooperation. They all had their job to do. Luckily throughout my tenure I enjoyed a very good relationship all round and was able to establish a mutual understanding of each other's day-to-day workings. I hope I managed to maintain a personal as well as professional understanding with the men of the press (it always was men back then). The reader can judge for his or herself, as several of the reporters I mentioned have their say elsewhere in the book!

I've talked elsewhere about some of the politics and machinations in the game. Sometimes the results could be brutal. Here though, I consider how sometimes a "I scratch your back, and you scratch mine" culture among people who knew each other affected the game. My very first player signing at The Lane saw me having to travel up to Scotland along with Chief Scout, Neville Briggs. It turned out to be quite a baptism. In December 1978 a young Dundee centre half (as they were known in those days: centre back being the current position) played on trial for the Blades reserves before an agreement was reached with the Scottish Club to sign him. His name was John McPhail. It seemed to be quite a straightforward proposition until the day of the journey, when my trip from home in Lincoln to Doncaster to catch the train proved quite difficult with deep snow on the ground. Departing Doncaster north to Edinburgh the conditions gradually worsened before easing off when crossing the border. Transferring on to the local Scottish Rail network, we arrived in Dundee, met by club officials in the presence of the player, and in a short while the player's terms and contract had been completed. Following a light lunch, we left about 3.00pm for the return journey. We arrived back in Doncaster about 8.00pm. I returned to my car to find it partly buried under snow. I cleared it best I could before setting off back home for what was probably my worst car journey ever, taking the best part of three and a half hours. Bed beckoned before the task of driving back the following morning to work. Pleased to say the snow ploughs and gritters had worked wonders and although the journey was difficult it was manageable. So, memorable, as it was my first transfer at The Lane, and for those atrocious conditions.

The story did not end there though. The weather conditions prevailed for some time and it was not until 6 February 1974 that John made his first team debut away to Fulham. Not unusually in that season we lost 1-4 with John picking up a booking. This resulted in the issuing of a FA disciplinary case to answer. The chairman, the manager and the then current club secretary kindly made themselves unavailable to represent the

166

player leaving the dubious honour to me. On the way down I discussed with John his past disciplinary record north of the border, with his reply being 'had a few bookings, the odd sending off, but nothing to get carried away with.' We were called into the meeting, chaired by Jack Wiseman and a couple of members of the disciplinary committee plus the FA's staff member serving as disciplinary secretary. Our case was based on the fact that he was a new player to the club and as a new player at the club had conducted himself in a dignified and responsible manner and his previous misdemeanours should not reflect upon the Blades. The chairman, as is customary, asked the secretary to read out his previous disciplinary record, which probably took longer than the length of the rest of the meeting! Having been asked to retire pending considerations, Jack Wiseman came to call us back in saying to John, 'You should be grateful for the case presented on your behalf, but next time try not to be so conservative with the facts.' Outcome: suspended one game. The conversation between John and myself on the way home was, you could say, "to the point and a bit frank!"

I must admit I was quite pleased with the outcome and believed both of us had done a pretty good job. It was not until sometime after that I found out that Dick Wragg and Jack Wiseman had done a deal whereby under Jack's chairmanship one of our players would be dealt with leniently and at a subsequent hearing, with Dick Wragg in the chair, a Birmingham City player would be treated in the same vein. Impartial in the corridors of power? Not sure about that. John went on to spend five good seasons with the Blades and formed a formidable pairing with Tony Kenworthy in the centre of our defence. I think it could be said that not all of their tactical prowess was always in accordance with the spirit of the game, but certainly no easy time was enjoyed by opposing strikers. I learned that it isn't always what you know, but sometimes it was also who you know.

One of the most unpredictable characters in the game earlier in my career was Brian Clough. At the beginning of the 1975/76 season a friend of mine, from years gone by, resided in the Nottingham area and was a member of St John's Ambulance service covering matches at both Forest and County. On a weekend visit to their home he mentioned that there were two players at Forest, Tony Woodcock and Bert Bowery, who needed league experience. Upon my return to work I mentioned these to Graham Taylor who instantly commenced a scouting mission, all of which came back very positive. Prior to deadline day that season, Graham obtained the authority of the board of directors to take Tony Woodcock on loan for a month and asked if I could prepare the papers and visit the City Ground to complete. On my arrival I reported to reception and asked for Mr Clough. Instantly he appeared and took me to his office, sat me down and went into the corridor and immediately summoned Tony Woodcock to come to his office. Upon his arrival, and with a very brisk tone to his voice, he simply said, 'Sign that f-----g form. You are going to Lincoln City for a month.' Without hesitation he signed. Getting ready to go Brian turned to me and said, 'Does Taylor want that other good for nothing striker, Bowery.' It was not my responsibility to give that sort of an answer, so he said, 'Pick that bloody phone up and ask Taylor if he wants him. If he does he can have him for the same month but you will have to complete the forms 'cos our fellow is no bleedin good!' The outcome was positive. I completed the transfer and Graham advised the board that he had signed two, and not just one as authorised. The following day the two players reported to Sincil Bank, underwent the usual training session, but when finished remained under one-to-one supervision with Graham discussing their roles and expectations. Within the current Lincoln City squad was a player called Dennis Booth, who was quite exceptional at mimicry. He stood against the fencing surrounding the training ground and called out to both players in an exceptional Brian Clough voice. Both players looked around believing that Brian Clough had turned up to watch them in their new surroundings!

Football gave me the chance to meet some very interesting people. Very early on in my days at The Lane Harry Haslam, who had enjoyed a very good relationship with the popular comedian Eric Morecambe during their days at Luton Town came into my office. On this particular morning he told me that Luton Town were playing at Blackburn Rovers on the coming Saturday, 13 September 1980, and that he took a phone call from Eric Morecambe asking if they could get together in Sheffield for a catch up. The invitation also included Derek Dooley and myself and the meal was to be at the Grosvenor Hotel in Sheffield. Eric was going to break his journey, enjoy an evening out, and travel onwards to catch up with the team in their Lancashire hotel. We arrived at the hotel reception almost altogether and were directed to the restaurant where we enjoyed a nice meal, but enjoyed even more the comedy of Eric reminiscing about days gone by. The restaurant, from being quite quiet when taking the table, had gradually filled up with many staring over towards Eric. Before coffee was served Harry said to Eric, 'What about a tune then, mate.'

'Can't do, there's nowt to play on.' Upon which I went to find the manager and request a piano for the dining room. He duly obliged within minutes. What followed was a hilarious, off the cuff, performance from Eric, with the restaurant now nearing capacity and a rapturous round of applause to follow. The evening ended with courtesies extended all round. Come Monday morning, Harry comes into my office saying he had a phone call from Eric on the Sunday thanking him for our hospitality, promptly saying it was a 'bloody sight better than Ewood Park' where they had lost 0-3! I consider myself very lucky to have been able to spend the evening with someone who many would say was a genius. All through sport.

During my days at The Lane I had the opportunity, along with Derek Dooley, to accept an invitation to be a guest of one of the sponsors for an England game at Wembley. We were to be the guest of our programme producers, Maybank Press Ltd, via their owner Eddie Buckley. The match in question was an England friendly fixture against Argentina on 13th May 1980. Part of our hospitality package was an overnight stay in a hotel adjacent to the stadium. Following the game, which ended in a win for the England team, we adjourned to the hotel for an evening meal at which members of both of the teams were invited to join sponsors at their tables. In our case the guests were Diego Maradona and his father. Having just seen him perform his magic on the field of play he, and his father, showed their skills in terms of friendliness and respect, making it an occasion to remember.

The story doesn't end there though. Having retired to bed at some god-forsaken time, I didn't take long to get to sleep in the twin room being shared with Derek. Fast asleep, I was awoken with all of the room lights switched on and with my eyes half open saw a shadow hopping past the end of my bed. Looking up, quite startled, it soon registered that I was not sharing a room with "Skippy" but my friend and colleague Derek, his artificial limb being propped up at the side of his bed. We were, however, able to share a few laughs at the breakfast table. Whether or not there was any connection between the presence of Diego at the table and the earlier relationship which existed between Harry Haslam and Eddie Buckley I am not sure, or any connection between Harry's attempts to sign him on his trip to Argentina I am not sure either, but it was a real pleasure to be in Diego's company and have the opportunity to talk to him about all things in his then quite short life. Another opportunity for which I am hugely grateful, and which would not have come to me without my involvement in the game of football.

Again whilst at The Lane through the good offices of Dick Wragg, the club were invited to stage the replay between Arsenal and Liverpool in the FA Cup, should another draw be recorded. The two clubs had been paired in the Semi Final, playing out a 0-0 draw out at Hillsborough. The replay was then held at Villa Park and a 1-1 draw was the end result. Yet another replay, again at Villa Park saw another 1-1 draw. Before the third replay, this time to be staged at Highfield Road, Coventry City's ground, Sheffield United had been approached to stage any further replay. As such it was necessary for the club to make all the arrangements for the printing of match tickets, allocations per club and for these to be available to hand over to the two attending club secretaries.

I travelled to Coventry to make the arrangements should the services of Bramall Lane be needed. This trip involved my first meeting with the late, great Bill Shankly. It was indeed an honour, but also quite a surprise, for I had not previously been aware of his diminutive stature, expecting him to be a commanding figure, given his dominance in his manager's role at Anfield. For this evening he was accompanied by Jimmy Tarbuck, the national comic icon. The ease of introduction was a real pleasure for me. Taking my seat in the directors' box, I was seated immediately in front of Jimmy Tarbuck and another Liverpudlian. I must say, whilst the game was quite interesting and close, the comedy coming from behind me was better than an on-stage performance! That aside, Arsenal secured the only goal in the later stages of the game and as a consequence I travelled back to Sheffield with all the tickets in the boot of my car. What I would have given to stage another replay!

Through my work in the game, therefore, I met great players, managers, and celebrities. I am sure that as Joe Bloggs in another profession I would not have had those opportunities. Sometimes my role gave me a view of the relationships between some of the characters of the game. Those characters are not always visible to the supporter's eyes as very often they are behind the scenes. One such story I witnessed in the 1984/85 season with the Owls. There had been some really ding-dong games against Chelsea, particularly in the Milk Cup, which unfortunately ended with the London side having the edge. Towards the end of the season our away league game was at Stamford Bridge – 6th May. At that time Ken Bates was their chairman. Both Bert McGee and Ken Bates revelled in banter, some of which I am not sure was banter or an element of one-upmanship. Detailed arrangements had been provided to us confirming the need for all visiting directors travelling by car to be parked up by 2.00 p.m. The team had travelled down the night before and had their pre-match meal in a Marble Arch hotel, the visiting officials joining them on their arrival to take their meals. The team coach left with the players safely on board with us still at the hotel. As our meal was coming to an end but the bottle of Chablis still had some left in. I reminded the chairman of the time. The Chablis had to be finished! When done, our journey in the chairman's car got underway. Needless to say, heavy London traffic slowed our journey down and on arrival at The Bridge we were later than requested. The police officer on duty at the entry gate stopped us and very politely said, 'Sorry, sir, the gates are now closed. You will have to leave your car over there,' pointing to a particular area. After some discussions and expressions of opinion our chairman, again very politely, asked, 'Do you know who I am?' To which the reply quickly came back 'Sir, I don't mind if you are Prince Phillip. You are not permitted to enter the directors' car parking area, but if you leave your car with me I will arrange for it to be parked in the designated area for your collection after the game.' The car was duly left with the officer but the look on the chairman's face was a picture: not at all happy, with his aim being to get to Ken Bates to offload his frustrations. Standing at the directors' entrance was indeed Ken Bates, and words were exchanged but quickly backed up with a friendly escort to the hospitality areas. Banter continued both at half-time and full-time, but the last word went to Chelsea with yet another victory under their belts. I never really got to the bottom of their relationship, and in fairness it was of no real concern.

A very close friend of Ken Bates was the chairman of Crystal Palace, Ron Noades. Prior to my engagement at Hillsborough, Sheffield Wednesday had transferred a striker called Andy McCulloch for a fee of £20,000. The deal was agreed on deferred terms with a deposit paid at the time of transfer and the balance in staged payments. The final payment had remained outstanding for some time and without reporting the matter to the Football League, Bert McGee was happy to speak on a chairman-to-chairman basis to reach a settlement. The chairman and I had set up a meeting in London to potentially conclude a commercial deal. Prior to setting off he had been in contact with Ron Noades and it was agreed we would do a detour to call in at their offices and collect the cheque. Duly arriving at reception, Ron Noades came through with an envelope, full of apologies and handed over the envelope. Getting back in the car, Bert asked me if the cheque had been signed, as he would bet his life it wasn't. Sure enough it wasn't, resulting in the immediate exit of Bert storming towards the reception area. After a while he came back, quite red-faced, relating much of the conversation, with the specific instructions to bank it first thing the following morning. He always worked on the principle "if you can't afford to pay for anything then don't buy." At the end of the season, at a meeting involving all clubs, he made a point of reminding Ron Noades of his attempt to take advantage of Sheffield Wednesday, doing so in front of many other chairmen.

I was also able to see during my time in the game how some of those within the sport saw themselves. During this period in football there was no doubt that the club at the helm was Liverpool. On 2nd February 1985 Liverpool were our visitors. On this day the chairman's wife was visiting family and was not available to host the ladies' hospitality area. Under normal circumstances this was a place with no entry unless personally invited, and the presence of men was definitely frowned upon. The wives of the Liverpool directors duly arrived and, not wanting them to be at a loose end, I took it upon myself to take them to their hospitality area and introduce them to the Hillsborough directors' wives. By way of conversation I asked if they travelled regularly with the team. One of the ladies said that at the corresponding fixture the season before those ladies who had travelled on that day had expressed their appreciation for the way they were hosted, so more or less a full complement of them travelled for this fixture. Other than that, she went on to say that normally they only travel in force when the team are in Wembley finals or European finals. A sign of supremacy if ever there was one!

Your involvement in a football club does give you some kudos within that town or city, irrespective of what division the club is participating in. Each town or city who have a football club have devoted fans including councillors equally as supportive of their club, having been brought up from a very young age to follow their family traditions. As a senior officer of that club you certainly learn to have respect and acknowledge that following, whilst at the same time trying not to abuse it. Many people have their restaurants or watering holes, and, whilst trying alternatives, will have that lingering desire to return to the place they nearly call home. I have been no different, with preferred options in both Lincoln and Sheffield. My first experience of the pull of the club was at Lincoln when, following Graham's appointment, he wanted changes to the away travel programme. When the game had finished and players were ready, the journey home was to be without a break, getting the players back to their regular haunts or their waiting families. Obviously with limited diets before the games, players needed feeding. On our personal visits to the Grand Hotel in Lincoln city centre we established an agreement with their head chef, Nev Rose, to provide us with suitable and substantial food packages to collect before leaving the ground to eat on the way home. These proved hugely popular, both in content and convenience. The establishing of this arrangement from my personal point of view ensured that when my home match duties had finished and the ground had been locked and secured, I only had to make a call to the Grand Hotel and ask, if necessary to speak to Nev Rose, and a table was always waiting, irrespective of how busy the dining room was at that time.

Similarly, days at The Lane saw very close relationships between one of the club directors, Albert Bramall, and his favourite watering hole, the Cosmopolitan Restaurant, literally in the shadows of the ground. Once hosted by Albert, and introduced to Tony, the owner, the pull of this eating house quickly rubbed off on me, with match tickets being put on one side for their use, and a more or less open invitation to visit as and when desired. At the north end of Sheffield is located Whitley Hall Hotel, within which was employed a head waiter absolutely mad on football –

albeit a Geordie and Newcastle United fan. After a few visits to the hotel it became clear that he wanted to attend home games at Hillsborough, as apart from games against the Geordie team he was an Owls fan, but many times he couldn't finish his lunchtime hotel duties in time for kick off. A simple arrangement to collect his paid-for tickets and ease of access into the ground ensured that once again, when finishing my match day duties, a table was always made available for my personal use. Even if told by reception that the restaurant was fully booked, Ronnie pulled some strings!

It was simply amazing, particularly during my Sheffield days, when I found the people to be so friendly and upfront, that many a time have I been visiting the bar for a refill, or I am simply present at a gathering, and someone wanted to come up and speak to me about whichever club. Very often expressing their views about topical issues or results puts you on the spot quite a bit. As a senior executive the last thing any supporter wanted was to be fobbed off or spoken down to and it was incumbent on you to deal courteously with them, show them respect, recognise what it meant to them and also for them to be able to return to wherever, feeling that they had been respected. If the club is desirous of engaging in deep community-based exercises then it is part and parcel of any of the serving officers or representatives to relay their commitment as well.

I have thought long and hard about this chapter. I imagine it is easy to become arrogant and used to the finer things when in a position such as the ones I held. I certainly met famous people, got preferential service in all sorts of areas, and saw the great and good of the game in action. I aimed throughout to stay true to the values I developed in childhood. Football gave me opportunities that I doubt I would have received in any other career. For that I remain grateful. I began by asking whether the people I dealt with in the sport saw me as Dick Chester the man, or Dick Chester the representative of a football club. That remains a difficult question to answer. I'm not sure if I am even the person to answer it. Maybe the comments included in the book from those I worked with and who worked with the clubs give some perspective. For the experiences relayed in this chapter, football was generally very good to me. The next chapter reflects on some more difficult times.

John Helm

I first met Dick Chester or "Richard Chester FAAI" as he was listed in the Rothmans Football Yearbook in 1981. For a chap with letters after his name I found him extremely approachable. That wasn't always the case with club secretaries in those days. I had just joined Yorkshire Television from the BBC where I was Network Football Producer and I had dealt with some very prickly customers.

Make no mistake in those days the secretary was THE main man at many clubs. Peter Robinson at Liverpool, Ken Friar at Arsenal, Les Olive at Manchester United. They were as well known as the managers and had as much if not more power. Nowadays you have chief executives, directors of football, managing directors, executive chairmen to say nothing of billionaire owners in the Middle East and all corners of the globe.

Dick was my first point of contact at Sheffield United. This once proud club had just been relegated to the Fourth Division finishing below the likes of Walsall, Carlisle, and Chester. Ian Porterfield, famous for a Cup Final winning goal for Sunderland against Leeds, had taken over as manager from Harry Haslam, and between them Porterfield, Chester and the legendary Sheffield cult hero Derek Dooley set about a revolution.

It didn't take long. Inspired by the goals of Keith Edwards, Bob Hatton and Tony Kenworthy they smashed their way to the title, unbeaten at home all season. While manager and players naturally grabbed the headlines, Dick Chester quietly played a pivotal role behind the scenes .

He continued to do so until being persuaded to cross the city and replace the equally formidable Eric England at Sheffield Wednesday. Time for another revolution as the Owls soared with Howard Wilkinson stamping his personality on a side including the likes of Mel Sterland, Lee Chapman, and Brian Marwood.

Over the years Dick worked with managers making a name for themselves. Graham Taylor went on to become England manager – as did Wilkinson for one match – and the coincidence should not be under-estimated.

A diligent and skilful operator, Dick Chester took a lot of the weight off the shoulders of managers who appreciated his support and loyalty.

His huge contribution to all the clubs he served is worthy of recognition.

Chapter Ten: Dark Clouds Hover
– Troubles in Football

For the most part I thoroughly enjoyed my career in football. That is not to say that there weren't issues and incidents that troubled me. In this chapter I consider the darker side of the game in my era. Some of this may make uneasy reading, but I feel it important that the reader had the opportunity to understand some of the difficulties and troubles that I, and football, faced.

The most common problem during my stay in football was unquestionably hooliganism, something that was spread across all clubs at the time. It was not concentrated in a select few. What was portrayed in the press was that this was a football-related issue and therefore it had to be tackled from within. When joining the inner sanctum of football management back in 1971 I was clearly aware that crowd disturbances were likely. They had in fact been within sport, including football, for many years – although not to the extent that the problem developed into. Between 1946 and 1960 it is on record that there was an average of 13 incidents per season whereas between 1961 and 1968 that had increased by 92.3% to 25 incidents per season.

Crowd incidents were not just confined to these periods or afterwards. Research reveals that problems were reported as far back as 1895 in football, when the referee in the Woolwich Arsenal and Burton Wanderers game was assaulted by a spectator and knocked unconscious. Before that, two English cricketers were assaulted on their tour of Australia with many other similar incidents occurring during further tours down under. Equally, disturbances of this nature were not just confined to football or cricket, with American League Baseball, Tour de France cycling, the Derby race, and Rugby Union all suffering from their share of the problem. At a 1936 Olympic football game between Peru and Austria a group of Peruvian fans invaded the pitch, with one armed with a revolver, assaulting Austrian players, officials and stadium security. This game finished up with Peru winning. The fixture was later declared null and void with a replay ordered, but Peru refused to play, with Austria declared winners. How sensible was that?

In my period in office, my recollections of any hooliganism began in the mid-70s. I recall Manchester United fans, following the club's relegation to Division Two, causing mayhem up and down the country. This was 1974/75. In the same Second Division season, a Bolton Wanderers fan stabbed a young Blackpool fan to death behind the Kop at Bloomfield Road. When Newcastle United hosted an FA Cup tie against Nottingham Forest in March 1974, hundreds of fans invaded the pitch, one of whom attacked a Forest player. In the 1975-76 European Cup semi-final between Real Madrid and Bayern Munich, a local Madrid supporter, not in full agreement with a refereeing decision, ran onto the field and punched the referee and Bayern's goal scorer Gerd Muller. As a consequence the home side were ordered to play all the following season's competition away from home. Leeds United were banned from European football as a result of their fans rioting after the 1975 European Cup Final against Bayern Munich. Manchester United were banned as a result of fans rioting before, during and after the 1975 UEFA Cup game against Saint Etienne. A couple of seasons later the FA Cup quarter-final game between Ipswich Town and Millwall in 1978 saw fighting break out on the terraces and spill into the streets around the ground with many injuries. In these early days many clubs had "hooligan firms" forming themselves as if they were supporting their club's best interests and creating threatening type names. Arsenal – the Heed, Birmingham City – Zulu Warriors, Derby County – Derby Lunatic Fringe, Chelsea – Chelsea Headhunters, Stoke City – Naughty Forty, Manchester United – Red Army, to name but a few. It was not at every game, but I would say that football hooliganism was commonplace in my early years in the sport.

In the same decade, two quality English players – later to make an impact in the English international team – Viv Anderson and John Barnes were subjected to racial targeting. In John Barnes's case, when playing for England in Brazil against their national side in 1984, he was abused by England supporters purporting to be members of the National Front. Racist abuse was unfortunately common in the 1970 and 1980s. I am grateful for the opportunity to have worked with people from all sorts of backgrounds, including one of the finest men I met in the game – the late Keith Alexander. Keith was the first full-time Black professional manager in the Football League, as well as being the first Black qualified referee in England. He symbolised to me that the game has moved forward in some ways from the abhorrent and open racism of earlier decades. Football has in the main steered itself away from the disease of hooliganism and crowd disturbances. In its place, with the emergence of new media platforms is the deplorable introduction of racist abuse to players picked out pretty much at random. I firmly believe that this will be a problem as difficult to control in its infancy as was hooliganism. There does seem to be a real emphasis on Black Lives Matter with many teams at the time of writing "taking a knee" before kick off as a symbol of solidarity. The game also shows its openness to all with the Rainbow Laces campaign supporting the LGBT community and the recently launched #HerGameToo which supports female fans. There are clearly issues to deal with – there would not need to be campaigns otherwise! It is my belief though that racism, for example, is not just confined to the national game of football. It is occurring throughout the sporting fields and like the early days of football has certainly bared its teeth into the game of cricket in particular. Ask Yorkshire!

Back to my era, things didn't subside in the 1980s. In May 1982, following a London derby game between Arsenal and West Ham United a supporter killed during the riot following the fixture. A 1985 FA Cup third-round tie between Burton Albion and Leicester City was ordered to be replayed as a result of a block of wood being thrown from the Leicester City contingent causing injury to the Burton keeper. Also in that same year Millwall supporters created mayhem when playing at Luton Town in another quarter-final tie and creating large-scale rioting. I believe it was this game which caused the Margaret Thatcher government to step in to set up a special working party to quell football hooliganism. Later in that same year Heysel Stadium, Belgium, hosted the European Cup Final between Juventus and Liverpool. Even before the game had started the report on the game revealed that Liverpool fans broke through the police cordon and headed towards the opposing supporters. It would appear many fans tried to get away from any trouble and fighting. The result was that a wall collapsed resulting in a reported 39 fans being killed and around 600 injuries. The outcome was the banning of Liverpool from all European competitions until 1990. Troubles were not confined just to match days, for, in 1986, Manchester United and West Ham United fans – better defined as hooligans – got themselves involved on a Sealink Ferry en route to Holland. Offenders involved in this instance were subjected to prison sentences. I am sure there will be others which the reader may well be able to quote, but these are the ones which registered with me.

Under the Margaret Thatcher Tory controlled government, attempts were made to introduce ID Cards for all supporters attending a game of football. She hoped for that system to have been instituted in preparation for the 1989-90 season. Indeed it was personally confirmed in a meeting with Graham Kelly, the Football League Secretary and Ted Croker the Football Association Secretary. They were advised that the minister appointed would be the Rt. Hon. Colin Moynihan. The football industry expressed their concerns and objections from day one and, in fairness, Mrs Thatcher came under immense pressure before backing down.

Football was being targeted as being both the cause and the potential curer of this "disease." I wondered how easy it would be to identify potential hooligans before they carried out their misdemeanours. It was suggested that there were two types of hooligans. One where the offender is driven by violence and fighting and enjoys showing off his prowess in whatever abusive manner he so decides at a sporting event. On the other hand there were people who simply did not want, or intend, to get involved but when they saw their side being subjected to abuse were not prepared to sit back and just watch. Not being privy to their character make-up you could only guess why. One obvious situation is the staging of that derby game between two teams from the same local area where each fanbase wants to show their supremacy. Controversial refereeing decisions can also spark other outbursts as well as any incident of violent behaviour between the players on the pitch. The one which has been identified as a prime cause is the consumption of alcohol before and, where permitted, during the game. Many changes were made in terms of crowd gatherings in my era. Segregation and perimeter fencing became a must to keep fans away from each other. At the same time there was a move to reduce standing terraces and replace with seated areas.

I am pleased to say that with the three clubs I served, the fans conducted themselves in general terms quite well. Both Graham Taylor at Lincoln City and Howard Wilkinson at Sheffield Wednesday used their programme notes to ask for good conduct by their fans. At the same time they made it clear that this problem was one for society to resolve, not necessarily the football industry. With bigger clubs like the Blades and the Owls there can be a bigger problem in trying to control it. Whilst I was not responsible for the editing of the club programme at Bramall Lane, I did have an input into it. Due to Harry Haslam's reluctance to do his own article I won the raffle and in discussion with him covered the points he wanted to make. One week I suggested that he devote space to reflect on the problems hooliganism was creating within the game. The philosophy aired was that if the press were banned from covering all such incidents there would be no gauntlet thrown into the ring to challenge one club's group to prove they were better than any other. There would be no coverage and therefore no proverbial badge of honour. The following Monday morning he arrived, as normal, into my office for his 'cuppa.' Harry told me he had had virtually every pressman in the country on to him questioning his view of banning such reporting and taking away their rights to open, unrestricted reporting. The disease was not receding at all and it was becoming something of a nightmare to establish positive controls to combat it. It was clearly of the utmost importance for the game that some kind of solution was found.

Working with the police was one potential method. During my time at all of my clubs a lot of time was spent with the police authorities and match commander planning and catering for any possible outbreak of any form of hooliganism. Certainly as Lincoln City it was beginning to become rife and had the potential to destroy the safety of the genuine football fan. Sincil Bank escaped fairly well, thanks in no small part to my request and approval for the use of police dogs within the perimeter fencing. It cannot be said that it was totally eradicated because it wasn't and certainly supporters arriving in the town and walking down the lower High Street, Portland Street, and Sincil Bank proved on more than one occasion to be troublesome. There were major incidents at FA Cup games between Newcastle United and Nottingham Forest and also a tie between Millwall and Ipswich Town. The latter game saw fighting breaking out on the terraces, spilled over into the streets and resulted in many injuries. Luckily Sincil Bank experienced nothing like that at all, but the disease was there with no cure on the horizon. This problem was to follow me in my career.

With hooliganism getting towards its peak, other forms of trouble came to light during my relatively early days at Bramall Lane. The then Labour Government had as an elected member for Barnsley, the Secretary of State for Northern Ireland, the Right Honourable Roy Mason. Not that he wasn't a true Barnsley Tyke but, with parliamentary duties permitting he very often, on his return home, used to arrange via his secretary, a ticket in the directors' box to watch a game at the Lane. He enjoyed the game irrespective of the opposition. On such occasions serious planning, in conjunction with the Police Authority's Special Branch, was needed covering every element from his arrival onwards. His car parking position was protected at all times until departure, he was escorted to his seat and a redistribution of seating arrangements was made to allow for his personal bodyguards. On such occasions it would be fair to say that our directors did sit and watch the game with some trepidation for fear of the unknown.

The 1970s and 1980s saw the peak of the so-called Troubles in Northern Ireland. The violence also reached the shores of England with horrendous incidents such as the Birmingham pub bombings of 1974. Safety was therefore always of paramount importance and seriously put to the test for one Central League reserve game in March 1979. A call was taken on reception with the caller asking to be put through to the person in charge with a security message. I took the call and in a strong Irish accent was advised that a bomb had been placed in the main John Street Stand. I was told it had been programmed to detonate shortly after kick-off. Worry? I would say so! Urgent calls to police authorities saw the ground invaded by an array of officers and dogs but after some lengthy searches they suggested that it was a hoax. The decision as to whether the game went ahead was left to me. Following more discussions and an escorted walk around the nooks and crannies of the area in question I trusted the judgement of their decision and, whilst advising the chairman of the happenings, allowed the game to go ahead. I can tell you now that there was one particular small room in the stand which had a regular visitor that evening and to say I was glad to safely travel home would be a severe under-statement. The crux of the problem was that the Irish National Liberated Army (INLA) had initiated a plan for the assassination of the Right Honourable Roy Mason, so security wherever he went had to be rigorously enforced.

There were many incidents during this epidemic, all seeking to bring the national game into disrepute whilst at the same time inflicting bad publicity on the clubs they were supposedly representing. The question is whether or not they were true football supporters or part of a fringe group hell bent on trying to impose those behavioural patterns on to all around. Over the years there have always been groups with far reaching views trying to impose them on the rest of us and it has to be said that some of these groups have had just cause to make their feelings known and to secure equality of rights largely designed for others and not themselves. In today's game things seem to have moved on with the emphasis strongly angled towards areas of discrimination.

The effect of those groups in my days relating to hooliganism and the associated behavioural patterns caused considerable additional work within the management of clubs. Constant liaison, discussions, planning, potential repercussions, and above all adherence to the requirements of the Safety at Sports Ground legislation, were all time-consuming but vital tasks. Regular meetings were held with Police Authorities, Local Authority, and both rail and coach companies, all collating their findings and the necessary cross-checking with visiting club management. At the height of the problem I would estimate that a good third of my working week hinged around this problem and my resolve to protect the good name of the club. As my career developed it could be said that the problem slowly dissipated but was still close to the surface.

A part of my job that was at times a delight, but on other occasions very difficult revolved around the contracts of players. Life as a footballer in my days was very much one of ups and downs, where limited squads made life quite difficult for managers. After the departure of Graham to Watford, his assistant George Kerr assumed that mantle at Sincil Bank. During his first week in charge he asked me to accompany him up to Wearside where he had three players to sign. All of the players, Micky Harford, Keith Laybourne and Micky Smith had been playing for a local team called Lampton Street Boys' Club and had been watched by George previously. The evening was like a party as we visited each home to find each player with his parents and family present, all to witness the registration signing and each household having a cuppa and eats to complete the celebrations. One other player not signed that night but later

181

to do so from the same local club was Alfie Eden. The looks on all their faces declared joy, admiration and optimism for the future. Of them all, it was Micky Harford who secured a positive future in the game and is still a respected member of Luton Town's management team.

At the other end of the spectrum I was nominated by the manager to meet up with one of the club's then current apprentices to confirm the club's decision on his future. Arrangements were made for Peter Sellars and his parents to attend my office across lunchtime. The decision I had to convey was that the manager had recommended to the board of directors that at the expiration of his current agreement he should be given his release. When I spoke those words the player and his family broke down in tears. His apprenticeship had meant so much to both himself and his family that it appeared the whole world had let him down. I am not sure, but I feel that he never secured a professional contract with any other club. Outcome – personal devastation.

Times were hard in mid-1980s South Yorkshire. The steel industry was in decline and unemployment high: 16.2% by 1986, among the highest in the country. So, what was a match-going supporter to do in such straightened times? Expensive tickets and difficulties at work may suggest that attendances would fall. The mid-80s were also a time of hooliganism and some awful disasters at football grounds in this country and overseas. The Sunday Times newspaper famously described football in 1986 as a "slum sport played in slum stadiums increasingly watched by slum people." Isn't it just the case that the press can get away using words and creating headlines and be unaccountable; they call it free speech! Attendances around the country did fall. Richard Crookes reproduces figures showing how Division One attendances fell from of over 24 million in 1979/80 to a low of just below 16½ million in 1985/86. Elsewhere in the country, attendances dropped, but not at Sheffield Wednesday. Average, home attendances grew from a low of 10,643 in 1978/79 to a high of 27,780 in 1984/85. Some might say that this is related to the dedication of the Owls fans. I take a slightly different view.

The success that Howard Wilkinson and his team brought to Hillsborough was mirrored in the support they got from the thousands of Owls fans who really enjoyed the visits of the "big guns" to do battle with – but purely on the pitch. They were so much in awe of Howard's level of discipline and commitment that they sought to steer clear of any confrontation visiting supporters may have in mind. It would be fair to say that these were few and far between. One would like to think that the friendliness of the Yorkshire folk combined with the detailed and intricate planning of the then match day commander made visiting fans feel welcomed. That does not go to say that we were immune from any problems – that was certainly not the case.

During my time in football, fans from all clubs expressed their indignation at the level of crowd disturbance, often interrupting the game itself and damaging the reputation of their club. For my part, at all my clubs, it took much of my time to put in place arrangements to quell such happenings. It certainly proved challenging trying to legislate for something which might happen whilst at the same time not knowing exactly what would happen. That's a bit like life in general. Thank goodness the game has generally cleared itself of this particular blight.

*

My first real headache in terms of crowd control came on the occasion of the visit of Newcastle United 30th March 1985. Arrangements had been made for pre-match tickets to be made available for sale from St James' Park to try and relieve any congestion at the turnstiles, which to a degree helped, but then the police received notice that some coaches carrying visiting fans had been stopped en route and a significant amount of alcohol seized and taken off the coach. Still well-fuelled up on the booze, several coach-loads of fans were dropped outside Leppings Lane. With the cooperation of the police they were escorted into the ground using the pens least occupied. A potential problem averted.

A later league game – 27th December 1986 – against Liverpool saw another near full house – recorded at 40,959. After liaison with my Anfield counterpart in the weeks before the game, pre-match ticket sales were available for their fans to purchase from the Owl's offices. On the day of the game we were confronted with every possible excuse under the sun as to how a supporter presenting himself to our ticket office had lost the ticket he had bought from his club. At the same time, a lot of fans had gathered in the local drinking-houses leaving it until the last moments before kick- off to make a dash down to the ground and hopefully get free entry. This information again came through the airwaves to the police commander and, in discussions with me, we decided on two possible courses of action. Firstly, to approach the referee to ask for a delayed kick-off. We did and were declined. Secondly to take the necessary steps to close the door into the central tunnel, place a police cordon in that position and then open gates and turnstiles to control orderly entry, which they did. In that instance the supporters not willing to pay for entry were the lucky recipients of some successful match day planning.

Other large gates during my tenure were: Liverpool, FA Cup 07/02/1984 31,073, Southampton, FA Cup 11/03/1984 36,762, Manchester City, Division One 06/05/1984 36763, Manchester United, Division One 09/11/1985 48,105, for which no match day problems were experienced. In the event of all-ticket matches being determined, and, personally aware, by being directly involved with the police on match-day management issues, I, on my own initiative – call it what you will – always retained some 200 to 250 tickets in my office. Being the one held to account in the event of a breach of safety measures I felt that this was a way of protecting the reputation of the club. Keeping these tickets to one side helped prevent overcrowding if some supporters did gain entry by less than legal means.

It would be fair to say, without casting aspersions on all supporters, the case of the few spoiling it for the majority certainly applied to Liverpool, Newcastle United, West Ham United and Millwall, who were the four clubs where pre-match planning was of paramount importance. I endeavoured to think ahead, to communicate with the visiting team's officials in advance of the fixture, and to keep in close contact with the police on match-day. I don't claim a perfect record, but this teamwork helped keep supporters safe and a positive atmosphere on match day.

With all of the above incidents taken into consideration, the worst was still to be reported upon. Firstly the tragedy of the Bradford City fire when during the visit of Lincoln City many supporters lost their lives. Then the Hillsborough disaster at the FA Cup semi-final tie between Liverpool and Nottingham Forest.

By the mid-80s Sheffield Wednesday's Hillsborough ground, with the recent renovation and development works, was once more deemed to be a ground worthy of consideration for major games. Hillsborough was selected to stage the replay for the 1984/85 League Cup Final in the event of a draw. The teams involved were Norwich City and Sunderland. To stage such a game the ground is chosen by the Football League, but the arrangements for the staging of the game is vested in their hands and not the club's. As a consequence they arranged for staff members to visit Hillsborough and to discuss with me the detailed arrangements and appropriate ticket distribution. After considering all the options, their delegated staff selected the use of the Kop for Norwich City supporters and the Leppings Lane end for Sunderland supporters. In my considered opinion I believed they had got the allocation the wrong way round and asked the chairman to write saying that if they proceeded along that course then the club would absolve itself from any responsibilities. The response was a call from their then secretary, Graham Kelly, asking me why that was the case. I duly advised him that Sunderland would require greater space in view of their average home gates and travelling from the North access to the Kop would be more conclusive. Graham accepted the reasoning given and alternative plans and drawings were returned to the Football League at Lytham St Annes. The outcome in the final was a 1-0 win for Norwich City so the plans were obviously aborted and filed away for future reference.

Following my departure from Hillsborough the principles behind the development of the stadium brought dividends with the ground being invited to stage the 1987 FA Cup Semi-Final between Leeds United and Coventry City. This was a success and Hillsborough was chosen again in 1988 to host that season's Semi-Final between Nottingham Forest and Liverpool. Prior to this, the stadium had been discounted since the 1981 Semi-Final when there were problems with overcrowding and crushing at the game. I remember relaxing in my lounge to watch the match of the day headlines and I was "gobsmacked" to see that the arrangements for the 1988 fixture included the allocation of the Leppings Lane End to Liverpool and the Kop end to Nottingham Forest. This was so much like an action replay to the objections I had given had the replay of the 1984/85 League Cup replay taken place. Not being present myself at the game I can only rely on after match reports where it was stated that the match went on uninterrupted. It seemed that many Liverpool supporters at the Leppings Lane end had been subjected to crushing with one fan immediately after the game writing to the FA expressing concerns for his personal safety. The then FA Chief executive, Graham Kelly, decided on the basis of an official report that "the identical 1989 tie was not regarded as a problem match."

We now know that 97 people died as a result of the events of 15th April 1989. The truth about what happened that awful day took decades to come out. Here I wish to lay as plainly as I can my experience. After protracted reviews, reports, and official enquiries the matter remained unresolved until Andy Burnham, Culture Secretary, set the wheels in motion for the March 2014 inquest, held in Warrington. Prior to the hearing, and arising from my days at Hillsborough and the work completed during that time relating to both the provisions of the Safety at Sports Ground Act and work undertaken at the Leppings Lane end I was interviewed on 5th November 2013, by an inspector with Operation Resolve. This was in preparation for the Coroner's Court hearing. The inspector was very courteous in his presentation and thorough in his questioning. At the end of a long meeting he thanked me for my frankness and responses and thought that the contents of his report would be sufficient to avoid any further visit. That turned out not to be the case as, following some additional information received by Operation Resolve, a further meeting took place on 18th March 2014 to clarify outstanding matters.

With the enquiry underway I was called to give evidence on 9th June 2014. Whilst comfortable in the knowledge that I had always tried to do my job properly, I was nevertheless somewhat nervous, but fully prepared to be open, transparent and sympathetic towards the families who had lost loved family members. I had stated previously that no one should expect to say goodbye to a family member following their interests, whatever they may be, and for them not to come back. Completely under different circumstances this was what had happened to me in my young days when losing my father. I have the utmost sympathy for the families.

Arriving at Warrington I parked in the allocated parking space where there was an attendant waiting to greet me. I was ushered into a private room where I was welcomed and advised by the Coroner's appointed solicitor how to conduct myself at such a hearing. I confirmed that I had never been in any such a situation previously. The advice on the one hand was what I partly expected in being specific and detailed in response to the questions presented and not to mention the behaviour of the Liverpool fans, the drinking culture of the day, anything about any match day incidents encountered by myself or any reference to the Heysel Stadium events. I spent almost three days in the witness box, cross-examined by thirteen Queen's Counsellors all of whom were addressing the many aspects of the case. At the end of my time in the dock I drove home, fully sympathetic to the loss of so many lives with deep feelings for their families. I also carried thoughts and worries as to how I would have coped with the trauma I would have experienced had I been the then responsible club delegate. Those worries and thoughts, combined with my previous and serious heart problems, resulted in me being referred for counselling – something I never ever believed I would have had the need to undertake. Such was the depth and concern of that treatment that it was necessary for my GP to send a letter to the Coroner asking for me to be excluded from any further involvement.

The enquiry was recognised as the longest ever undertaken and whilst any decision is open to public comment, the declared result has been the subject of massive amounts of time, costs and decisions made by professional persons. I bow to that and to its findings. At the same time, as I also included in my statements to Operation Resolve, I am confident that, had the allocation of designated areas been reviewed and amended and the services of Chief Supt. Brian Mole been in place as match commander, such a tragedy could have been avoided. The one final thing I would add is that whilst the game was staged at Sheffield Wednesday's ground the match in actual fact is under the direct control of the authority responsible for the staging of the FA Cup.

The events of 15th April 1989 cast a shadow over football for a long time. Rest in peace the 97 souls who lost their lives as a result of the events of that day. We will always remember.

Chapter Eleven: After Football

Why did I ever leave football? That is a question I have asked myself several times, particularly considering what I felt I had achieved, the apparent respect I had gained and the potential remuneration I could have gained from any other engagements within the sport. I had entered football as a naive young man. I came into the industry aged 31 years as then the youngest secretary in the Football League. I left as a well-respected administrator who, on the evidence of the earlier clandestine meeting with the Football Association, could possibly have moved from Hillsborough to a position even higher. Others in the industry had spoken highly of my work. I include letters here from Arsenal and Liverpool to illustrate that point.

ARSENAL FOOTBALL CLUB LTD.

Secretary: K. J. FRIAR
Manager: G. GRAHAM

ARSENAL STADIUM
HIGHBURY, LONDON N5 1BU
TELEPHONE: 01-226 0304
TELEX: 298083 ARSNAL G.

KJF/MM

14 October 1986

Mr D Chester
Sheffield Wednesday Football Club
Hillsborough
Sheffield
S6 1SW

It was with some sadness that I read your letter this morning confirming your impending departure from the Club.

One of the great benefits of our business is that over the years one meets some great people and friendships form and I am truly sorry that we will no longer be able to see your smiling face when we make our annual pilgrimage to Hillsborough.

Your own contribution to the game we all love has been considerable and I know that you will be greatly missed not only by me but by the many other friends you have made over the years. The game is going through a difficult period just now and frankly we cannot really afford to lose people of your own standing.

I do sincerely hope that you will keep in touch with us and send to you the very sincere wishes for a successful future career from everyone here at Highbury.

With kindest regards,

Yours sincerely

Ken Friar
Managing Director

Company Registration Number 109244 England

LIVERPOOL FOOTBALL CLUB
AND ATHLETIC GROUNDS P.L.C.

ANFIELD ROAD, LIVERPOOL L4 0TH
051-263 2361/2
Telex 627661 LFC G
Registered No. 35868, England

Match Information Service Only 051-260 9990

Mr. R.H. Chester,
Secretary,
Sheffield Wednesday Football Club PLC,
Hillsborough,
Sheffield,
S6 1SW   16th October 1986

Dear Dick,

      Thank you for your letter of 13th October.

      I am extremely sorry to hear that you have
decided to leave Sheffield Wednesday F.C., but nevertheless
wish you every success in your new chosen career.

      Football is going through a very traumatic period
at present and it can ill-afford to lose such an able and
experienced administrator as yourself.

      I have greatly enjoyed knowing you and have, in
recent years, valued the personal friendship which has
developed between us. I sincerely hope that I will not lose
contact with you and would like to take this opportunity of
extending an invitation to you to visit Anfield at any time.
You will always be very welcome as my guest at any game.

      With kindest regards and all good wishes for the
future.

           Yours sincerely,

           Peter R.

           Chief Executive/General Secretary

Registered   K.M. DALGLISH, M.B.E.,   P.B. ROBINSON,
Trade Mark   PLAYER/TEAM MANAGER   CHIEF EXECUTIVE/GENERAL SECRETARY

As readers may remember, I left my initial role after football, feeling that I was worth more than picking up fish and chips for Dennis Bocock. This decision left me in a conundrum, though. I began to rack my brains as to how I could ensure a future and cover my responsibilities in life. Between my Blades and Wednesday times I had started some consultancy work. Through a third-party introduction, I continued this sort of work during

1986. I paid particular attention to Scarborough Football Club who were aiming for Football League status. Peter Gargett, their then owner, commissioned me to provide a report advising the board of the necessary processes to secure a successful future for the club and, if endorsed by their board of directors, I was to become directly involved in the processes and procedures needed to secure a successful profile for the club and the town as a whole.

The club secured their membership of the Football League and was progressing satisfactorily under the control of Peter Gargett and the then manager, Neil Warnock. Soon though, business pressures meant that Peter decided to take a break from football. He sold his controlling interest to a Leeds-based businessman, Geoffrey Richmond, some eighteen months or so later. Richmond made the decision that he would dispense with the services of a knowledge-based consultancy arrangement (me) and use his own management team to control the affairs of the club. This, therefore, left me with a void in my portfolio and the need to fill that gap. At this time I well-remembered Bert McGee's comments on leaving Hillsborough when he said, 'Don't worry if the move doesn't work out. You have the ability to succeed under whatever circumstances prevail.' The establishment of Scarborough Football Club as a member of the Football League had been quite satisfactorily undertaken with the club showing their worth on the field of play, and the town were also beginning to show they had much more to offer than just its reputation as a leading seaside holiday resort. I, however, was in need of gainful employment.

Within six months of my involvement with Scarborough FC I was approached by a Lincoln-based company – Aquix Holdings Ltd – to discuss the possibility of me aiding their expansion into the football industry. Their experience was in Electronic Point of Sale tills – EPOS. The aim was to include that type of technology into gate counting systems like I had introduced during my Hillsborough days. After some initial discussions, considerations and development, a programme was developed and launched within English and Scottish football. The match day administration was handled by staff in their Lincoln offices. The company also had existing outlets with the EPOS technology in Spain. Via their representative based in that country they promoted the potential of gate-counting technology to some of the leading clubs.

The outcome was an invitation from the Spanish Football League to attend a function at the Bernabeu Stadium to make a presentation. Along with staff from Aquix Holdings we arrived and were hosted by Real Madrid personnel. We were given a tour of the ground, feeling completely bewildered by the size and content of their trophy room. Before sitting down for lunch I was asked where my overnight bag was so that someone could take it down to the airport in readiness for my flight back to the UK in time for a family holiday the following day. Taking my place at the top table, having been allocated the guest speaker's role, I was quickly under the impression that this was going to be a long affair. I realised that I needed to keep an eye on the time for my flight home. It was the last one available to ensure my itinerary for the following day. Time drifted on and on until I spoke to the Chairman and asked if I could make my presentation there and then. Duly granted the permission I completed the honour, answered several football-based questions, received some very warm applause, sat down and then instantly left the room. A driver was waiting to take me to the airport, which was quite a hair-raising ride. I was glad for the driver's sake that it was before the days of speed cameras! Such was the shortage of time that, when I arrived at the airport, I was escorted straight to the waiting aircraft without ever seeing customs or ticket control desks. I boarded the plane, heard passing comments about the person who had held up departure, immediately took my seat and put my seat belt on ready for departure. To this day I am pretty sure that the influence of Real Madrid, and maybe an incentive or two, got me back home on time. More evidence of the power of football. I'm not sure it was the name of Dick Chester that earned me such treatment.

Away from football, and following my return to the Lincoln area, I followed my brother's interests and tried my hand at flat green bowls. Whether it was because of my involvement as a football referee or not I soon became interested in the finer points of the game. After attending some courses, I qualified as a county coach, following which I dedicated some of my Sunday morning leisure time to teaching beginners at the Lincoln Indoor Bowling Club.

It was a real pleasure to be able to help others to come into the game and I distinctly remember one elderly lady who wanted to learn how to play, mainly due to the hospitality such an involvement in a club can provide. In the kindest way possible she was never going to make a bowler but was a good sport determined to do the best she could. We used to enjoy a laugh from time to time and in one conversation I jokingly said to her if you ever get a bowl on that little white pot I'd show my bum in Woollies shop window! Lo and behold we enjoyed another laugh about two weeks later when she achieved that particular feat, instantly asking when would I be up town in Woolworths! Joke back on me but I saved Woollies from the embarrassment – mine as well I would add.

I have listed below a few comments that might be given some thought as they relate to your performance while taking the Course and while you were being assessed :-

A very good performance. Showed the right qualities when working with a beginner & humour, patience, encouragement. Hope you will all go your name to go forward for testing at coach level.

May I wish you every success in your future Instructing and I look forward to the day when you might let your name go forward for consideration as a Coach (minimum of eighteen months experience required as an Instructor).

Many congratulations on your achievement.

Yours sincerely,

Philip Jones

Philip Jones
Honorary Federation National Coaching Co-ordinator

A real highlight during my time playing bowls was the annual bowls tour, generally lasting for seven days, and taking in venues in southern England, Cornwall, Scotland and other locations. All of these were via coach travel with pretty much a full coach-load each time. It became an integral part of the holiday for a last night, end of tour event to include a presentation by myself, as tour captain, made up of all the funny things tour members had either said or done. These always came with a double-meaning slant put on them – generally depicting my sense of humour and delivered by me in some sort of fancy dress. Good times were had by all and those who joined the tour with a more reserved air very soon became the prime target for mention at the last night dinner. Each one finishing the tour was subjected to some light-hearted humour either to do with their bowling or things that had been done or said. All twisted into humorous double-meaning lines but creating a good laugh all round, so much so that it was a "look forward to" moment on each and every tour. Whilst I played for three differing bowls clubs in the Lincoln area I really found my time at Branston, the village where I grew up, to be my most satisfying in terms of direct involvement and satisfaction, playing with many of my earlier pals.

Away from the direct participation in sport, and following my return to Lincoln, I was invited to attend various functions as a guest speaker and on one particular occasion I was guest at the annual prize-giving evening of Aubourn Football Club, which saw me present the player of the season award to my son, Mostyn.

191

Good job one of us got dressed up for the evening

Whilst managing the consultancy, the time arrived for me to subject my business affairs for the annual auditing procedures. Visiting my appointed auditor I presented him with my accounts, correctly balanced, including both draft Income and Expenditure Accounts and Balance Sheets. A short time afterwards I was summoned to collect the completed accounts and sign the relevant declarations for submission to Inland Revenue. At the same time I was handed a sizeable invoice charge. Upon inspection I noted that the only difference between my draft accounts and those professionally completed, was that there had been a transfer of a figure from one column to another but other than that they were exactly the same. I felt quite pleased, but then I considered the charges submitted. I felt bitterly aggrieved at the expected payment. Having previously battled to get the best possible deals for my employers I was not averse in expressing my views about the amount being charged. During some fraught discussions it was said that his invoice was "par for the course" for that type of work, apart from which the sizeable tax to be paid was non-negotiable as he had not been consulted before final audit. When I also questioned this tax liability a stock answer came back to the effect that if he had been consulted beforehand something could possibly have been done. I reminded him that he had not offered or suggested any such help. My reactions were quite explicit, leaving the meeting confirming that he had in the first year of trading with me found a new client, lost a new client and now found a new competitor in business. I had quite hastily decided that there was an opportunity for someone to dedicate a business specifically aimed at helping the small businessman to have his affairs managed on a regular quarterly basis, at a sensible level of charging. I felt that I was the man for this job.

This resulted in me opening a business under the name of Summa Business Management in 1988 with one other client other than myself. Very quickly that escalated, to the extent of needing new premises and staff to aid the processing of all of the client work coming in. Those premises opened on Canwick Road, Lincoln, and such was the nature of the work and confidences placed in us that in some cases we actually held client cheque books and were nominated as approved signatories on the respective bank accounts. These clients came from all areas of the business world including the motor trade, publicans, food processing, building trades, consultancies and small shops. Within three years of beginning operations, the marketing experiences and integrity gained in my football career had served me well. All seemed to be going well.

In my capacity of chairman of the Branston Bowls Club

Life has a habit of taking turns for the unexpected. From the starting blank canvas almost five hundred clients had been secured. This additional client intake resulted in a new partnership arrangement, but not long after I was taken ill at work. Having dined out the previous evening I was working at my desk on 12th February 1991 when I was hit with excruciating chest pains. Believing it to be the result of the previous evening meal, I put it down to indigestion but not long after with no signs of easing, my then business partner called for an ambulance. Admission to Lincoln County Hospital, Johnson Ward, was the next port of call. Shortly after admission I suffered a cardiac arrest. Whilst there is natural concern surrounding people sustaining heart problems, let alone cardiac arrests, the after-care, support and prescribed medication, by my G.P. Dr John Wade meant that I made a good recovery.

THE FOOTBALL ASSOCIATION
16 Lancaster Gate, London W2 3LW. Tel: 071-402 7151. Fax: 071-402 0486

18/2/91.

Now if this picture doesn't make you feel better – nothing will !!

Best wishes my old mate !

Graham

ENGLAND TEAM MANAGER

To Dick Chester – who helped me into this position !!

GRAHAM TAYLOR
ENGLAND
TEAM MANAGER

Postcard and photo sent to me following my illness

During this rehabilitation period my G.P. said to me, 'I will prescribe whatever medication is required, no problems whatsoever, but take my advice and have a drink of whisky each evening as it will do you as much good as any of the tablets.' Funnily enough those words still linger in my ears when I am sitting having my evening ration. Since sustaining that illness I have maintained a steady work pattern, some would say too much, but my determination was such that I wasn't going to let myself become a couch potato. I wanted to achieve something more. I continued on a lower-scale basis to render a personal accountancy service to a select few clients but at the same time combining these with more football-related consultancy work. I suppose it was a shock to the system and a time to reassess what I wanted to achieve. I felt that I still had more to give, but knew I needed to look after myself. I wanted to focus more of my efforts on the business of sport.

Tony Willis and myself winning Club pairs competition and being presented by Fred Brummitt, Club President

Being both an active player and also a committee member of Branston Bowls Club, I processed grant applications for financial assistance to secure both a new mower and a new pavilion via the Foundation for Sport and the Arts. These proved successful and during the necessary inspection by the area delegate the project received their blessing with an acknowledgement of the accuracy of the application and end product. During one of the on-site meetings their representative who was responsible for the East Midlands area stated that he was leaving and

I should consider applying for his position. The Foundation for Sport and the Arts was funded entirely by donations from the football pools companies – yes, there used to be somewhere where with eight draws on your coupon you could win the magical sum of £75,000 – big changes since then! The pools companies ran into quite a problem when the new National Lottery started. Of course prizes into the millions are a much bigger draw than what the pools could offer, never mind the business advantages handed to Camelot on start-up.

On the recommendations of the regional representative I did put a letter together for the attention of Gratton Endicott, Secretary to the Foundation. I received quite a blunt, condescending reply basically saying what makes you think you are the right person for the job. Following a later approach from them I did eventually take the job in 1994, despite my concerns. Having been the appointed East Midlands representative for only a very short period of time I, along with the other 16 representatives, received confirmation of a meeting in Liverpool. This was not the usual annual meeting which representatives attended, albeit certain processes were retained. An unexpected announcement was made by Gratton to the effect that with the emergence of the National Lottery the trustees had decreed that due to significant decline in funding from the football pools companies there had to be some redundancies. The aim was to enable a sensible continuation. The new format was to consist of not less than six and not more than eight representatives to cover the entire UK. Although no final decision had been arrived at, the announcement put everyone on alert. I was worried that a rule of "last in, first out" would apply and began to think of ways that I could salvage a job I was really enjoying.

On my way out of the meeting I picked up a copy of their annual report and statement of accounts to try and piece together how the operation had been constructed. Having only been in position for some six months and the last one engaged I was of the opinion that I would be the first one out. I had also picked up from their staff members that they were under pressure from the Revenue Authorities. Although all consultants were engaged on a self-employed basis they were being regarded as employed by virtue of the fact that the Foundation for Sport and the Arts were dictating the way of working, imposing certain rules to follow and basically performing as employers. After analysing the accounts and ascertaining some additional facts from their appointed staff I believed it was possible to offer a workable alternative. I asked for a meeting with Gratton during which I suggested that I could put together a business to manage all of their awarded grants throughout the UK, excluding southern Ireland. I felt that a central hub controlling all of the awarded grants would not only consolidate their operations but create

196

efficiencies. The ultimate outcome was the awarding of a five-year contract and the start of a most enjoyable experience.

I had previously and discreetly enquired amongst their Liverpool-based staff, and ascertained that not all of the area consultants were, shall we say, putting themselves about to any degree. It seemed they were happy to submit their monthly accounts for settlement. I was also advised that the national pools companies had been given a raw deal as compared to the National Lottery in terms of taxation and VAT advantages. Sounds typical I suppose! It appeared evident to me that they were in a position where they didn't want to see the Foundation decline but were an organisation given money without needing to work hard for it. They were really devoid of answers as to how they could survive. My experience to date was solely restricted to the East Midlands area but I had worked out a pattern for delivery of service allowing for the fact that I was still operating my other consultancy work, meaning that organisation and planning had to be spot on otherwise some customers would not get the service they were expecting.

Looking at the UK as a whole, disregarding for the moment the Northern Ireland patch, I believed that with some staffing in place a workable solution could be found. I believed that following some in-house, self-administered training, appointed staff who had no such previous experience could manage the internal processing but it was obvious that assistance was needed with the "on the road" business. On that basis I met again with Gratton and offered him a proposition – his words still resonate with me: On your way back to Lincoln bear in mind that you and I have a deal and I want to get the paperwork ready for signing as soon as possible.' I called back to Liverpool within three days with my solicitor in attendance, who had been fully appraised of what I was requiring. Whilst Gratton and I were discussing things in general, in particular how he was going to serve notice on the existing consultants, the legal documentation, as agreed by the solicitors, was presented to both of us for signature. Sport and Arts Consultancy Services was born in 1998.

Beginning the consultancy was like the proverbial whirlwind. Notices were duly served on all existing Area Consultants, new offices were opened in Branston, the village where I was brought up in my younger days. Office staff, all ladies, who had been eagerly waiting in the wings were employed. A new centrally controlled customer-facing, computerised system designed by myself but programmed and installed by a locally based IT development company was installed. It catalogued all correspondence, every telephone call, cheque request, payment and provided a detailed history of each and every project.

The last cog in the wheel was to find the right person to support me on the road. My son, Mostyn, who was at that time working on an assembly line for a Lincoln-based engineering factory with no office experience whatsoever, was my target. I spoke with him about the job specification, potential pit-falls and the risk I was taking with someone with no associated experience. Having got the initial nod of approval I insisted that he accompanied me on some case work before making his final decision . It would mean he was to give up a job providing support to his family if he took the ultimate step of tendering his notice. It would mean him placing all his eggs in one basket.

Mostyn came with me on what turned out to be the last accompanied visit prior to his full-time employment when I had to conclude a case file for a project awarded to Nottingham City Council. On arrival I introduced him to their appointed officer who had been responsible for the management of the project. I informed him that my son was there as a watching observer. Generalising during the early part of the meeting I said to the officer, 'Sir, this is my son who is hopefully going to learn the ropes and then join me in the business. Would you object to me making myself scarce whilst you and he complete the necessary processes to sign the project off.'

'Certainly not. What a good way to teach a new recruit.' I returned almost half an hour later to a big smile across my son's face and a re-assuring comment from their officer to the effect that if you don't wish to employ him, can I have first refusal please? Welcome on board my ally. Now you can travel the entire UK, with only a conventional map and handwritten notes to get to the destinations. Life really started in the fast lane. Only a fortnight prior to starting he had to take his son to a junior bowls competition in Scunthorpe. Naturally it was of interest to me also to go and watch. Before setting off in my own car I was asked not to get too far in front as my son didn't know the way and did not want to get lost . What a change in store for him.

Our initial responsibilities under the terms of contract included everything from the initial award of grant, ongoing support and advice, all correspondence, interim cheque releases, through to a final site visit, satisfactory post-completion report and the final release of withheld funds. Each office-based administrator had responsibility for a pre-defined geographical area caseload. They were at all times required to be courteous, open with advice but quite pedantic in terms of detailed conditions of the award. All of this was in accordance with their previous training programmes.

The paperwork from the previous sixteen consultants was drip fed into our office and it would not be an under-statement to say there were times when it was difficult to clean the floor for boxes of case files, all requiring close scrutiny and validation! Initially there were a couple of weeks for Mostyn to come with me, not only to learn the ropes but to develop a degree of confidence. He was, after all, presenting in many instances, to senior personnel. One of the things instilled into him from day one was "if you are asked a question and you don't know the answer, don't try and bluff your way through it. Apologise – say you don't know the answer but when you get back to the office you will find out and return a call with the correct response.'

'If you bluff it and get found out to be giving wrong information, your reputation and credibility will go down the drain.' During our five-year contract we completed some 5,500 cases covering 100,000 miles a year and it has to be said that we could count on one hand the number of occasions we were late for any appointment. Sounds an awful lot like my own up-bringing, where timekeeping was compulsory and respect for others paramount.

The vast majority of those cases came to a positive conclusion. The Foundation for Sport and the Arts provided funding for everything from the restoration of church bells and church organs to training grants for pupils attending the likes of RADA, the Royal School of Music and Royal Ballet School. Funding would cover the travelling costs for parents taking their children to intermediate training schools for sport, classical music, and many other similar vocations. One example that springs to mind is climbing the many steps to reach the bell tower in St Paul's Cathedral and inspecting the completed renovation work. At the other extreme I clearly remember visiting a family in Devon where three of their children were all pupils with the National Youth Orchestra. On the occasion of my final visit the parents expressed their appreciation for the help and support given that they arranged an afternoon tea for me. Little did I know but as we were coming to the end of a delicious Devon cream tea the three children asked if I would like to go through to their practice room where they could perform on their individual instruments for me. I was humbled in both cases with how the Foundation had positively affected lives.

Of course not every case was as positive. An early case dating from my time covering the East Midlands was one where an award had been made to a brass band organisation. There had been a couple of issues during the processing of the application, but nothing which you could actually put your finger on. The lady handling the project on their behalf had to keep going back to her superior to get answers. When I arrived to complete the post-completion audit process and tie everything up with their own accounting records I was met by their guvnor: 'Sorry about earlier difficulties,' was his opening gambit. 'If you want to know anything about this band just ask me. I know it all.'

'OK, thanks a lot, can I start with your financial records and bank statements please.' Guess what? They weren't available.

'I must have mislaid them or left them at home.'

'Right I'll view the instruments and new uniforms you have purchased then.'

'Yes, OK, come this way. They are in the band room.' Guess what they weren't there.

'Ah the bands people must have taken them home after practice last night.'

'OK. I tell you what: you now know what information I need, get them in place, let me know and I will re-visit, but in the meantime I will not be signing off your project and any balance of funding to be paid will be held to order.'

At the time there were rumours circulating that it was common practice for brass bands to seek funding from The Arts Council of England and also the Foundation for Sport and the Arts for the self-same items, meaning that there was surplus funds to put into the kitty. After speaking with the Foundation I was given the contact details for the Head of Arts Council England, Nicole Penn Symons, who confirmed their award for the same project and expressed some reservations, without anything definite. It was decided that she would arrange a meeting between all three parties at the band's headquarters, but she, I and a representative from the Foundation for Sport and the Arts would meet earlier to agree upon the processes to be taken at the meeting. Neither she nor the representative from the Foundation wanted to chair the meeting so asked if I would undertake that responsibility – which I duly did. Whilst it was conducted in a friendly atmosphere the level of questioning was quite direct and served to produce the necessary evidence to show that there was a case here of double-funding, where both grants had been used for the purchase of one set of instruments and uniforms. The balance after purchasing those goods was deposited in general funds. The outcome was a severe rebuke, confirmation that no further applications for grants would be considered by either body and that surplus funds were required to be deposited within seven days to avoid any potential legal action being taken.

I mention this story because shortly afterwards whilst visiting a Foundation award case in the Soho area of London Nicole Penn Symons telephoned, and asked if I could arrange to meet up with her in their offices later that evening. She very kindly thanked me for my astute handling of the case. She went on to offer me all of their casework to undertake on a similar basis to that which I was currently handling for the Foundation for Sport and the Arts. I apologised, declining the offer on the basis that it was far too soon for us to handle the task properly and professionally. I felt that it would be foolhardy for us at that time to take on such a volume of work and not to be able to deliver it to the standards we had set ourselves. We still had mountains of work to complete to get everything in order with our current obligations. She understood, but was somewhat disappointed, and then went on to ask if I would promise to go back to her when I felt I was in a position to contract for them. She suggested that they did not have on their books any outside contractor offering such a unique level of service. This I did shortly after and took into our portfolio a significant volume of additional casework, all of which was very competitively priced, as most of our travel costs were provided for in our existing operations.

This award brought our casework up by about another 500 but with it came some prestigious, multi-million pound awards. I can honestly say that there was never ever any preferential treatment to anyone. A grantee claiming travel money for a child in the family to attend specialised artistic training was treated just the same as a client who was handling a full refurbishment of a theatre venue. Our remit was quite easy to define. All projects should be completed in accordance with the original application detail and, unless formally amended during the programme, to be completed totally in accordance with the same with a full and final appraisal of the costs incurred.

When the Trustees made their award they did not expect to recover any of that money. That was unless we, as their appointed representatives, found that original estimates used for the application had been bettered, or the grant had not been properly managed. In those cases the grantee was required to repay those sums to the awarding organisation. During our time we were responsible for the return of some two million pounds, all of which were re-distributed to other deserving causes.

Whilst all of this was going on, two of my earlier colleagues, Robin Bradley who had done some design work for me on properties in Branston Village and Keith Roe, a classmate in our days at Lincoln Grammar School, were now sitting on the board of directors at Lincoln City Football Club. They were in the position in 2001 to offer me the chance to return to the club initially as chief executive and later managing director. This move saw me come full circle, having started my career at Sincil Bank and now coming out of football retirement to go back into the game – an opportunity I had discounted in my own mind. The announcement in the *Lincolnshire Echo* was headed "The man for all reasons" with a quote from the chairman, Robin Bradley, saying, 'I've known Dick for many years and I know the personality of the guy and he is exactly the kind of person we want at the club.' With the pleasantries over, the real task was opened up when it was made known that the club were hovering around maximum bank borrowings and life on the field of play was not that exciting either. Did that bring back some memories? You could certainly say it did! The whole thing seemed reminiscent of the early 1970s when I originally joined, but this time the club was effectively being run by the Supporters Trust, who had been granted the major shareholding originally held by the late chairman, John Reames. Almost identical to my 1971 baptism into football, the directors' main suggestions about raising income revolved around how they could increase charges to supporters. I distinctly remember one board meeting when attention to budgets and finances were of paramount concern that I suggested emphasis be transferred to areas of spending where in one particular area directors could personally fund their hospitality arrangements within the boardroom. The suggestion went down like a lead weight. There was clearly a difficult job to be done.

From the day that Alan Buckley scored the deciding penalty for Walsall to condemn Sheffield United to Division Four, to me rejoining Lincoln City, I hadn't come across Alan, by then the Imps manager. You can imagine the sort of banter exchanged, which helped to form a good working relationship. The team, under his management, had dragged themselves out of the lower reaches of Division Four the previous season and were hopeful of a better campaign. That proved not to be the case with some disappointing results, diminishing attendances and no surplus funds to make any sort of impression in the transfer market.

At this time the rules and regulations of the Football League prohibited leading First Division clubs having any sort of financial control over any one of the lower division clubs. However, I had several conversations with ex-colleagues from my Division One days and struck lucky with a conversation with Michael Dunford, CEO at Everton FC. The result was an expression of interest on their part of forming a relationship between the Imps and the Goodison Park club. It was envisaged that this sort of an arrangement would produce all-round benefits for both parties. The first exploratory meeting was held at their stadium with their Chairman, Sir Phillip Carter, who I had worked with years previously when considering the formation of the Super League. Also attending were Michael Dunford, my chairman Robin Bradley and me. Parking our car and wandering round to reception, Robin asked if he could just pause for a moment to take in what was happening, not believing that this proposal was within his grasp, and also asking what he was to say or do. My advice was quite simple, 'Be yourself, speak from the heart and speak the truth and you will be fine – these are nice people.' The meeting went so well that it was only too apparent that another meeting was required to both allow for such developments to drop into place and for the two managers to become acquainted, as at that time they had had no professional association.

The second of these meetings took place at their Bellfield Training Headquarters leading up to the Christmas period when there were some in-house celebrations going on. What appeared most strange, though, was that the younger players were enjoying the celebrations, whilst the more senior pros were in the gymnasium performing head tennis routines. With formal introductions out of the way it soon became clear that there could be a very good understanding between Walter Smith and Alan Buckley with the host performing "tea making skills par excellence." What was said in professional terms between the two managers was of no consequence to others. It was, and always should be, private and professional. The only thing to break up those intense discussions was when their Centre of Excellence Manager, Ray Hall, came on to the scene to wax lyrical about a young striker who had just scored two stunning goals for their U18 team. That player, confirmed to me in a later phone conversation with Michael Dunford, was none other than Wayne Rooney, record England goalscorer and currently manager of Derby County.

So much progress, goodwill and friendship had been formed that it was agreed that Everton FC would visit the Red Imps and that Sir Phillip Carter would pilot his own plane, with their entourage on board, down to Lincoln. All that remained was for me to seek the clearance of RAF Waddington to permit landing. Easier said than done, particularly with Vulcan Bomber training exercises in operation. After much discussion, clearance was obtained thanks to the cooperation of leading RAF officers. On the day in question the Everton party were met by a good representation of Imps' senior personnel and, on arrival at Sincil Bank ,hosted to lunch by the club, shown around the facilities, given the opportunity to address any issue raised, albeit there were none of any due concern. After shaking hands on an agreement I escorted the guests back to RAF Waddington, clearing themselves from any exercise routines for take-off.

Sufficient headway had been made to reach an agreement whereby in preparation for Season 2002/03 Everton FC would allocate players not currently featuring in their first team but in need of continual match day exposure, to spend their time at Sincil Bank. The Toffees would continue to pay their wages and expenses. Lincoln City being responsible only for any incentive scheme entitlements. Prayers answered on two fronts: firstly, quality players with no payroll commitment, secondly, if we had a player attracting attention from any other Division One club we would advise Everton and provide them with the first option.

Prior to those discussions with Everton, ITV Digital had seemingly thrown a lifeline to Championship, League One and League Two clubs by offering a staggering £315 million pound deal to screen games from all of these divisions. Their negotiations did not go according to plans and they themselves went into administration with Sky picking up the pieces for a much lesser sum. This collapse was reported to have the potential of putting scores of clubs into financial difficulties and in fact it is recorded that within four years of the ITV collapse, fourteen clubs had gone into administration. Lincoln City were operating up to their maximum £60,000 overdraft and, presumably because of the whole uncertainty surrounding the football industry, Barclays Plc called in their overdraft leaving the Imps with no alternative other than to call in the administrators, Begbies Traynor of Nottingham.

Administration meant the termination of services of both Alan Buckley and me, as is the norm in these sorts of events. The administrators fully believed they had all the necessary expertise to run the company. I suppose cynically I could also argue that such actions would go a long way to protecting their fees! Following meetings with the board, Alan left with his outstanding contract settled in full and, in my case, I simply returned to my business full-time. Before leaving, Robin Bradley thanked me for my work and apologised for the outcome, which I acknowledged. At the same time I advised him that whilst he was the chairman he should ensure that at all times he was fully aware of all the negotiations and dealings with the administrators. If the club went under it was his name above the door and it would be he who would take the flack. I have to this day continued to hold Robin's commitment to the Red Imps and my personal relationship with him in the highest esteem.

In total the club were facing a bill for total liabilities of some £1.5 million and such was their case that in the first instance the appointed insolvency practitioners declined to handle their case in court, but after an agreed delay the case was eventually submitted and adopted by the courts. Unlike today there was no provision for the imposition of penalty points by the Football League and the club was free to start the season with a clean sheet. That was not the end of it, though. With the passing of time, Everton FC had replaced their manager, Walter Smith, with David Moyes who had decreed that no player would be leaving Goodison Park until he had had the time to properly assess all players on the books. Outcome – the previous deal was dead in the water. It can only be left as a "what might have been." A postscript is that some years later the Imps current benefactor, Clive Nates, was looking to invest in a club and, as an Evertonian, was suitably impressed with the earlier potential link with Lincoln City that he threw his lot in at Sincil Bank. Something of a happy ending, therefore.

The one real memory I have during this latter spell was the professionalism of the Assistant Manager, Keith Alexander. If ever there was anybody with a better player knowledge than Keith I hadn't had the privilege to meet them. Alan Buckley, resident in the Grimsby area, was much dependent upon Keith, his knowledge and his hours spent watching players in action and many was the time he put Keith's knowledge to the test but never once was Keith caught lacking. Keith's expertise in football was matched if not exceeded by his quality as a person. His death in 2010 was tragic for his family, friends and colleagues. It was also a huge loss to the game of football.

My five-year contract with the Foundation for Sport and the Arts had now reached maturity but was not renewed. By this time, apart from a few awards, their existence was shrouded in doubt, and in fact very shortly after the organisation closed down. The Arts Council of England had a change of direction within their top management. They to transfer all of the grant monitoring processes to their regional offices. This had previously been their practice but failed to deliver the comprehensive service which we had delivered. Business decisions of this nature are made by their appointed officers and it is no use crying over spilt milk when there is nothing you can do about it. So stop crying over spilt milk and get on with life! Our engagement had been very successful and acknowledged by their head office. The decision brought to an end a relationship enjoyed by all those participating. It is my fervent belief that there was a feeling of some discomfort within their ranks. Whatever the reasoning, decisions were taken for me to cease trading. I was again at a bit of a loose end and wondering where to go next.

Along with myself, the closure of the business affected other people. I had to make difficult and painful decisions necessitating the closure of the offices and release of the staff who had performed a really excellent level of service. There was, however, the need to properly conclude the uncompleted caseload held on file and this was undertaken by me and my son, working from our home bases. At a difficult time, I needed something to keep me gainfully occupied.

Whilst this work was being attended to, I received a telephone call from David Richards (now Sir David) who had assumed control over the Football Foundation – an organisation dealing with grants predominantly designed to aid the football industry. The Foundation had been provided with funds from the major footballing authorities in the UK. I met with him in his east Sheffield-based business premises when, after some discussions as to the precise nature of my work and his precise requirements, it was agreed that he would send a couple of case files for me to review and advise on the findings. He was particularly keen to discover some anomalies which he could use to stamp his authority on the future workings of the Foundation. The first case he asked me to review was one awarded to a County Football Association, which, at the end of our work, showed impeccable management and control, prompting a report to say that "if you ever wanted to hold a case up as an example for others to follow this was the one."

The second case brought out a completely different outcome and was one where the intentions of the newly appointed chairman could be well and truly used to deliver his intended message to all. It was in respect of a non-league West Midlands-based football club, involving new facilities for the benefit of aspiring young players and community users. Whilst levels of delivery, as expressed in the original application and award papers, were delivered, it also revealed that some of the funds had been used to cover first team player travelling and out-of-pocket expenses for the non-league club. Furthermore, the appointed project manager had been less than professional with the submission and payment of his fees. Maintaining telephone contact with the Association's chairman, I was asked to urgently complete a full report for his consideration and action. This was submitted as requested but lay dormant for some time. Later, a further on-site meeting with the grantee, chief executive of the Football Foundation, me and my son (who had worked with me throughout) convened to consider all elements of our findings. Prior to this meeting we had spent many hours following up what seemed at the time to be gossip-mongering, but, as time revealed, there was clear evidence of misappropriation. The ultimate outcome was surprising in as much as no actions were to be taken other than additional financial assistance to help them bridge the shortfall in finances. These had occurred because of the fundamental flaws in the project management! To this day I am not aware of any material changes made by the Football Foundation to eradicate any such future practices, as communication between us has dropped off the radar and no further work has been forwarded for our completion.

As my work in grants was coming to an end I needed something to keep the old "grey matter" working. Over my years in football I had developed an interest in the collating of match data. I wanted to create a total database of football results. A huge task, but one which I believed was possible. In the late 1990s I began a partnership with Michael Ward who, apart from being an expert in IT, proved his experience beyond all recognition and became a competent, trusted partner but more importantly a true friend. I wanted to develop a database consisting of comprehensive match-by-match information for both English and Scottish football from the late 1800s to date. This break provided me with the opportunity of concentrating on this project. The long and tedious task soon became an obsession! In the very early days I could call upon the services of my son, who was still with me pending his take up of alternative employment. My daughter, Nicola, based in Birmingham, also helped, with her services being used to good effect in the main Birmingham City Library. The now completed database from the inception of the game to present day contains: results for both league and cup competitions, half-time scores, attendance, league tables – where applicable, club histories, full managerial details per club, and a host of other ways of questioning the data to provide statistical reports and summaries. It has been a monumental effort to collate all that information.

The original start point was purely for me to be able to include some facts for inclusion in the match day programmes I edited. Since then with Football League help, input and agreement, the project has never stopped growing or developing. In fact it is a programme which will never be out of date. Information is updated on a seasonal basis with ever-changing summary data and, I am told, represents the largest computerised record of English and Scottish football. The object at the moment, and God knows there have been many discussions, is to develop the project with a third party for a variety of commercial markets.

The football industry has enough funding to develop its own version of the database if it so wished. My commercial experience suggests to me that the database could serve the world outside of football, commercially or socially. From my perspective, time is running out with the prospect of me pushing up the daisies before seeing it in its operative state. It is free of any copyright infringement and has its own Intellectual Property rights. Data has been secured from the public domain, involving visits to many libraries – both national and local the length and breadth of the UK – to secure any missing information with no material ever being copied with every single entry being inputted into a specially designed in-house programme thereby ensuring exclusivity. That has been an endless task and certainly kept the cogs turning. It now needs third party, technically and commercially savvy partners to bring it as a product to market.

In between all of that, I once more linked up with Reg Brealey to help design a project to benefit disadvantaged youths, circa 18 years of age. That absorbed an immense amount of time, researching, designing and producing training programmes to accommodate many different disciplines of work. Well-trained youngsters are more likely to be involved in society, so the aim was to provide the user the best possible training for his or her preferred discipline. The financial benefit to me was once more a promise of an equity stake. This was another promise which failed to deliver. Only a short period of time ago when an official launch was anticipated, Reg delivered a statement to me saying that: 'There is only one person to manage this project and it isn't you.' At least at that moment he came straight to the point! Maintaining friendship for me was the priority – back to childhood lessons! Were there lessons to be learnt or should one value friendships in terms other than monetary. I opted for the friendship angle believing that at some time in the future all would come good. Such was the strength of my feelings that on the occasion of my re-marriage I asked and accepted Reg's involvement as best-man.

Good relationships do serve the test of time. I found that out when undertaking duties for the Foundation for Sport and the Arts. Whilst catching up on some admin in the office, mid to late 1995, I took a call from a respected contact from my Sheffield days. During my days at The Lane my senior ticket office staff member was Elaine Bland, whose husband happened to be Michael Bland, the manager at the Yorkshire Bank. He stepped in to help me out when encountering problems with the club's existing bankers, and with whom I had developed a close and trusted business association.

At first I thought the call might be a general catch up but to my utter surprise it was a straightforward enquiry asking if I would be interested in a return to Bramall Lane. It transpired that he had established sufficient interest from his senior executives that the Yorkshire Bank could be interested in securing a deal to take over at Sheffield United. If successful he would be required to be their lead officer but wanted me to return to effectively run the club on his behalf. There was of course work to be done to get to that stage, so I was duly asked if I could establish the current position at the club, keeping the 'powder dry' at this stage. I called on my long-standing friendship with Derek Dooley and he kindly provided me with two years' completed accounts and the current year's budgets with an open invitation to ask if there was any more detail I required. I advised Michael that, surprisingly, I had sufficient info to put together a reasonable assessment. Meeting up with him we collectively prepared a report for presentation to their head office. We duly submitted and seemingly gained the nod of approval. Unfortunately, at their board level meeting it was declined, not on the strength of the report but more on the effect such a takeover would have in terms of upsetting Wednesdayite account-holders – such would be the likely outburst of opinion, to be quickly followed by an exit to other banking organisations. Blue and white, or red and white. Never the twain shall meet!

Michael Bland rang to apologise for any inconveniences caused and expressed his personal disappointment at the outcome and an ambition thwarted for himself. Knowing that I had a personal relationship with Reg Brealey, the then current chairman at the Lane, he said he could introduce me to another businessman who he knew was interested in securing a football club. That businessman was Mike McDonald, the successful boss of a Manchester-based engineering company. That approach was made, at the back end of 1995/ early 1996 and he quickly confirmed his interest in Sheffield United, duly asking if I could make the introductions.

This I quickly arranged. The meeting thrashed out the basis of the deal, which was to be the exchange of two Lincolnshire-based hotels owned by Mike McDonald in return for ownership of Sheffield United FC. The actual details of the negotiations were handled privately and confidentially but if successful I would be entitled to claim brokerage fees for both the sales and purchase transactions. The deal, I believe, was concluded with one hotel, The Petwood Hotel, Woodhall Spa and cash for the transfer of holding shares. Completed at the back end of 1995 Mike McDonald moved his entourage into The Lane – as for me the brokerage fees still remain outstanding.

Friendship is significantly built up on trust and the recognising of spoken words. This is as true in football as in any other walk of life. There is also more to life than money. Whilst I continued to retain my friendship with the defaulting offender, I found it disappointing that it appeared to be so one-sided. I buried my grievances back then but found this was not to be the last time either. My re-marriage was held at the Petwood Hotel for which I paid the full-going rate. I did not ask for, nor was offered any perks or discounts. Friendships, I was always told, are two-sided, so why have I been taken for a ride so often? I have asked myself numerous times. I'm not sure that I have an answer. I made many friendships and long-lasting professional relationships through football and am grateful for the many people who have seen fit to add their comments to this book. So, I bear no grudges as life is too short for those. I still have that nagging question of why, though. Why? Why?

It wasn't long before Reg came knocking again – 2009 in fact – with a request for me to undertake a due diligence exercise on behalf of an investor aiming to secure control of one of the clubs I had served previously. Signings of confidentiality and non-disclosure agreements prevent me from telling the full story, but it provided me with a first insight into the methods of workings in football clubs coming up to the twenty first century. I was amazed at the relaxed manner in which company secretaries and CEOs were allowing their club to operate in such a manner, particularly when their owners were making it perfectly clear that they were looking for an escape route and reaching the end of their continual financial "prop up."

The office provided for me was directly off the main management operating area with an array of computerised and IT technology on view.

Many of the seats were empty not just for minutes but for most of the time I was involved. The then CEO had difficulty answering questions about the day to day running of the club, asking for such information to come from one person or another. Delegation was of the highest order but responsibilities for the duties contained within his employment contract were sadly missing. Of course things in business develop and I for one would welcome any new innovation or streamlining to improve company performances but at each stage the person in charge needs to be on top of his job and not just occupying a seat in his ivory tower.

RJB CONSULTANTS

RICHARD CHESTER

It is a pleasure to write this reference for Richard Chester who I have known for 45 Years, initially from my appointment as a Director and Vice Chairman of a Football League Club where he was Secretary. He undertook the transformation financially of this company by the establishment of a Rights Issue in the share capital thus saving the club from extinction.

Following his move to a larger Football League club at which I was the Finance Director and Vice Chairman, Richard once again performed the same documentation for one million pounds which again resulted in a second club out of its difficulties.

His knowledge of company law and stewardship of management can only be described as perfection and his documental presentation in all aspects of administration was always described in basic, simple terms , easily understood by whoever had the task of decision making.

I have attempted to describe in the simplest of terms, Richards natural talents incorporating the three requirements of Ability Integrity, and Loyalty, but as each of these could easily with Richard be a number one, I have written them in Alphabetical Order.

I wish him well in whatever his objective, but know someone is going to make an appointment of which they will forever be grateful.

R J Brealey.

Brealey

RJB CONSULTANTS
Newfield Welbourn Lincoln LN5 0ND
Tel/Fax 01400 273079 Mobile 07960 412205
Email rjbconsultants@gmail.com

This particular deal was declined in preference to an alternative party. A further request came my way from the same source but this time relating to a lower-level club. A similar story prevailed as the CEO did not know the precise financial position of his club simply saying, 'When I know that there isn't enough money to pay the wages then I ask the chairman to put more money in.' The club in my opinion had a real opportunity to stem the flow of their decline by simply stabilising and managing the financial leakages. Then, not unlike my earlier clubs, improvements could be sought not only on the park but, just as importantly, in terms of better management control and marketing. The ownership of this particular club was also transferred to an alternative bidder and in a fairly short period of time sold again as a result of sustained losses.

Not to be put down in his efforts to get back into football – the subject of widespread media coverage at that time – Reg Brealey became heavily involved in an attempt to secure control of Chesterfield F.C. Largely because of the club's proximity to Reg's days at the Blades, and general geographical location, favourable for his home base, this seemed an ideal opportunity. Again, bringing in a new potential investor, recommended from the business sector within the City of London, a team was put together to advise and formulate another due diligence exercise. I joined forces with Tony Kenworthy, the ex-Sheffield United defender, plus a third party introduced by the potential investor, to review both on and off the field performances with recommendations for change. What transpired was a fairly heated meeting at the premises of the then owner, Dave Allen – ex Sheffield Wednesday chairman – who had financially committed himself to the club for a period of time – when he simply said to both Reg and the newly introduced investor, 'Here's the keys to the club put your money on the table and you can have them now' – or words to that effect. Outcome no money, no deal, move on.

Having undertaken previous due diligence exercises, and meeting up with other professionals along the way, the team was strengthened to encompass all business disciplines to provide a "one stop" consortium. Even with the newly formed team being recognised by several clubs seeking a take-over deal, the outcomes were identical. "No money to back up your interest. Sorry. No deal." Generally, other than the meeting re Chesterfield FC, I was not privy to, and did not want to get involved with, the detailed financial transactions involved within any such deal. In my view they were purely of a private and personal nature and needed to be conducted accordingly. I can truthfully say that I do not have any such detail for any of the clubs involved but I do wonder, particularly in view of the dreadful financial positions of those clubs involved, if the main thrust of the negotiations wasn't "Buy now, Pay later – I have the team who can do the job for you." Excluding the previously mentioned attempts to secure a take over deal in football, there were some other sixteen enquiries where the services of either myself or Tony Kenworthy were called upon to provide detailed background of those clubs being expressly targeted.

Quite a sensible approach in all fairness for, who, in their right minds, would lodge a substantial investment on the table to then find that the losses causing the sale could not be stemmed? At the same time, why should the owner adopt the usual approach of being optimistic about its future when all of his investments have failed to deliver such returns? A problem from both sides which I doubt will ever go away. The present-day state of the game really hasn't changed in terms of those owners wanting to sell and those investors wanting to buy but the numbers involved get bigger and bigger. All of those exercises were done by members of the appointed team on the basis of an involvement in the running of the clubs after completion of purchase with no one receiving any sort of reimbursement for time or expenses incurred

My time after football did not entirely leave the beautiful game and sport more generally behind. I thoroughly enjoyed being able to make a difference from the smallest level to large multi-million pound schemes in my work with grant-making organisations. I was fortunate to be able to work alongside my son and in having both my children behind me with the huge amount of research needed for my database. I am grateful to them both! If I am to leave a legacy to the footballing world, it may well be the database. The contacts I made earlier in the game came in use to me in my consultancy work. I am grateful for the opportunities to complete due diligence work. It would have been more pleasurable if I had been paid for it though! The work was interesting on its own terms, but also provided me an insight into the world of modern football.

Would I return to football now? I am, as I write, in my early 80s. From my own point of view I feel I have all my marbles intact and still have a work ethic in my mind. I certainly would not want to go back to the old working days of 70 to 80 hours per week. A consultancy involvement could be a possibility. Experience in life counts for a lot and I am sure the experiences gained could still serve a club well. Working knowledge and experience is something not to be discounted. Football, never mind which club you speak about, is not a toy, it's an integral and important part of many people's lives, and it would be immoral if those running the game today overlooked that. I'd be happy to support clubs, owners and CEOs with any of my knowledge, realistic thinking, and management skills. I am convinced that the building blocks of success have changed little since my day, even if the sums involved have.

Michael Dunford, former Everton FC CEO

The Premier League and the English Football League comprises 92 clubs who have basically created a competitive trade association. Yes, we may well have a deep desire to topple everyone we play, but many football clubs have over the decades become very insular and deeply protective of their own interests. The current financial crises many clubs now face can to some degree be put down to these Dickensian practices.

When I joined Everton in 1994 they had been one of the prime movers in the creation of the Premier League. The supposed "big" clubs demanded a higher share of the financial spoils and wished collectively to have a greater voice in how our national sport should develop. Some clubs were all too eager to forget their roots and in fact some could be said to have sold out to the financial devil.

Luckily there were a few administrators, and indeed directors, who wished to protect the game and ensure that all clubs prospered whilst respecting the rich tradition that the great game had developed over generations. Dick Chester was one such person who was a visionary and was always eager to see progress and tradition work in harmony. I first met Dick in his early days at Lincoln City and as I was starting out in the game. We maintained a strong relationship throughout our careers up to and including his time at Hillsborough.

When he returned back into the game at Lincoln City in 2001 Dick suggested to me that he had the germ of an interesting idea which might just prove of benefit to his own club and mine, Everton. Whilst the FA rules prohibited lower clubs becoming nursery clubs for the "Big Boys" there must surely be a way of working together for mutual benefit. The more we explored this subject it soon became clear that there could be huge advantages for both clubs. A meeting was held at Goodison Park involving our respective Chairmen, Dick, and myself. The plan was that if Everton's developing youngsters spent some time at Lincoln then they may benefit from the experience of playing in the combative lower division. At the same time, our coaching staffs could undertake exchange visits as indeed could members of our administrative and commercial teams.

Most clubs' operation structures were in essence very similar, albeit there were huge differentials in the numbers of staff employed. There was never any suggestion of either club being able to influence the other but simply a pooling of ideas was only going to be the basis of our informal relationship. In fact Everton tried to develop a similar like-minded relationship with Fergus McCann at Celtic FC. To create such an arrangement the paramount ingredients would have to be based on integrity, honesty, and trust. From my point of view all of those had been reflected in Dick's career.

Today's loan system has embraced much of what we set out to achieve and whilst the venture between our two clubs eventually petered out it was not for the want of trying from both sides.
We can learn so much from each other and removing the over-protective insular views held by many at that time was indeed a challenge. Hopefully, with a few more like Dick Chester in our midst then the great game will continue to provide so much enjoyment to so many.

Chapter Twelve: Reflections

Do I miss football? Of course I do! Although the challenges were immense and variable; the respect shown to me by all around me will register in my mind forever

Do I miss the day-to-day involvement in helping to provide a club worthy of fan base support? Of course I do! To be on the inside and try to work for the benefit of those on the outside trying to deliver a better all-round product was so rewarding. At the same time, everything you did was open to public and press scrutiny. Not many jobs are quite like that.

Did my senior managerial experiences provide for me a better standard of living and prepare me for other career opportunities? Of course it did! There can be no telling what your life holds in store for you but for me it turned out quite well. Dedicated to all of the tasks expected of me, I think I gained the confidences of those around me and it certainly provided me with good all-round experience in virtually all of the management disciplines which, indeed, helped me later in life.

Would I welcome a return to the industry as it is presented today? That is more difficult to answer. It is not until you are inside the business, and you have the chance to gather all the facts and figures on show, that a question like that could be answered with any degree of certainty. In my final chapter I reflect on my experiences and consider the state of the game today. I invite readers to consider the purpose of the English game and how clubs and the authorities could move closer to what I would consider a game fit for all.

Even before I became involved in the game, English football had gone through some significant changes in terms of style of play and approach to the game. November 25th 1953 was really the day that brought English football back down to basics. Having used Wembley Stadium as a fortress for visiting teams to overcome, this day saw the visit of Hungary in a friendly international game. Hungary brought into the game a new formation the likes of which the England national team had not encountered before. The formation of English teams with one goalkeeper; two full backs (right full back wearing number two and left full back number three); three half backs (number four right half, number five centre half, number six left half) and FIVE forwards (number seven right winger, number eight inside right, number nine centre forward, number ten inside left and number eleven outside left) had been the order of the day from the late 1880s until the 1950s. It would be fair to say that some clubs had tweaked it a bit, but the general formula remained the same.

The Hungarians came and introduced a new formation of one goalkeeper, two full backs, three half backs, three inside forwards and two forwards. Numbers on the shirts seemed to count for nothing for the number nine (centre forward) basically played a wandering game with the English centre half getting nowhere near him all the game. The result was a resounding 6-3 win for the visitors – a game also remembered for the hat-trick scored by Ferenc Puskas. From that day forward managers and coaches considered their options and formations, and for a period from the late 1950s through to the 1970s, teams played mostly 1-4-2-4 or 1–4–3-3. Since then, whilst not a rule, games have been played in all sorts of formations but what has changed is that the fan can no longer judge the playing position of any player by virtue of the number appearing on the back of their shirts, as, instead, the shirts reveal their squad number – some of them so high it makes you wonder how they have been derived!

Away from the pitch the world of football has also changed considerably and is a far different place than when I was part of it, but the principles remain broadly the same. Whilst my working input was significant I would hasten to add that, had it not been for the commitment of some excellent support staff, this could have been significantly more. The supporter is keen to have access to all of the club's services at a time to suit them. The staff meanwhile were mainly made up of family people, all of whom would have enjoyed being at home enjoying weekends and bank holidays but had committed themselves to work for the club. The unsociable hours put in by the staff were part and parcel of their contract, with no enhanced payment for overtime or unsociable hours. A big ask, therefore. For my part I tried to recognise this level of commitment and I can truthfully say, not one member of my staff approached me for a salary review. I tried to recognise their commitment and performances and where appropriate I called them into my office and advised them of a salary increase. Additionally, on a personal level, I treated my staff to a pre-Christmas meal at a chosen local venue and on some occasions used the club's minibus – generally used for transportation of the apprentices for training and playing purposes – to pick the staff up, allow them to enjoy themselves and then drop them back home

The duties relative to crowd control are not just a Football League requirement as contained within their regulations, it is also part and parcel of the provisions of the Safety at Sports Ground Act and accordingly, in my opinion, takes on a whole new meaning especially when you are the appointed officer accountable for such onerous responsibilities. During my time in football I managed a total of 360 League and Cup home games where I witnessed 1018 goals being scored in total, with my teams coming out on top scoring 710 of those. At the same time the total number of spectators passing through the turnstiles was 4,471,231, with each and every one of those expecting due care and attention at all times. Luckily I can say that I cannot recall a single incident which related to a breach of my duties and responsibilities. For the benefit of the differing sets of supporters at each of the clubs served, the breakdown in terms of games and attendances is; Lincoln City 173 matches, attendances 1,056,646; Sheffield United 130 games, attendances 1,988,302 and Sheffield Wednesday 57 games, attendances 1,426,283.

During my time I had the opportunity to attend several pre-match banquets hosted by my clubs but never on any occasion did I accept. Many times I have been in discussion with my counterpart from the visiting club, particularly when in the First Division, and been told that these duties could be handled by delegated staff with a "reporting back procedure" in place. That was never an option for me. If anything was to go wrong the buck stopped with me, which in my mind means your presence is required. Close liaison at all clubs with the police authorities was an essential part of ensuring controls and, should events crop up needing attention, which they do many a time, then with time being of the essence, a search for the responsible officer before actions taken is not an option – in my mind.

The responsibilities associated with the positions I held did not stop at crowd control. It is the responsibility of the company secretary to ensure that all procedures and processes associated with both the industry regulations, and also company law matters, are vested in you. To take the position seriously, as is required by the governing boards of directors and industry regulations, I also regarded it my task to ensure that all other processes were appropriately under control. At the time of my involvement, it was a stipulated requirement that, with all transfers, clubs were not permitted to talk to the player until the agreements of both selling and buying clubs had been confirmed in writing and signed accordingly. Discussions between the signing club and the player could then begin, and once satisfactorily concluded, contained within the player's contract, whereupon no payments could be considered or made. All transgressions reported would be dealt with quite vigorously by the relevant authority. Any similar irregularities of a company nature would equally find their way into the hands of those controlling authorities and again fall back into the lap of the company secretary. To maintain a clean bill of health, I found, at times, that it could be a very lonely existence and whilst there was a natural friendliness in both the game and with the community an "arm's length" approach was a virtual pre-requirement. Again, without any feeling of arrogance, I encountered no problems –

keeping my employers in the clear.

What I do feel, however, as an outsider looking in, as is my position today, I am not at all sure of the commitment of those running the game. I am unsure whether they are doing so in the best interests of the game or in their own best interests. I have mentioned my observations on the commitment of those CEOs I came across in my due diligence work on behalf of potential investors and on the staff levels which clubs deem necessary to stage a game at three o'clock on a Saturday afternoon. This is an area, without any personal direct experience in the running of a club today, which I find difficult to understand. The maximum number of administrative, ground and maintenance staff I had working under me to deliver the required service at any one of the clubs I served was probably not more than thirty to forty. Looking at the same three clubs and using the data as included on LinkedIn, it seems to suggest that the comparative figure would be somewhere in the region of 200. From various information released via the press, the Covid-19 pandemic did bring about redundancies in clubs but still left them with plenty of capacity to function. As an example, Arsenal announced the loss of 55 jobs, aimed at saving some £2million – an average of £36,500 per employee. With money pouring into the game, with each new contract negotiation producing bigger and bigger sums of money, it seems that the relevant share outs (where the club is handed money from above rather than having to work for it) find their way into the monthly payroll system with the supporter still faced with demands to foot shortfalls in club finances .

More and more expensive season tickets is one answer. Richard Crooks in his excellent books *Grandad what was Football Like in the 1970s*, and his 1980s sequel, detail how prices rose rapidly at Sheffield Wednesday. In 1970/71, the price for an adult in the centre of the North Stand was £11 in the old Division Two. This had risen to £16 by 1973/74 – though "ladies" did gain a one-pound discount. By 1979/80, although the team were now plying their trade in the old Division Three, a season ticket in the same place cost £41.40. By the time of the team's return to Division One in 1984/85 the price was £80, and £85 for the following campaign. Of course, this was a time of rampant inflation. The Bank of England's inflation calculator tells me that the £11 ticket would have cost £53.06 if the price had risen with inflation. As it was, the cost went up by more than £30 over and above that.

It is well known that the heavily industrialised areas of Yorkshire and the North East have a great number of workers who were renowned for working hard and living hard. As a youngster I saw it first hand when visiting family in Middlesbrough at times when there was nothing on the table, but the working member had enough for his fags, the pub, a bet, the club in the evening and the match on a Saturday. Living within the Sheffield area, with its heavy steel and manufacturing industries, I was able to recognise similar traits where many male supporters placed a similar emphasis on their lives. Too many men who felt that they must have their season ticket or tickets. If it's the man of the house, then the wife can't buy her new dress because it was too expensive, for example. Men who found the increased price for tickets as OK, but who insisted the family scrimp and save elsewhere. Men who felt the family might have to have a review of their holiday arrangements. Men who wouldn't do anything if there is a match on that day. Men who told their wives they needed a few pints before and after each game, so put the meal on the back burner. Men who told their partners that they would need to spend a few bob on betting on the result. Men who suffered terribly if results did not live up to pre-season hype. Families who were treated as second best due to the demands on those men – driven in part by the financial demands of their club.

These are all things which the industry could address if there was sufficient thought put into true supporter values. Even by the 1980s ticket prices were rising faster than was reasonable. I use Sheffield Wednesday as my example, but the need to keep ticket prices in check and to look after match-going fans was common throughout the game. It would not change the mindset of the fan I describe above, but might give some help or respite to his family at little cost to the game overall.

Lincoln City will always register with me in terms of getting things consolidated into a good pot. Not in terms of any priority, the club had during my service, transformed itself both on and off the field and considerably enhanced their standing with the fan base. After my leaving, not that I could have done much about it, but it reaffirmed the views expressed between Graham and myself when Heneage stated he didn't want Second Division football under his chairmanship and that aiming for mediocrity was a dangerous policy. The club seemingly reverted back to the days of mediocrity until along came Danny and Nicky Cowley who, it would seem, achieved similar outcomes as during the period under mine and Graham's watch. Success on the field again, but combined with a significant upturn in taking the club back to its fans.

Clearly I am not privy to the current inner workings or policies of the club and can only look in from the outside and draw conclusions like any other fan. Yes, Lincoln City have enjoyed another successful season on the field, but it would appear that the policies of fan-based promotions and valued recognition are passing them by, which is beyond my instant comprehension. With more staff at their disposal – development, or retention of, young local talent is out of the picture, as is positive, football staff involvement in the community. As I pen this autobiography results are slipping away also – a time if ever there was one when supporter trust and confidence is required.

In all my time in football I have never understood the need for new managerial appointments, within any club, to launch a clear out of players signed by previous incumbents. This worried me most when those players were from the local area. I will take some convincing that those being signed from all parts of the country are more committed to the cause than those being brought through the ranks to support their own local professional club. That was highlighted beyond all reasonable doubt with the local youngsters coming through the ranks at both Sheffield Clubs.

Yes it will be more difficult for managers to pick up local talent when both the grass-roots game is evaporating around them, and players' loyalties are seemingly governed by their agents rather than from within their own hearts and heads. There seems to be a significant void between players of today who seem to rank personal rights and privileges higher than obligations, responsibilities and loyalties, as was present during my involvement. I am not sure that many clubs will be faced with supporting fund-raising games for a long serving player enjoying a testimonial for ten years unbroken service.

I have made reference to my feelings regarding the non-development of English talent – both apprentices, junior players and coaches or managers. Whilst compiling this book there was an article appearing in the national press which highlighted those views. The article was published in the *Daily Mail*, written by Ian Herbert and relating to a young footballer who was released by Manchester City two weeks after his 18th birthday. Such was the level of disappointment that he took his own life. At the subsequent inquest the parents were advised that it would be highly unusual to have any legal representation only to find on the day of the hearing that Manchester City were represented by four lawyers. The biggest problem as I see it is that the clubs cast their nets over the up and coming brigade, land as many as possible to give them the strongest chance of securing best talent in the market, and then stick them in the current academy system. If they show the necessary talent, they sign them up as a junior pro but if not simply discard them. The motive really is quite simple: "let's look after ourselves, mate. That's what we are here for." In my mind this simply highlights the greed syndrome which has captivated the big boys – it's no different than paying the exceptionally high salaries which have become commonplace at the top level. Once a player signs the relevant registration form he basically hands over his freedom to the club and is dictated to as appropriately required by the respective development coaches. Of course parents are going to be excited at the prospect of their young son ultimately becoming a highly talented, successful professional. Their career could potentially transform a family's standard of living. It is easy to be oblivious to the statistic that 70% of the young kids never have the opportunity to sign a professional contract. Tracey Crouch, in her football governance report published November 2020, cited that 99% of the 10,000 to 12,000 boys in the youth development system at any time are released even before being given a scholarship. It is difficult to come to the conclusion that the might and power of the big clubs since the emergence of the Premier League has brought enhanced benefits to the game as a whole. Wouldn't it make more commercial sense to be specific in selection, more professionally astute in development and more sincere in their dealings? This, in my opinion, is one area where some significant changes are needed, with the Football Authorities stepping up to the plate and not hiding behind their comfortable existence.

Certainly not trying to be wise after the event but, in giving my decision not to take the position offered to me by the Football Association all those years ago, it was my belief at the time that the main thrust of my duties would be moving from committee room to committee room with no positive commercial role to play. Within the hierarchy of today's game there will undoubtedly be some highly qualified professional servants to the game but on reflection I do feel it is now time to break-away from the machinations of committee work and handouts from highly negotiated media deals and adopt a more commercial approach, fully designed to secure the future of the game. After all, "meetings are events where minutes are taken but hours are lost!"

This unquestionably means the control of foreign influences both on and off the field either by a regulation restricting the number of foreign players on the match day team sheet for any one game, or seeking government intervention with whatever legislation possible to return the game to its foundations of being the envy of the world. True feelings of ownership of one's club need to be returned to that community. Unfortunately, this is not the case, otherwise comments made by television pundits, during the proposed Super League breakaway, of the "attempted murder of English football" would not have been uttered. Let that not be just words but a positive policy of all English governing bodies, combining and working diligently to give us our game back.

In terms of the modern game, therefore, I believe that there is work to be done both at club level and more importantly through the various organisations. The changing nature of the game in terms of ownership, sponsorship, money and players has transformed the nature of football in many ways that are not always for the better. It is not of course possible to travel back in time, even if it was even seen as a good idea! Clubs though should look for methods to become closer to their fanbase. In my ideal world this may be done through some form of local involvement. Leicester City have shown, however, that foreign owners can develop close and mutual links with the local fanbase and community. The national organisations seem, from the outside, to have become both top-loaded and over-staffed and therefore inflexible and slow moving. It seems to me that the Football League needs to redouble its efforts to support its 72 members by possibly using their power in the commercial world to create and develop new forms of income. The finances of football are skewed towards the teams in the Premier League. The Football League should maximise their ability to support those at the lower levels. The Football Association has a different job. Clearly at the moment they are unable to stem the flow of both foreign owners and players so they should seek to work closely with the government to establish some form of restriction to encourage a greater proportion of English representation both on and off the field. Again, from the outside, it seems the FA has lost track of what is important. It must look at the game as a whole and secure the grass-roots alongside the national game. A big job, but a vital one.

I am not convinced that the changes needed to the sport require extra funding from the government. As I write, the UK Chancellor of the Exchequer has recently announced a national investment in grassroots sports. With all the money that is currently swimming around the game of football one has to ask the question "What has all the money in the game been spent on?" Which sections of the industry could have managed with a bit less and invested those savings in the grassroots game? Certainly the availability of the right standard of facilities to accommodate grassroots development is lacking and does in fact relate more to the management of the same by local authorities, which, over the years, has been lacking. Clarity of thought and planning from all the institutions involved in the development of our national game could have avoided any need for further government investment to spend directly and could have benefited all levels of the game.

My life has moved on from football and, of course, all things eventually change – they call it evolution. That has always been the case with the world in general. I can remember my parents saying to me, 'You don't know how lucky you are. If you'd only gone through what we went through at your age you would know what life was really like.' Modern technology has come into our lives to a level which I doubt would ever have been contemplated some 40 years ago. I recall my mother and aunty – who used to live together – coming to visit me in Sheffield at a time when I had purchased a new television with a remote control. This particular evening I was going out to a function and beforehand showed them how they could sit in their chairs and control what they watched. I did however take the micky a bit with the remote in my hand. I got my mother to move her arm up whilst I increased the volume on the remote and then to move her hand down whilst I did the same with the controls. I then asked her to move her arm to the left and I used the remote to change channels down and similarly moved her arm to the right to change channels up. The look of bewilderment was one I will never forget but when my aunty said to my mother, 'We shall have to get one of these it will save us getting up and down,' I didn't have the nerve to leave the house without admitting that I had been messing about. My mother was always careful with her words but this time she had to let herself go. I will not put on record those few choice words! Having reached the ripe old age I have, it is now the turn of the younger generations of the Chester clan to have the odd laugh at my expense.

When you look back to my start in football in 1971, Kevin Keegan was transferred from Scunthorpe United to Liverpool for £33,000, and negotiated what I believe was the first fifty pound a week contract with additional appearance money and win bonuses adding a further £80 per week to provide earnings of £130 per week, for someone who at that time was regarded as one of England's best players. One wonders what he would be worth today! The average working man's salary was quoted at £1,484 per annum, which in 2021 was worth £30,422. The average price of a pint in 1971 was 8.75p whereas today that same pint can cost an average of £3.69. *The Sun* newspaper did report only recently on a London pub who increased their price of a pint from £6.40 to £7.00. I am sure readers will point out that costs to watch their favourite club have been hiked by similar levels with the Premier League being at the forefront of this policy. That mid-80s £85 season ticket inevitably seems a bargain given some of the eye-watering prices charged today. It has to be said that the hardcore support from the rank-and-file working class has either diminished considerably over the years or the clubs themselves have lost faith in realities.

The game itself in terms of its management structure and technological advances in terms of performances, health, fitness, and dietary controls has to be applauded. In my very early days at Lincoln the structure was 1 x Manager, 1 x Assistant Manager, 1 x Physio and 1 x Youth Coach looking after all of the training, coaching, scouting, fitness and youth development elements. The physio acted as the sponge man on match days – complete with smelling salts and the cold sponge to deal with whatever. He would also complete treatments on injured players during the following week. At that time they were mostly self-taught with the clubs happy to release them on their valuable assets. The manager and his assistant did all of the scouting, opposition assessment, training and coaching including goalkeepers.

Today each club has a dedicated team of advisors, coaches, and scouting networks doing the self-same work, but no doubt in terms of health and well-being much better qualified. My only doubt about the marketing of players today is who within the signing club has the qualifications and skill to set values way above levels of investment they have ever made in their lives? A player is like a major capital expenditure item in a commercial company which appears on the balance sheet as an asset for which in depth analysis, valuation, lifespan and income generation is determined before purchasing. With a player it seems that the agent plays a major part in fixing valuations and deals, which removes the need for the manager to track around the football scene, watching, analysing, seeking references and making the judgement totally on his own findings. Assuming that happens. Why the agent? Where does all the money go? I have no knowledge of this, but my understanding of human nature, and experience of dirty, murky and clean deals during my career makes me ask the question at least.

Was my life in football a benefit to me and do I feel I served the community and fanbase satisfactorily? In terms of the many responsibilities granted to me by various boards of directors I do believe I honoured my obligations to the full. One of my real dilemmas when asked about writing this book was my conscience and whether I should breach the confidences entrusted to me during those years. Since leaving the game I have neither sponged off any club seeking "match day freebies" nor spoken about elements of my work. I can also say that there has been some disappointment felt by me, in as much as having given all three clubs total commitment, and elements of achievements with each one, I have never been granted the privilege of accepting an invitation to return either to "old boys" gatherings or any other such event.

The role of the senior administrator is one of diligently performing the tasks necessary to ensure full compliance rather than floating around, looking the part with a piece of paper in your hand or seeking publicity, and I think I performed my duties well. There may have been situations where it was not unlike my annual school report: "worked hard but still room for improvement." I really can't give a definitive answer, as that has to come from others. Thinking back to my childhood, the words of wisdom handed down to me by my father: "don't expect respect to be handed down to you, you have to work for it and earn it" stuck with me and I think served me well. Apart from the introduction of computerisation in my Sheffield Wednesday days, where I employed someone to deliver information I required, I have never asked anyone to do any work which I couldn't do myself. That remit took me into all areas of business management and whilst I wasn't master of them all, I gained sufficient understanding which certainly helped me later on in my career. I don't think I created any enemies, and I don't think anyone would say that I "put one over them." At all times I always tried to conduct affairs in the best interests of my employer and would, if necessary, push the rules to breaking point but never fully break them. In all I did, I tried to remember the needs of the match going supporter – memories stemming back to my childhood when the family went to all lengths to ensure the Saturday afternoon match was affordable – if only just. Again, I suppose I was not always 100% correct all of the time, but I can assure all of the many fans who I have had the privilege to serve that I tried my best, sometimes against a lot of obstacles thrown in the way.

As far as my time in football is concerned I can honestly, hand on heart, say that I tried to adopt a three-pronged approach to each and all. Firstly: ensure there was a clear understanding of the financial situation. Secondly: ensure management controls were in place to deal with any situation effectively. Thirdly: that relationships and understandings at all levels were clear, with the board of directors fully appraised, commercial partners respected at all times, employees fully aware of their obligations in proper performance of their duties, and supporters at all times respected. My ultimate aim was always to gain respect and not demand it. Also in my younger days my father used to tell me never to forget where you come from because if you are to be at all successful in a career and disrespectful to any on the way up they will be waiting for you on your downward slope.

In private and family life I have at all times tried to adopt similar standards and, here again, I don't think anyone can turn round and say they have had a raw deal – in fact there are times when I do believe I could have come out of things better than I did but at least I could always live with my conscience. My family has in some ways suffered from my commitment to work, from trying to do my best to achieve life's benefits. If I was to turn the clock back a bit, I could possibly have done things better but having said that, everyone has a degree in hindsight and for my part I now want to enjoy what family time is left for me and hope that I have set standards which others may feel confident of following.

It is only left to say that I hope that readers have enjoyed the book and learned a little about me, and plenty about what goes on behind the scenes in football. If so, then the book did what it set out to do.

Acknowledgements

I will be forever grateful to my experiences both in work and life and thank everyone who has been part of that journey, allowing me to record my memories in an autobiography which I never ever dreamed was a possibility either in my childhood or earlier working career. I am convinced that had I chosen not to listen or learn from the lessons given by both Mum and Dad, I doubt I would ever have attained the standards I believe I achieved. In my early days it was my dad that I looked up to, dealing with any issue that cropped up in a quietly spoken way. Later on in my life those feelings were equalled towards my mother who performed virtual miracles to provide all that was deemed necessary for a stable up-bringing for my brother and myself.

My thanks also to Steve Ellis for the provision and approval for his Sheffield Wednesday pictures, as seen throughout the book. Also, whilst representing a Chester family connection, I have to thank my granddaughter, Charlotte, who as proprietor of Luka Photography has helped me with her professionalism and design capability. Charlotte is making great strides in the early part of her career. I am delighted that she has been able to support me, and more than happy to recommend her work. Her website https://lukaphotography.co.uk/ provides further details.

Finally I have to pass on my personal thanks to both John Dyson who has offered invaluable assistance and guidance in helping to put my story together and of course Steven Kay at 1889 books who had the confidence to support the publishing of this book.

Lightning Source UK Ltd.
Milton Keynes UK
UKHW020911180822
407485UK00009B/360

9 781915 045096